W9-CAJ-377

Bloom's Modern Critical Interpretations

The Adventures of
  Huckleberry Finn
Alice's Adventures in
  Wonderland
All Quiet on the
  Western Front
As You Like It
The Ballad of the Sad
  Café
Beloved
Beowulf
Billy Budd, Benito
  Cereno, Bartleby the
  Scrivener, and Other
  Tales
Black Boy
The Bluest Eye
Cat on a Hot Tin
  Roof
The Catcher in the
  Rye
Catch-22
The Color Purple
Crime and
  Punishment
The Crucible
Darkness at Noon
Death of a Salesman
The Death of Artemio
  Cruz
The Divine Comedy
Don Quixote
Dubliners
Emerson's Essays
Emma
Fahrenheit 451
Frankenstein

The Grapes of Wrath
Great Expectations
The Great Gatsby
Hamlet
The Handmaid's Tale
Heart of Darkness
I Know Why the
  Caged Bird Sings
The Iliad
Jane Eyre
The Joy Luck Club
The Jungle
Long Day's Journey
  Into Night
Lord of the Flies
The Lord of the Rings
Love in the Time of
  Cholera
Macbeth
The Man Without
  Qualities
The Metamorphosis
Miss Lonelyhearts
Moby-Dick
Night
1984
The Odyssey
Oedipus Rex
The Old Man and the
  Sea
On the Road
One Flew Over the
  Cuckoo's Nest
One Hundred Years of
  Solitude
The Pardoner's Tale
Persuasion

Portnoy's Complaint
A Portrait of the
  Artist as a Young
  Man
Pride and Prejudice
Ragtime
The Red Badge of
  Courage
The Rime of the
  Ancient Mariner
The Rubáiyát of
  Omar Khayyám
The Scarlet Letter
A Separate Peace
Silas Marner
Song of Solomon
The Stranger
A Streetcar Named
  Desire
Sula
The Sun Also Rises
The Tale of Genji
A Tale of Two Cities
The Tempest
Their Eyes Were
  Watching God
Things Fall Apart
To Kill a Mockingbird
Ulysses
Waiting for Godot
The Waste Land
White Noise
Wuthering Heights
Young Goodman
  Brown

Bloom's Modern Critical Interpretations

Franz Kafka's
The Metamorphosis
New Edition

Edited and with an introduction by
Harold Bloom
Sterling Professor of the Humanities
Yale University

BLOOM'S
LITERARY CRITICISM
An imprint of Infobase Publishing

Bloom's Modern Critical Interpretations: The Metamorphosis—New Edition

Copyright © 2008 Infobase Publishing

Introduction © 2008 by Harold Bloom

Bloom's Literary Criticism
An imprint of Infobase Publishing
132 West 31st Street
New York NY 10001

Library of Congress Cataloging-in-Publication Data
Franz Kafka's The metamorphosis / [edited and with an introduction by] Harold Bloom.
— New ed.
    p. cm. — (Bloom's modern critical interpretations)
  Includes bibliographical references and index.
  ISBN 978-0-7910-9827-1 (hardcover)
  1. Kafka, Franz, 1883–1924. Verwandlung. I. Bloom, Harold. II. Title: Metamorphosis.
III. Series.

PT2621.A26V4283 2008
833'.912—dc22

                                        2007046277

Contributing Editor: Janyce Marson
Cover designed by Takeshi Takahashi
Cover photo Digital Vision/Getty Images
Printed in the United States of America
Bang EJB 10 9 8 7 6 5 4 3 2 1

This book is printed on acid-free paper.

Contents

Editor's Note   vii

Introduction   1
   Harold Bloom

"The Metamorphosis"   5
   James Rolleston

The Liberation of Gregor Samsa   23
   John Winkelman

Insect Transformation as a
Narcissistic Metaphor in Kafka's *Metamorphosis*   35
   J. Brooks Bouson

"The Judgment" and "The Metamorphosis"   47
   Allen Thiher

Competing Theories of Identity
in Kafka's *The Metamorphosis*   63
   Kevin W. Sweeney

Sliding Down the Evolutionary Ladder?
Aesthetic Autonomy in *The Metamorphosis*   77
   Mark M. Anderson

Sounding Out the Silence of Gregor Samsa:
Kafka's Rhetoric of Dys-Communication   95
   Robert Weninger

The Sense of an *Unding:*
Kafka, Ovid, and the Misfits of Metamorphosis   117
   Michael G. Levine

Kafka's *Metamorphosis* and the Search for
Meaning in Twentieth-Century German Literature   145
   Margit M. Sinka

Metamorphosis: Defending the Human   155
   Michael Rowe

Chronology   171

Contributors   175

Bibliography   179

Acknowledgments   181

Index   183

Editor's Note

My Introduction finds invalid the ideas that Kafka's *The Metamorphosis* is either an allegory of the writer's destiny or a theological fantasy of death and resurrection.

James Rolleston centers upon the *inner* changes that Gregor undergoes, while John Winkelman sees the story as a contrast between Gregor's inward purification and his outer degradation.

For J. Brooks Bouson, Gregor's transformation is a narcissistic metaphor, after which Allen Thiher couples *The Metamorphosis* with Kafka's *The Judgment*.

Kafka's evasive interplay between different theories of identity is explored by Kevin W. Sweeney, while Mark M. Anderson counts the costs of an achieved aesthetic autonomy.

Robert Weninger analyzes the language of failed communication in the story, after which Michael G. Levine brings Ovid to the grim feast of Gregor's ending.

For Margit M. Sinka, Kafka's foreclosed quest for meaning is allied to other twentieth-century writers in German, if only as a more extreme study of isolation than those given by Hermann Hesse and by Thomas Mann.

The volume ends with Michael Rowe's argument that Kafka defends the human in his parable of suffering.

HAROLD BLOOM

Introduction

What can it mean to trust in the Covenant, not between Yahweh and the Jewish people, but between writing and a writer? Gregor Samsa is a solitary (his last name, in Czech, can be translated "I am alone"), a commercial traveler, and a kind of family pariah or outcast, at least in his own tormented vision. His celebrated metamorphosis, into a kind of huge bedbug, is completed in the story's first sentence. Gregor's fate is certain but without hope; there is plenty of hope, for writing as for God, but none for Gregor. The Law, which is the way things are, including one's parents' huge debt to one's employer, is essentially a universal compulsion to repeat. No irony, however well handled, can represent repetition compulsion as the Law of the Jews. Samsa's employer is therefore not Yahweh, but another version of the Gnostic Demiurge, ruler of the cosmological emptiness in which we dwell.

The only rage to order that Kafka knew was his implicit rage not to be interpreted. There can be no ultimate coherence to my Gnostic interpretation (nor to Scholem's, nor Benjamin's, nor Heller's, nor to anyone's) because Kafka refuses the Gnostic quest for the alien God, for one's own spark or *pneuma* rejoining the original Abyss somewhere out of this world. The huge bedbug is neither the fallen husk of Samsa nor his potentially saving *pneuma*. It can hardly be his spark from the original Abyss because it is a horrible vermin, and yet only after his transformation into a bug is Gregor capable of aesthetic apprehension. Like Shakespeare's grotesque Caliban, the insect Samsa hears the beautiful in music, and so for the first time apprehends another sphere.

1

Kafka refused an illustration for *The Metamorphosis* that would have portrayed Gregor Samsa as a literal beetle or bedbug: "The insect itself cannot be drawn. It cannot be drawn even as if seen from a distance." This is not to say that Samsa suffers an hallucination, but only reminds us that a negation cannot be visually represented, which in turn reminds us of Kafkan nostalgias for the Second Commandment.

Is Gregor accurate in his final consciousness that his death is a liberation, an act of love for his family? Wilhelm Emrich, elsewhere so wary a Kafka exegete, fell into this momentary passion for the positive, an entrapment all readers of Kafka suffer sooner or later, so exhausted are we by this greatest master of evasions. Because the insect is inexplicable, it does not necessarily contain any truth. *The Metamorphosis* like all crucial Kafkan narratives, takes place somewhere *between* truth and meaning, a "somewhere" identical with the modern Jewish rupture from the normative tradition. Truth is in hope and neither is available to us, while meaning is in the future or the messianic age, and we will not come up to either. We are lazy, but industry will not avail us either, not even the industrious zeal with which every writer prides himself upon accepting his own death. If *The Metamorphosis* is a satire, then it is self-satire, or post-Nietzschean parody, that humiliates Kafka's only covenant, the placing of trust in the transcendental possibility of being a strong writer.

The story then cannot be interpreted coherently as a fantasy of death and resurrection, or as an allegory on the less-is-more fate of being a writer. Gregor's death is not an effectual sacrifice, not a self-fulfillment, and not even a tragic irony of any kind. It is another Kafkan negation that refuses to negate the given, which is the world of Freud's reality principle. Gregor does not become a child again as he dies. Yet we cannot even call him a failure, which might guarantee his upward fall to the heights of redemption. Like Gracchus, like the bucket-rider, like the country doctor, like the hunger artist, Gregor is suspended between the truth of the past, or Jewish memory, and the meaning of the future, or Jewish messianism. Poor Gregor therefore evades the categories both of belief and of poetry. How much would most of us know about this rupture without Kafka, or Kafka's true heir, Beckett? A Gnosticism without transcendence is not a knowing but is something else, and there is no transcendence in *The Metamorphosis*, or anywhere in Kafka. To transcend in a world of rupture you only need to change your direction, but that is to adopt the stance of the cat (or Gnostic archon) of Kafka's magnificent and appalling parable, "A Little Fable":

> "Alas," said the mouse, "the world is growing smaller every day. At the beginning it was so big that I was afraid, I kept running and running, and I was glad when at last I saw walls far away to the

right and left, but these long walls have narrowed so quickly that I am in the last chamber already, and there in the corner stands the trap that I must run into." "You only need to change your direction," said the cat, and ate it up.

(Translated by Willa and Edwin Muir)

JAMES ROLLESTON

"The Metamorphosis"

A common error in Kafka criticism is to align individual works under
a single rubric. Because "The Judgment" relates the destruction of a falsely
based individuality, Gregor Samsa is forced into the same mold, with guilt
and parasitism read between the lines of the text; because "The Judgment"
shows the resurgence of a father, crucial importance is attached to the
uniform and bearing of Herr Samsa. But Gregor has little in common with
Georg Bendemann. For one thing, his life is not notably successful. For
another, if he has "exploited" his family, Kafka would surely have indicated
the fact more clearly; the father's depressed state is simply explicable in
terms of the collapse of his business five years earlier. And the person who
affects Gregor's outlook decisively in the course of the story is not his father
but his sister Grete. True, Kafka wanted to publish "The Stoker," "The
Judgment," and "The Metamorphosis" under the collective title "Sons (Die
Söhne)"; but the plural noun is just as suggestive of essential differences as it
is of a common pattern. "The Stoker" presents Rossmann's emergence from
anonymity, with no preordained tendencies except a recreative commitment
to an ordered world. "The Judgment" shows the dramatic and instantaneous
collapse of a man who has carried the idea of order to the point of aspiring
to replace reality itself by his elaborately staged mental categories. "The
Metamorphosis" begins, in a sense, where "The Judgment" leaves off. Georg

From *Kafka's Narrative Theater*, pp. 52–68. © 1974 by The Pennsylvania State University.

Bendemann has so alienated himself from the process of living that the functional bond between self and world is severed; his individuality is, literally and figuratively, submerged in the organic substance of life. Gregor too has become alienated, but not, like Georg, through an active combination of will and imaginative distance. Rather, Gregor is deficient in both qualities; his life resembles that of an automaton, and the organic world invades him in the form of the transformation, not to kill him, but to compel him to live. In the compulsion laid upon Gregor to develop a new identity, Kafka has in one sense returned to the zero point of "The Stoker." But while Gregor, like Karl Rossmann, is effectively cut off from his own past, he is, unlike Karl, surrounded by that past both physically and mentally. His new life, by definition lacking a future, impels him to a reanimation of his past that effectively amounts to living that past for the first time.

The theatrical analogy, which has been shown to be essential to the structure of "The Judgment," is here so obvious as to be for the most part unnoticeable. The split between human mind and insect body compels Gregor to look at his existence from the outside, to formulate a role, a pattern of living, for himself. Gregor's conscientious, if objectively hopeless, struggle for an identity is what gives the story its human breadth; if "The Metamorphosis" is nothing more than a "punitive fantasy,"[1] then Kafka's only purpose is to portray Gregor's obtuse slowness in recognizing the need for his own death. As Lawrence Ryan says:

> According to Sokel, Gregor becomes a "true son" through this affirmation of his own death, indeed it is only by doing so that he realizes his "own being." But it seems to us to border on inhumanity if one claims to hear in this something like the voice of life itself, affirming the instinctual, biologically conditioned sequence of generations as opposed to all emancipation of the individual. Kafka is not recognizable in such an interpretation.[2]

The development of Gregor's quest for an identity can be divided into six stages, each section of the story containing a kind of caesura, a point at which the nature of Gregor's responses noticeably changes. Each change is correlated with a shift in Gregor's relationship to his sister. Her role is structurally analogous to that of the friend in "The Judgment." We have seen how, as Kafka's commentary emphasizes, the friend is the axis on which Georg's relationship to his father revolves: without the friend, the father would have no power over Georg. So it is here: although the father causes Gregor's death physically, it is the sister who opens the way to this development and to Gregor's acceptance of it. Gregor is never under any illusions about his father's attitude, taking it fully into account in his attempts to form an identity; about the sister he achieves clarity only gradually. His relationship with her is both analogous and antithetical to that of Georg Bendemann with the friend in Russia: Georg exploits his friend, Gregor is exploited by his sister. We are told that she has always been "close" to him, a phrase expressive of her mirroring function. Although Kafka goes far in suggesting independent motivation in the sister, the result is always to counterpoint and broaden the scope of Gregor's inner drama, which is increasingly focused on her; of prime importance is the fact that Grete represents the "world," the exclusively human realm as symbolized in its positive form by her violin playing. Her negative function lies in her unyielding hostility to Gregor's efforts at achieving a median identity between the human and the animal. This is not to say that she "destroys" Gregor any more than the friend (or indeed the father) destroys Georg Bendemann; Georg destroys himself, and Gregor's death is inevitable from the moment of the transformation, inherent in the impossibility of "human beings living with such a creature (ein Zusammenleben von Menschen mit einem solchen Tier)" (Grete's words). The role of both Grete and the friend is that of catalyst, bringing into the open, for the hero himself as well as for the reader, the movement of the hero's consciousness.

It is only partially true that, as is often asserted, Gregor refuses to accept his transformation in the first part, talking about the office as if nothing had happened. Upon first awakening he responds quite directly to his condition—"It was no dream (Es war kein Traum)"—and when he first starts thinking of his job ("Oh God, he thought, what an exhausting job I've picked on!"),[3] there are extremely easy transitions between his thoughts and his exploration of his body, as the sentences about his "itching place (juckende Stelle)" make plain. The negative thoughts about his work are, as it were, induced by the transformation and harmonize with it. There is, I think, critical unanimity that Gregor has in some sense "willed" the transformation as a release from the inhuman monotony of his nominally human life; the animalistic suggestiveness of the fur-covered lady in his picture confirms this initial hypothesis. What deserves greater attention is the significance of the picture frame; we are told shortly by Gregor's mother that he had made it himself, indeed that carpentry, that basic manifestation of *homo faber*, is Gregor's only activity as an individual. If the picture in its frame is as important as its position in the story suggests (both here and in the furniture-removal scene), it indicates that, by slipping into the organic world, Gregor is also gaining a chance to reassert his individuality. The transformation leads inexorably towards death, to be sure, but it also gives Gregor the opportunity, not available to untransformed humanity, of building, within strictly circumscribed limits, a fresh identity from a zero point. Just because the scope of his activity is so limited, it is knowable in every detail and translatable into an "ordered" way of living; the self-dramatizing talent that destroys Georg Bendemann enables Gregor to continue living, as he absorbs every statement and gesture of his family into a new self-image.

But this is to look ahead. Part One of the story details the simultaneous movement of Gregor outwards, towards the "world," and inwards, to his new nature. This process has a rise and a fall, with a climax at the point where his culminating effort on behalf of his old identity (unlocking the door) coincides with a sudden calm awareness of the irrevocable change. Three tangible pressures push him away from his initial state of inquisitive self-absorption: the sight of the clock, the anxiety of his family, and finally the job itself in the person of the chief clerk. The geographical position of Gregor's room already suggests the dominating hold his family has over him; but in the sister's exhortation to open his door there is a hint that her demands on him are more total, less concerned for his residual humanity, than the others'. Gregor's response conveys a surprising brusqueness that already implies an ambivalence in his professed regard for her:

> However, Gregor had no intention of opening the door, but felt thankful for the prudent habit he had acquired in traveling of locking all doors during the night, even at home.[4]

The sister's influence on Gregor is strong; here, as elsewhere, the effect of her intervention is to take a decision for him that he does not really want to take. The sentence quoted suggests an almost petulant rejection; nevertheless, Gregor now decides to get up. Two words, in a repeated counterpoint, evoke the conflicting impulses in Gregor during the remainder of this section: "quiet" (*ruhig*) and "sensible" (*vernünftig*). Clichés of virtuous conduct derived from his old identity, these words take on new dimensions as they seem to point him in opposite directions. As he decides to get up they still operate in unison in his own mind—but only because his plan, a hasty response to his sister's insistent "normality," is a ludicrous fantasy:

> His immediate intention was to get up quietly without being disturbed, to put on his clothes and above all eat his breakfast, and only then to consider what else was to be done, since in bed, he was well aware, his meditations would come to no sensible conclusion.[5]

Gregor has in effect opted for reason rather than tranquillity, as the uncontrolled response of his "little legs" (*Beinchen*) indicates; as he tries to compel his body to conform to the dictates of his old identity, he fills his mind with the appropriate cliché: "But what's the use of lying idle in bed (Nur sich nicht im Bett unnütz aufhalten)." When the first attempt fails and it begins to dawn on Gregor that "peace" (*Ruhe*) is attainable only through self-adaptation to his new body, Gregor desperately reiterates the precepts of his old identity, especially the twin key words, as if to compel order by unleashing the full force of the moralizing rhetoric that has ruled his life hitherto:

> But when after a repetition of the same efforts he lay in his former position again, sighing, and watched his little legs struggling against each other more wildly than ever, if that were possible, and saw no way of bringing any order into this arbitrary confusion, he told himself again that it was impossible to stay in bed and that the most sensible course was to risk everything for the smallest hope of getting away from it. At the same time he did not forget meanwhile to remind himself that cool reflection, the coolest possible, was much better than desperate resolves.[6]

With the withdrawal of the props of his old life, symbolized by the blotting-out of the window by fog, such talk is mere incantation, the magic of "rationality" (*Vernunft*). One is reminded of Georg Bendemann's grasping at such straws as his identity crumbles. Gregor, however, has a more frankly magical option, the option of "peace" (*Ruhe*), which has an unexpected kind of potency:

> And for a little while he lay quiet, breathing lightly, as if perhaps expecting such complete repose to restore all things to their real and normal condition.[7]

On a superficial level, of course, this magic is no more effective than the rhetoric of "rationality"; but it is no longer so clear what "normal conditions" are. The peaceful posture does induce a degree of calm in Gregor, the calm of beginning self-acceptance. When he now tries to get out of bed it is "more a game than an effort (mehr ein Spiel als eine Anstrengung)"; and he even "smiles" at the thought of asking for help.

The arrival of the chief clerk (*Prokurist*) puts a temporary end to this. But Gregor's "agitation" (*Erregung*) is succeeded by a new awareness of his body as he crashes to the floor. While he continues to respond on a "normal" level, the dimensions of this "new" version of his old life begin to be suggested. The idea crosses his mind that his fate could befall the chief clerk, an idea whose presumption and breadth of perspective would have been inconceivable in his normal state of servitude. And after the mother has sketched his earlier life-style, Gregor reacts with a new calmness, an apparent awareness that, amid the banalities of his family's remarks, he will have to seek the pattern of a past as yet without meaning; carpentry had been his earlier avenue of self-expression, now he will be confined to listening and observing: "'I'm just coming,' said Gregor slowly and carefully, not moving an inch for fear of losing one word of the conversation."[8] This movement culminates in a resounding "No," wholly natural to Gregor, unbelievable to everyone else.

Once again the movement inwards is reversed, this time by the sister's weeping. In his newly achieved calm Gregor does not understand why she is crying, when he has achieved his own synthesis of "peace" and "rationality": "And it seemed to Gregor that it would be much more sensible to leave him in peace for the present than to trouble him with tears and entreaties."[9] However, his irritable, agitated self-questioning shows that his "No" does not really apply to her, he cannot exclude her. She has reopened the gap between his mental and physical selves which the chief clerk then greatly enlarges. A key to the effect he has on Gregor lies in his appropriation for his own viewpoint of the two attributes with which Gregor has been grappling, restoring them to their old status as clichés: "I thought you were a quiet, dependable person (Ich glaubte Sie als einen ruhigen, vernünftigen Menschen zu kennen . . .)." His demolition of Gregor's old identity before Gregor has fully emancipated himself from it causes panic. Gregor's total concentration on the feat of opening the door is not so much an effort to regain his old identity as a desperate urge to be rid of all responsibility for himself.

At the same time, the transformation itself is proceeding uninterrupted, and a strong indication of its "meaning" is offered in the parallel development of self-acceptance in Gregor. The caesura in this first part occurs when the sister departs for help and Gregor realizes his words are no longer understood. With the paragraph beginning "But Gregor was now much calmer (Gregor war aber viel ruhiger geworden)" a new phase opens, in which Gregor's mind is functioning largely on a different level from his body; but as the body's autonomy grows, Gregor's thoughts often seem in a significantly inverse relationship with his actions. Thus it is said of Gregor, "He felt himself drawn once more into the human circle (Er fühlte sich wieder einbezogen in den menschlichen Kreis)," at the moment when the loss of verbal communication entails his definitive exclusion. And yet the feeling is true on other levels: the family, which had previously been fragmented, will now become a unit again in its affliction; and Gregor, through his intense involvement in the trivia of daily life, will become a part of that unit as he never has been as the breadwinner.

When the door is finally opened, Gregor continues to speak as if his old identity were still functioning—but he also feels himself to be "the only one who had attained any composure (der einzige, der die Ruhe bewahrt hatte)." Clearly this speech is different from the earlier panicky outburst, when we were told that he "hardly knew what he was saying (kaum wusste, was er sprach)." Now he is, as it were, speaking experimentally, presenting both his identities simultaneously, the one visually, the other verbally. Moreover, what he says, although in polite terminology, is as open, as aggressive as what the chief clerk had said to him; at the moment of finally losing his old identity, he allows the entire underside to emerge within the framework of an organized personal plea. The chief clerk is right to feel threatened by Gregor. While Gregor's conscious mind persists in developing rationales for his pursuit of the chief clerk, his actions strongly suggest that he is in fact attacking this most resented representative of "the world": "Gregor made a spring, to be as sure as possible of overtaking him (Gregor nahm einen Anlauf, um ihn möglichst sicher einzuholen)." Indeed the imagery of the chief clerk's departure is extraordinarily reminiscent of Georg Bendemann's final moments: "[He] was already ridiculously clinging with both hands to the railing on the landing . . . with his chin on the banister he was taking one last backward look."[10]

But because Gregor cannot communicate, his unleashed aggression appears indiscriminate. The arduous task of controlling his instincts is not yet begun and his involuntary movement in the direction of the spilled coffee makes drastically clear that any literal notion of a "human circle" is illusory. Rejected by both mother and father, Gregor is forced back into himself, both physically and figuratively. At this point the banality of Gregor's mind, the lack of "imagination" which Kobs has shown to be a conscious goal of Kafka's narrative style, begins to acquire thematic force. By doggedly adapting mind to body, Gregor reestablishes the kind of rudimentary communication with the human world that makes a temporary but nonetheless temporal existence possible. That is not to say that Kafka is merely building a naturalistic structure upon an antinaturalist base; Benno von Wiese has pointed to the stylization implicit in the family's behavior:

> Significantly, no one around Gregor reflects upon the amazing, inexplicable quality of this transformation. They accept it as a fact, albeit a repulsive one, just as Gregor himself and even the narrator accept it.[11]

The stylized reactions of the family have the same purpose as the transformation itself: to remind the reader that the strict alignment of narrative perspective with Gregor's viewpoint is designed to focus attention exclusively on his responses. All that is arbitrary and undignified in his initial situation becomes, through Gregor's "unimaginative" persistence, the source of dignity, almost of coherence. As in the case of Georg Bendemann, though to very different fictional ends, the "ordinariness" of the hero's thoughts is the necessary modality of an extraordinary mental theater; because of this "The Metamorphosis" has a concreteness of texture that tends to refute Lukács's fundamental charge against Kafka that his "artistic ingenuity is really directed towards substituting his angst-ridden vision of the world for objective reality."[12]

In the second part the work's central drama is played out. On the one side two forces are ceaselessly driving Gregor towards his death: the trivializing game the sister plays with his existence, which represents an irrevocable denial of his humanity; and the continuing process of Gregor's transformation itself, drawing him ever further into the organic realm, a process his "human" component cannot accept. This conflict manifests itself, almost in passing, in a sentence referring, without further explanation, to Gregor's increasing reluctance to eat: "When he had not eaten, which gradually happened more and more often...."[13] On the other side there is the overt drama of the second part, Gregor's efforts to achieve a modus vivendi. Because the reader sees things from Gregor's perspective he is constantly invited to agree that Gregor's aims are eminently reasonable, perhaps even practicable. At the same time the conclusion of the section, obviously paralleling the conclusion of the first part, introduces an element of ritual that forcibly reminds the reader that Gregor's existence is an impossibility, that the "drama" is only in his mind.

The last speech of Georg Bendemann's father begins: "So now you know what else there was in the world besides yourself; till now you've known only about yourself!"[14] Here lies the significance of Gregor's "inner" transformation; both he and Georg gain this insight only at the cost of definitive exclusion from the human realm, but Gregor has the opportunity, denied to Georg, of rearranging his consciousness. That Gregor views what lies before him as a form of task is made explicit at the start of the section: "so he had plenty of time to meditate at his leisure on how he was to arrange his life afresh."[15] He concludes that the situation requires "patience and the utmost consideration (Geduld und grösste Rücksichtnahme)." It is easy to overlook these sentences, because they sound like mere clichés from the life of a repressed traveling salesman whose past "consideration" has prevented any human warmth from entering his life. But in context they have a twofold meaning: Gregor is just learning how to feel "comfortable" (behaglich) in his new body, and such sentiments directly contradict the instinctual freedom he is now experiencing. The presence of clichés has the same kind of negative significance as the family's lack of amazement, noted by Benno von Wiese; it directs the reader's attention to a tenacious struggle for equilibrium within Gregor. Further, Gregor is now aware of his family as he had never been while they were his dependents; he feels "pride" (Stolz) at what he has achieved for them and, for perhaps the only time in his life, asks the kind of ultimate question forced upon him by his transformation: "But what if all the quiet, the comfort, the contentment were now to end in horror?"[16] The idea of "patience and the utmost consideration" is an indirect response to this question. The ironic opportunity of the transformation is that it has made Gregor fully "human," aware of the several contexts of his own being. Hitherto he has "partly lived," his only positive feelings, acceptance and resentment, canceling each other out. Now that communication is impossible, he realizes its paramount importance. He observes his family intensely, both to enlarge the picture he has of his previous existence and to glean hints about how he should behave now. Reduced to a minimal theater of mime, Gregor stakes everything on making comprehensible his "good intentions." Georg Bendemann erected the rationalizations of mental theater upon a life of ruthless self-absorption. Gregor attempts to use the most simplified modes of physical gesture to impose a human meaning on a body that has its own laws and increasingly insists on following them.

But the static, "experimental" world which both Georg and Gregor need for the acting-out of their adopted roles is available to neither. As suggested earlier, two unrelenting forces doom Gregor's efforts to achieve a modus vivendi: one is his own increasing animality, the other is embodied in the pivotal character of the sister, Grete. The sister is seen by Gregor in three different guises, each of them modifying and calling into question the other two as the story develops. Her reactions to Gregor are, on the surface, those of an adolescent girl, both intrigued and repelled by Gregor, eager both to be useful and to explore the unknown, but above all narcissistic, referring everything to her developing sense of self. But when the reader pieces together hints which Gregor drops but, because they are irreconcilable with his own enterprise, does not develop, a more complicated picture emerges. The sister is herself experiencing a "transformation," parallel to and in growing conflict with Gregor's.[17] Stages of this transformation, presented independently of Gregor's perspective, are her hostile "Gregor! (Du, Gregor!)" at the end of the second part, and her assertion that the insect cannot be Gregor in the third. At other points the reader identifies himself strictly with the interests of the transformed Gregor; from this third point of view Grete's personality is nothing more than an instrument through which the world rejects Gregor's efforts at self-adaptation. Put in the form of a theorem, a human being strong enough to deal with Gregor directly is bound to be insensitive to Gregor's efforts at communication (conversely the person able to "understand" Gregor, namely the mother, is not strong enough to deal with him directly). Significantly, the inclinations of Gregor quickly understood by the sister are purely behavioristic, desires he has made no effort to communicate: standing by the window and crawling on the walls. The theorem is graphically demonstrated when the ambivalent sister is supplemented as Gregor's "keeper" by the frankly hostile charwoman.[18]

Gregor's blood tie, his personal limitations, and the imperatives of the role he is endeavoring to play combine to prevent any of this from being articulated intellectually; nevertheless, the three elements in Grete's function rise gradually to the surface of his consciousness. At first he sees her adolescent character, flighty but benevolent, and does everything he can to turn her into a permanent channel of communication. From the first a note of impatience is struck, when the sister's horror at her first glimpse of him makes Gregor half-aware of her fundamental alienation from him: "well, he had to be somewhere, he couldn't have flown away, could he? (Gott, er musste doch irgendwo sein, er hatte doch nicht wegfliegen können)." But at once Gregor covers up this feeling, emphasizing the positive in the person he realizes is his only bridge to the world, imputing an elaborate sensitivity to her brusque gestures:

> And with fine tact, knowing that Gregor would not eat in her presence, she withdrew quickly and even turned the key, to let him understand that he could take his ease as much as he liked.[19]

Adapting himself to the fact that he will see no one but his sister, Gregor strains desperately for "a remark which was kindly meant or could be so interpreted (eine Bemerkung, die freundlich gemeint war oder so gedeutet werden konnte)." It is at this point, while reviewing the shape of his past life, that Gregor reflects, "With his sister alone had he remained intimate (Nur die Schwester war Gregor doch noch nahe geblieben)," and dwells on his plan to send her to the conservatory. Without doubting the "truth" of these intangible thoughts and feelings, one is entitled to see Gregor as to some extent revising the pattern of his past in order to lend meaning to the identity he is now building around his relationship with Grete. Repeatedly the alienness of her attitude becomes abundantly clear to Gregor, as elaborately "considerate" sentence structures are negated by brusquely factual statements:

> She certainly tried to make as light as possible of whatever was disagreeable in her task, and as time went on she succeeded, of course, more and more, but time brought more enlightenment to Gregor too. The very way she came in distressed him.[20]

But having nowhere else to turn, Gregor submerges these painful insights in still more tortuous sentences as he seeks still more extreme ways of effacing, through "consideration" (Rücksichtnahme), what cannot be effaced; only the sister's acknowledgment can make these efforts worth while, and so intense is Gregor's longing for it that he can hardly help receiving it, if only in his imagination:

> Had she considered the sheet unnecessary, she would certainly have stripped it off the sofa again, for it was clear enough this curtaining and confining of himself was not likely to conduce to Gregor's comfort, but she left it where it was, and Gregor even

fancied that he caught a thankful glance from her eye when he
lifted the sheet carefully a very little with his head to see how she
was taking the new arrangement.[21]

Gregor's total absorption in the sister's convenience, his desire to accept
everything she does as "right" and hence supportive of his identity as a member
of the household, leads him to remain passive when she proposes the removal
of his furniture.

With the mother's words concerning the furniture we reach the caesura
of this central part. Gregor suddenly realizes the falsity of the premise on
which he has tried to erect an identity. Within the framework of a single
sentence we can see him moving to a new view of the sister: not merely
an impulsive adolescent, she is a developing personality whose urge for an
identity is fundamentally antagonistic to Gregor's own:

> Another factor might have been also the enthusiastic temperament
> of an adolescent girl, which seeks to indulge itself at every
> opportunity and which now tempted Grete to exaggerate the
> horror of her brother's circumstances in order that she might do
> all the more for him.[22]

The hopeless contradiction underlying Gregor's efforts is revealed: to
fight for his humanness he must behave like an insect. But even as everything
is falling apart, dissolving into a struggle for existence Gregor is certain to lose,
the worthwhile basis of his "identity" is thrown into striking relief. As Gregor
contemplates his intervention, he is conscious only that it must be done "as
kindly and cautiously as possible (vorsichtig und möglichst rücksichtsvoll)."
When his mother enters, all thoughts vanish from Gregor's mind except the
need to spare her the sight of him:

> His mother however was not accustomed to the sight of him;
> it might sicken her and so in alarm Gregor backed quickly to
> the other end of the sofa, yet could not prevent the sheet from
> swaying a little in front.[23]

That Gregor has made "consideration" into his basic impulse, stronger than
all his developing animal urges, is clear throughout the dissolution of his
tenuous modus vivendi at the end of the second part. His pathetic attempts
to assert his rationality, at a moment when it is of no value to him, stand
in sharp contrast to the self-centered meanness of the sister and the sheer
animal hostility of the father. An enigmatic but much-quoted dictum of
Kafka's seems applicable to Gregor at this point, as his identity, cleansed of

the self-deception on which it had been built, survives the moment of its destruction: "The light on the grotesquely grimacing retreating face is true, and nothing else."[24] It is paradigmatic for the Kafka hero to glimpse a desired goal at the moment when it is denied him forever; Gregor's goal has been to rejoin his family by literally acting himself, imposing human behavior on an animal form, and the symbolic "complete union (in gänzlicher Vereinigung)" of his mother with his father on his behalf can be seen as the momentary realization of that intimate "human circle" (*Familienkreis*) towards which the transformed Gregor has been striving, but which is in fact a kind of mirage, visible only to him who is excluded from it.

In the third part there is no trace left of the anxious relationship with the sister upon which the central section hinged; for Gregor the sister now is simply the abstract representative of the world which is withdrawing from him. As his family all take jobs, the apartment is filling up with strangers and Gregor's existence has become a fact without meaning. Gregor no longer attempts to unite the human and animal sides of his being, oscillating between unrealistic concern over the family's situation and instinctive rage at the universal inattention to his needs. The only common factor now is the indifference that betokens his coming death: Gregor neither eats anything nor cares at all about the fate of his furniture, which had seemed so vital when the possibility of an identity had not yet been foreclosed. The complete separation of mind and body means that the Gregor of Part Three, while doomed to increasing self-alienation, is also completely "free" in the sense that what remains of his mind, now beyond all responsibilities, is open to the kind of impressions that are normally submerged by the struggle for existence. Gregor himself notes this final stage of his transformation as he begins to respond to the violin:

> He felt hardly any surprise at his growing lack of consideration
> for the others; there had been a time when he prided himself on
> being considerate.[25]

Although the premise of Gregor's vision is thus the emancipation of his mind, and the shape of that vision strongly suggests a "fairy tale in reverse" [*Antimärchen*], yet Clemens Heselhaus's formula is not quite fulfilled: "Nature must be destroyed in order that the spiritual can free itself (Die Natur muss vernichtet werden, damit das Geistige frei werde)."[26] For the startling thing about Gregor's "plan" is the degree of self-acceptance it involves. The ambivalence of the rhetorical question "Was he an animal, that music had such an effect upon him? (War er ein Tier, da ihn Musik so ergriff?)" has been noted; the paradox is that only as an animal, indeed only as a mortally wounded animal, are such emotions accessible to him. Gregor has virtually ceased to exist, survived only by a tranquil affirmation of his past in all its aspects. He accepts his physical shape, indeed "his frightful appearance would become, for the first time, useful to him (seine Schreckgestalt sollte ihm zum erstenmal nützlich werden)"; he accepts his mental limitations, salvaging only the plan to send his sister to the conservatory; and he accepts Grete's independence, asking only that she understand him. Gregor does not dream of the reversal of the transformation, only that the barrier of communication that had doomed his rational efforts to achieve an identity be somehow removed. The music makes this seem easy.[27]

If Gregor's words are not taken at face value, a quite different interpretation can be placed upon his vision. But there is every reason to take them at face value. For although Gregor can only achieve these images at an extremity of his life, they do not clash with his common sense, which has by no means deserted him. The striking thing about the very sharp caesura in the third part, which occurs when the lodgers break in upon Gregor's imaginings, is that it does not in any way change the direction of Gregor's thoughts. The first sentence about Gregor after the break expresses not confusion but resigned continuity:

> Disappointment at the failure of his plan, perhaps also the weakness arising from extreme hunger, made it impossible for him to move.[28]

By continuing to refer to his vision as a "plan" Gregor stresses its naturalness, its compelling logic as he confronts death. In the vision Gregor affirms the experience' of the transformation, pressing it to the point where it would yield a synthesis, his human self turned to the sister, his animal strength unleashed on the "intruders" (*Angreifer*); the image of himself at the center of the family's life is succeeded, as he detaches himself from his body, by the equal and opposite affirmation of what the real sister says—he must disappear. Jürg Schubiger is dissatisfied with Kafka's presentation of death:

> In Georg Bendemann's last words . . . we meet the same banal and unfruitful emotion which also fills the empty, peaceful meditation of the insect before his death. Everywhere Kafka leaves us in the lurch. In none of his works did he portray death believably; when it comes to dying he's not really involved. As a spectator he stands to one side.[29]

The last sentence, to which one can assent, throws into relief the misunderstanding implicit in the remainder of the passage. Kafka's heroes do indeed observe their own deaths. This is because they are always aware of death as something that can be willed, and as the roles they allot themselves in life fail to bring them to their goals, the temptation grows to redeem the whole losing game by a "successful" death. Gregor Samsa in effect experiences his death before actually dying; the word "empty" (*leer*) denotes the willed replacement of his being by the consciousness of his family.

A more serious argument against Gregor's death is the implication in Günther Anders's view that such affirmative emptiness is a dangerous illusion, the slave's acceptance of his slavery:

> Whereas in the history of the emancipation of the individual it was precisely the undetermined psyche, that is, one subject to neither restraints nor controls, that was seen as the essence of being ("being" therefore equals "freedom"), for Kafka only the determined, controlled psyche has "being."[30]

That Kafka was aware of this tendency in his writing is shown by his direct treatment of it in "In the Penal Colony." Here he has embedded Gregor Samsa's death so thoroughly in its context that it is impossible to make an unqualified statement about its meaning—e.g., that Gregor has or has not gained "freedom." This is what troubles Jürg Schubiger: the thematic movements of the story—Gregor's continuous decline from the human to the organic and finally to the inorganic, and the counterpointing transformation of the sister from "a somewhat useless girl (ein etwas nutzloses Mädchen)" to an emblem of self-contained humanity—both are fulfilled by Gregor's death and the family's liberation. And yet both have become encrusted with so much experiential data that a straightforward reaction to the story is no longer possible. The structural simplicity of "The Metamorphosis" demands such a reaction; but the experience of seeing the world from Gregor's viewpoint refutes it, the more so because Gregor's explicit attitude to the world is wholly positive. Thus the moment of Gregor's death epitomizes the complete hollowing-out of his identity, the ultimate working-out of self-negating tendencies already far developed in his life before the transformation; the subsequent emphasis on his shrunken physical shape underlines the finality of his disappearance. At the same time the positive elements inherent in the notion of "living one's life for others" are also brought into the open by the transformation: the dignity of Gregor's doomed struggle for self-adaptation, the self-mythologizing scope of his musical vision, both surpassing and strictly consistent with his life as we have come to know it, finally the conviction that his death will free his family—all this can be seen as an affirmative development, a "raising of the consciousness." A comparable ambivalence pervades the picture of the family after Gregor's death. They have a new self-assurance, an appreciation of life born of genuine suffering, a strength of which they had been unaware throughout Gregor's life. And yet, this independence can be seen as Gregor's final gift to them, anticipated and prepared for by him; moreover, the banality of their aspirations no longer seems convincing after the levels of experience reached by Gregor. Emrich, whose view of Gregor is too tautologous to be very useful—"He can be interpreted only as that which cannot be interpreted (Er ist interpretierbar nur als das Uninterpretierbare)"[31]—accurately conveys the impression left by these final pages:

> When Gregor dies (*krepiert*), the idyllic lie proceeds unimpeded at an intensified level: "three jobs" call them and a marriageable daughter "stretched her young body." The "horrifying end" overwhelmed only Gregor, just because he only wanted to care for his family.[32]

The transformation, by separating Gregor's mind from his body, compels him to act out the personality he had previously taken for granted. In the process that personality comes to seem larger than it ever had been in "life," without losing its inner logic; the banal goal of providing for the family acquires a metaphysical aura—and at the same time the life to which Gregor sacrifices himself is called into question. The logical connection between Kafka's use of the theatrical analogy (here rooted, not in any character's mind but in the story's premise, the transformation itself) and his youthful fascination with the problem of perception is now clear. The fact that we are compelled to view the insect's behavior from both within and without, automatically adding our "objective" image to Gregor's own reasoning, means that a constant process of evaluation is going on in the reader's mind. Is Gregor behaving intelligibly? Is he telling us the whole truth as he sees it? How far is the sister's behavior pardonable? Can we imagine the various scenes ending differently? The simple "inevitability" of the story provokes a constant questioning of all its ingredients until it becomes as enigmatic as the "tree trunks in the snow." The "Play of Gregor," as it might almost be called, dissolves into a series of interdependent layers: the quality of Gregor's life, Gregor's attitude toward his family, the family's attitude toward Gregor, the quality of the family's life. Each layer of the action has a claim to being uppermost in the reader's mind; and each culminates in a parablelike clarity that serves only to generate questions without end.

I have discussed "The Judgment" and "The Metamorphosis" very much in terms of themselves and each other, without ongoing references to my structural thesis. But the heroes of these stories, to a greater extent than elsewhere, come into being through the intimate detail of their stories. To other Kafka characters one can attach at least one essentially valid abstraction—with Karl Rossmann it would be the theme of "order," with Josef K. that of "innocence"; but with Georg and Gregor all such abstractions are embedded in the texture of their lives; their ambitions have no resonance beyond their immediate existence. Only through unprejudiced close reading can the motive force of these lives, of which the characters themselves are often (sometimes deliberately) unaware, be isolated and given coherence.

Additionally, there are uniquely private elements in these works which propel the reader's response into the realm of the psychological. At this turning point in his career Kafka was utilizing the powerful emotive connotations of family relationships to produce a central character of "substance"; insubstantiality has, precisely, been both the theme and the problem of his early writing. By no means does he abandon the achieved tension between hero and world: rather he incorporates an extra dimension of alienation between hero and reader which enables "substantial," even irrational aspects of the hero to be evoked without destroying the dispassionate balance of his art. As the title of the "breakthrough" story suggests, he wants the reader to *judge* the hero. If I have seemed to be "for" Gregor and "against" Georg, it is because the ethical implications of these stories cannot be bypassed. Without establishing any kind of abstract framework, Kafka is clearly making use of moral categories to fuel the functional tension between hero and reader. The hero ignores, misunderstands, or represses a truth that the reader sees and must respond to. Once Kafka has developed, in the closed structure, a way of incorporating such tensions into his narrative texture, the reader, while still tempted to "judge" the hero, will be denied the superior knowledge necessary for success in doing so.

Finally the question of structure. In these stories the two "elements" are perfectly fused, and hence not prominent as fictional devices. As my readings have shown, the recreative function of Karl Rossmann as "author" of his world is developed even further by Georg and Gregor. Both of them establish mental versions of the world, which they attempt to defend against the forces of disruption inevitably summoned into being by their enterprise. At the same time they find themselves cast in the story's central role, partly through their own volition. Simultaneously they strive to uphold the validity of their fictions and to evade the logic of their destruction. The outlines of the closed structure are thus emerging from the open rhythm generated by the authorial hero. The functional use Kafka makes of family relationships ensured that the aesthetic balance achieved here could not be repeated. But then, repetition was something Kafka never sought.

NOTES

1. Sokel's term.
2. Lawrence Ryan, "'Zum letzten Mal Psychologie!'," pp. 165–66.

3. *E*, 72.

4. "Gregor aber dachte gar nicht daran aufzumachen, sondern lobte die vom Reisen her übernommene Vorsicht, auch zu Hause alle Türen während der Nacht zu versperren." *E*, 75. Again I have altered the first phrase of the Muir translation, which simply misses the force of "dachte gar nicht daran."

5. "Zunächst wollte er ruhig und ungestört aufstehen, sich anziehen und vor allem frühstucken, und dann erst das Weitere überlegen, denn, das merkte er wohl, im Bett würde er mit dem Nachdenken zu keinem vernünftigen Ende kommen." *E*, 75.

6. "Aber als er wieder nach gleicher Mühe aufseufzend so dalag wie früher, und wieder seine Beinchen womöglich noch ärger gegeneinander kämpfen sah und keine Möglichkeit fand, in diese Willkür Ruhe und Ordnung zu bringen, sagte er sich wieder, dass er unmöglich im Bett bleiben könne und dass es das Vernünftigste sei, alles zu opfern, wenn auch nur die kleinste Hoffnung bestünde, sich dadurch vom Bett zu befreien. Gleichzeitig aber vergass er nicht, sich zwischendurch daran zu erinnern, dass viel besser als verzweifelte Entschlüsse ruhige und ruhigste Überlegung sei." *E*, 77. My point about the frequency of "Ruhe" and "ruhig" is perhaps inevitably lost in the translation.

7. "Und ein Weilchen lang lag er ruhig mit schwachem Atem, als erwarte er vielleicht von der volligen Stille die Wiederkehr der wirklichen und selbstverständlichen Verhältnisse." *E*, 77.

8. *E*, 81.

9. "Gregor schien es, dass es viel vernünftiger wäre, ihn jetzt in Ruhe zu lassen, statt ihn mit Weinen und Zureden zu stören." *E*, 82.

10. *E*, 90–91.

11. Benno von Wiese, "Franz Kafka, 'Die Verwandlung'," in *Die deutsche Novelle von Goethe bis Kafka*, vol. 2 (Düsseldorf: Bagel, 1962), p. 334.

12. Georg Lukács, *The Meaning of Contemporary Realism* (London: Merlin Press, 1962), p. 25.

13. "Im gegenteiligen Fall, der sich allmählich immer häufiger wiederholte." *E*, 100.

14. *E*, 67.

15. *E*, 96.

16. "Wie aber, wenn jetzt alle Ruhe, aller Wohlstand, alle Zufriedenheit ein Ende mit Schrecken nehmen sollte?" *E*, 95.

17. Politzer stresses this parallelism, but regards the story's final symmetry as an aesthetic error: "The title of the story might apply to Grete with greater justification than to Gregor, for it is her metamorphosis which is developed in the course of the narrative, whereas we have to accept Gregor's as an accomplished fact. More and more she plays herself into the foreground: the end will show her transformation completed, very much to the detriment of the story." *Parable and Paradox*, p. 74. Hartmut Binder's investigation of the problem of perspective, however, leads to the conclusion that Kafka has broadened Gregor's viewpoint to such an extent that the caesura of his death is more apparent than real: "The epilogue is by no means inorganic, but merely the continuation of the second narrative strand which was always present and which had already, although from Gregor's perspective, been presented with the same neutrality: a fact that reveals itself, for example, in the reader's experience that the change of perspective at the conclusion of the story involves no change in the modalities of perception." *Motiv und Gestaltung bei Franz Kafka* (Bonn: H. Bouvier, 1966), p. 295.

18. Stanley Corngold stresses the charwoman's role in this dialectic; the very strangeness of her hardened "normality" propels the reader into reevaluating the effects of the metamorphosis: "The cleaning woman does not know that a metamorphosis has

occurred, that in this insect shape there is a human consciousness, one superior at times to the ordinary consciousness of Gregor Samsa." "Kafka's *Die Verwandlung*: Metamorphosis of the Metaphor," in *Mosaic*, 3 (1970), 98.

19. *E*, 98.

20. "Die Schwester suchte freilich die Peinlichkeit des Ganzen möglichst zu verwischen, und je längere Zeit verging, desto besser gelang es ihr natürlich auch, aber auch Gregor durchschaute mit der Zeit alles viel genauer. Schon ihr Eintritt war für ihn schrecklich." *E*, 105.

21. *E*, 106–7.

22. *E*, 111.

23. *E*, 112.

24. "Das Licht auf dem zurückweichenden Fratzengesicht ist wahr, sonst nichts." *H*, 46.

25. "Er wunderte sich kaum darüber, dass er in letzter Zeit so wenig Rucksicht auf die andern nahm; früher war diese Rucksichtnahme sein Stolz gewesen." *E*, 129.

26. Heselhaus, "Kafkas Erzählformen," p. 357.

27. Politzer's interpretation of this scene is diametrically opposed to mine: "Even in this moment of dedicated listening he cannot accept music for what it is; he has to translate it into images of concrete possession which is all that he understands. . . . We have arrived at the vertex of the story which, thanks to Kafka's masterful counterpoint, is also the low point in the insect's development. We feel the icy breath of an existence fatally gone astray." *Parable and Paradox*, p. 77. But if this is the low point, where are the high points? Despite Politzer's lip service to the story's structural movement, basically his view of Gregor is statically behavioristic; he sees only one aspect of a situation where Kafka's systematic deployment of antithesis has invariably built in a counter-element. Above all, he does not distinguish between the banal substance of Gregor's life and the "transformation" of that life through the hero's reenactment of it: "The metamorphosis has failed to change him. He dies, as he lived, a thing" (p. 79). And yet Gregor's death is the moment at which the reader feels most strongly the ambivalence of the story's physical outcome. By positing some unrealistic, quasimystical notion of "inward change," Politzer fails to notice the substantive change that is actually taking place in Gregor, through his unyielding fidelity to his own past.

28. *E*, 132.

29. Jürg Schubiger, *"Die Verwandlung"—eine Interpretation* (Zurich: Atlantis, 1969), p. 52.

30. Günther Anders, *Kafka Pro und contra* (Munich: C.H. Beck, 1951), p. 20.

31. Wilhelm Emrich, *Franz Kafka* (Bonn: Athenäum, 1958), p. 127.

32. Wilhelm Emrich, *Franz Kafka*, p. 123.

JOHN WINKELMAN

The Liberation of Gregor Samsa

Ifit could be established with a given degree of probability that Franz Kafka's *Die Verwandlung*[1] is a conscious and intentional adaptation of a particular work of literature, this fact could become the basis for correspondingly cogent inferences as to the meaning of this enigmatic but intriguing story which has been, in the words of Stanley Corngold, "the commentators' despair."[2] No effort has been made to establish such a relationship between this story and any other work of literature, although various works have been suggested as "sources" in a more superficial sense that permits no such inference.

Idris F. Parry[3] and Victor Erlich[4] saw Gogol's "The Nose" as a source for *Die Verwandlung*. Mark Spilka perceived sources for the story in Dostoyevsky's *The Double* and Dickens's *David Copperfield*.[5] Heinz Politzer proposed instead Grillparzer's *Der arme Spielmann*.[6] Evelyn T. Beck suggested that Kafka was influenced particularly by the Yiddish play "Der wilde Mensch" by Jakob Gordin.[7] None of these approaches has been successful in clarifying the story as a whole.

Another suggested source has been the medieval epic *Gregorius* by Hartmann von Aue. This approach dates back to Klaus Wagenbach's discovery that in 1902 Kafka attended, while a student in the Prague university, a course of lectures on Hartmann von Aue.[8] Following up on this lead, Heinz Politzer suggested that the name of Kafka's hero, Gregor,

From *Crisis and Commitment: Studies in German and Russian Literature in Honour of J. W. Dyck*. Edited by John Whiton and Harry Loewen, pp. 237–246. © 1983 by the University of Waterloo Press.

might be based on that of Hartmann's protagonist; however, Politzer merely made this suggestion in a footnote and did not base his analysis of the story on the possible relation between the two stories.[9] Kurt Weinberg pursued the matter in greater detail and took note not only of the similarity of the names but also of the fact that the age of Gregor's sister Grete, seventeen, corresponds to the number of years that Gregorius was chained to the rock on his island and that the motif of incest, so central in the medieval epic, recurs in the relationship of Gregor and his sister. He also suggested that the brutal cleaning woman in Kafka's story was modeled on the (first) fisher's wife in *Gregorius*. Thereafter, however, Weinberg shifted his ground and sought parallels in the Bible and church history, with the result that no clear relational between *Gregorius* and *Die Verwandlung* emerges from Weinberg's discussion.[10] Finally, Klaus Köhnke noted additional similarities between Gregorius and his modern namesake: like the former at the end of his ordeal, Gregor is a horrible sight; both are outcasts; Gregor conceals himself behind a sheet just as Gregorius hid his nakedness from the Roman legates with leaves; both are deprived of food; Gregorius was for a time a knight, and Gregor a lieutenant of the reserves; Gregorius saved his besieged mother, and Gregor saved his economically beleaguered family from their creditors; and like Gregorius, Gregor is a "guoter sündaere" who is punished for unwitting transgressions.[11]

The similarity of the names Gregorius and Gregor is perhaps the most striking common feature of the two works to emerge from this discussion. However, other hypotheses regarding the name of Kafka's hero have been put forward. Edmund Edel pointed out that the name Gregor could almost be arrived at by transposing the letters of Georg, the name of the hero of Kafka's *Das Urteil*.[12] Ruth K. Angress theorized that Kafka may have based the name Gregor on that assumed by the hero of Leopold von Sacher-Masoch's novel *Venus im Pelz*, which she also viewed as the source of the picture of the fur-clad woman represented in the print which occurs in Kafka's story.[13] Franz Kuna suggested that Gregor Samsa's last name could have been derived from that of Sacher-Masoch himself, by reversing the letters "mas" of Masoch and adding the first two letters of Sacher.[14] Finally, Hartmut Binder pointed out that the name could also have been derived in its entirety from Jakob Wassermann's *Die Geschichte der jungen Renate Fuchs*, a novel known to Kafka, in which a minor character named Gregor Samassa appears.[15]

More decisive than any of the arguments seeking to link Kafka's story with Hartmann's epic or other sources is the fact, hitherto unnoticed, that Gregor Samsa is imprisoned in his room for seventeen months, just as Gregorius was chained to his rock for seventeen years. This chronological similarity is built into the very fabric of the narrative and therefore links it inextricably to *Gregorius*.

Kafka began writing *Die Verwandlung* on November 17, 1912,[16] and the story likewise begins on November 17. Binder comments merely that the season of the year is the same in both cases, but the correspondence of the very date may be demonstrated from the story itself, which in this respect at least does not seem to be any "revelation of a dream-like inner life" but is quite consciously contrived. Kafka establishes the time as November by the fact that the weather is at first cool (E 92) and after one month cold weather has set in and storm windows have been installed (E 105). Moreover at the beginning of the story it is a slack period in Gregor Samsa's line of work, that of a traveling salesman of yard goods (E 82), an allusion to the pre-Christmas slump in textile sales with which Kafka would have been familiar because of his father's involvement in the business of fashion accessories.[17] The precise date is established by the chronological details of the opening scene. Perhaps a quarter of an hour after awakening, Gregor looks at his alarm clock and sees that it is 6:30 or rather, the light still being rather dim, he corrects himself and realizes that it is almost 6:45 (E 73). Later he sees that it is 7:00 (E 77). Thereafter it continues to grow ever lighter for perhaps another quarter of an hour (E 87). Now in Prague on November 17, 1912 dawn occurred at 5:43 and sunrise at 7:16,[18] which corresponds exactly with these circumstances of the story.

Having gone out of his way to establish this chronology, Kafka continues throughout the story to inject details respecting its duration. On E 106 we learn that one month has elapsed. Section II ends with the father's wounding Gregor by hurling an apple at him, an incident occurring two months after the opening of the story (E 110). Section III begins after the lapse of a little more than one additional month (E 118).

Thus, to recapitulate, Section I takes place on November 17. By the end of Section II it is January 17. At the beginning of Section III it is a few days after February 17.

Section III abounds in details suggesting the lapse of much time. Both the mother and Grete secure gainful employment (E 119). The father's uniform gets dirtier and dirtier (E 120), an implausible detail having no apparent purpose besides suggesting the passage of time; for the bank in which the father works in a minor capacity would scarcely tolerate his slovenly appearance. The father, mother, and sister are "abgearbeitet und übermüdet." The servant girl is dismissed and replaced by a cleaning woman. Family heirlooms are sold (E 121). Gregor spends his "Nächte und Tage fast ganz ohne Schlaf." He remembers his employer and fellow-workers as well as other details of his life before his metamorphosis "wieder nach langer Zeit" (E 122). Grete ceases to select Gregor's food with care or clean his room conscientiously. "In der ersten Zeit" Gregor protests against Grete's neglect but later he is forced to resign himself to it (E 123). The family takes in boarders. Gregor's room becomes the repository for excess furniture and other trash (E 125 f.). At some time during the period covered by Section III the mother thoroughly washes and scrubs Gregor's room (E 123), but by the end of the section it is in a filthy state, full of masses of dust, lint, hair, and garbage (E 129). At the conclusion of the story it is the end of March (E 138) and Grete, who in the first two sections was seventeen years of age (E 104) and "nur ein Kind" (E 107), has matured into "einem schönen and üppigen Mädchen" of marriageable age (E 142).

The text of Section III, unlike that of the other two, employs many words or phrases denoting repeated or habitual action and thus suggesting duration of time. The door between Gregor's room and the living room "die er schon ein bis zwei Stunden vorher scharf zu beobachten *pflegte* [wurde] *immer* gegen Abend geöffnet." Thus he is permitted to listen in on the family conversations "ganz anders als *fraher.*" These conversations are unlike those "der *früheren* Zeiten." Life in the Samsa home "ging *jetzt meist* nur sehr still zu." As a regular part of the new evening routine the father "schlief bald nach dem Abendessen in seinem Sessel ein" and "die Mutter nähte . . .; die Schwester . . . lernte . . . *Manchmal* wachte der Vater auf . . . und sagte zur Mutter: 'Wie lange du heute *schon wieder* nähst!'" The usage of the past tense is represented in English by "would fall asleep, would sew, would study, would wake up and say, etc." (These and a few similar examples are found on E 119; emphasis added.) "Gregor sah *oft* ganze Abende lang auf dieses . . . Kleid," "[Er] bestand *immer* darauf," "trotzdem er *regelmässig* einschlief," "[Der Vater] *pflegte* zu sagen" (E 120, emphasis added; most of the verb tenses again express habitual action: "would sleep, would try to rouse and persuade, would always insist, etc.") Every page thereafter through E 127 provides many similar examples.

Section III also expresses the passage of time by the frequent use of the past perfect tense, which denotes action preceding a past point of reference and thus suggests an added dimension of temporal depth: "verloren hatte, gedacht hatte, hatte werfen müssen, angenommen hatte" (E 119). This device also continues to E 127.

This constant and detailed temporal reference makes *Die Verwandlung* unique among Kafka's stories and novels. It is not a typical stylistic mannerism but a device adopted only here in line with Kafka's purposes in this particular story.

Now if we designate the date of the opening scene as November 17 of year N and interpret the text to mean that at the conclusion of the story it is the end of March of year N+1, the elapsed time of Section III would be approximately five weeks, insufficient time for all the events and changes described above and out of keeping with the stylistic devices which have been described. Furthermore, Gregor's musing "vergangene Weihnachten—

Weihnachten war doch wohl schon vorüber?" (E 130) cannot refer to Christmas of year N, for the fact that at the beginning of Section III it is past February 17 of year N+1 is, like everything else preceding Gregor's death, told from Gregor's point of view. Hence at that point Gregor *knew* that Christmas was past; only later does he lose track of time (the fact that the story ends in late March is stated by the author himself). And finally, the process of Grete's physical and sexual maturation could not have been consummated in five weeks.

It therefore follows that the story begins in November of year N and ends in March of year N+2; hence the total elapsed time is seventeen months.

This provides us for the first time with a solid link to Hartmann von Aue's *Gregorius*. Just as Gregorius was chained to his rock for seventeen years, Gregor is confined to his room and to the prison of his insect shell for seventeen months. This is no superficial link like the mere similarity of names which alone, as has been shown, is not conclusive. It is a link which permeates every aspect of Kafka's story and therefore must have been consciously and intentionally built into it by Kafka in order to identify it as a version of the Gregorius myth. The argument based on this analogy is supplemented by additional similarities between the two stories, to wit: the correspondence of the names Gregor and Gregorius; the shared theme of incestuous love, explicit in Hartmann's epic and clearly implied in Kafka's story (E 123 f., 130); the fact that Kafka made his sister Ottla, twenty years old at the time, over into the seventeen-year-old Grete; the fact that Kafka, to avoid the incongruity of a Jewish Gregorius, made the family Catholic (on E 99 Grete calls on the saints and on E 138 the entire family make the sign of the cross); the fact that he caused the beginning of the story as well as the writing of it to fall on November 17; and the fact that the story takes occasion to note the length of elapsed time on December 17, January 17, and February 17.

Why, we may then ask, does Kafka model his story on Hartmann's *Gregorius*? Is *Die Verwandlung* in the nature of a parody, in which case the narrative would be obviously similar but the message the opposite, or a disguised retelling, in which case the narrative would be altered almost beyond recognition but the message remain the same? The latter is the case.

The Prologue of Hartmann's *Gregorius* states the message of the epic: God will forgive any repentant sinner, however heinous his sin, provided that the sinner does not despair of God's mercy. To illustrate this moral Hartmann lays a twofold burden of sin on his hero, who is both the product and the unwitting perpetrator of incest, to the medieval mind one of the greatest sins. Discovering his guilt and filled with a sense of his worthlessness, he seeks to atone for his sins by having himself chained to a lonely rock where he endures exposure to the elements with no sustenance except for water provided by the Holy Ghost (*Gregorius*, ll. 3114–3131).[19] After seventeen years, almost as horribly emaciated and as gruesome a sight as Gregor at the time of his death (*Gregorius*, ll. 3449–3465), he attains God's forgiveness, is rescued, and is elevated to popehood.

All these narrative details Kafka distorts almost but not quite beyond recognition. The lonely rock becomes an equally lonely Prague bedroom. The sea surrounding Gregorius's island takes the form of the doors which cut Gregor's room off from the rest of the apartment.[20] The key to Gregorius's lock, so prominent and necessary in Hartmann's epic, becomes the key to Gregor's room and there takes on a prominence which in purely narrative terms it does not deserve (E 85 f.). The loathsome sinner becomes an even more loathsome insect, which is not only horrible to the sight but also sickening to the sense of smell (E 92, 105). The rain which pelted Gregorius now beats against Gregor's windows. The office of the Holy Ghost is assumed by Grete. Just as Gregorius was for a time a knight errant, Gregor before his metamorphosis was the modern equivalent, a traveling salesman. The elements of incest and near-starvation are carried over, with modifications, from one story to the other.

Whereas the narrative as such is changed, the message is retained: redemption may be achieved through repentance and atonement.

The story of *Die Verwandlung* may be summarized as one of ever greater outward degradation accompanied by ever greater inward purification. Immediately after Gregor's metamorphosis into an insect he craves spoiled leftovers as food (E 98). After approximately one month no food appeals to him (E 108), and thereafter he scarcely eats at all (E 122 f.). As his appetite for food in a material sense atrophies, a yearning for spiritual sustenance takes its place (E 128). This corresponds to the water which in Hartmann's *Gregorius* is supplied by the Holy Ghost and keeps the "guoter sündaere" alive for seventeen years; for Hartmann too must have meant the water to symbolize spiritual sustenance. Hearing his sister playing the violin, Gregor is surprised by the fact that he has come to respond to music whereas formerly, even in his human phase, he had not had any feeling for it. He now senses in music, which alone among the arts is not bound to any visible or tangible substance and so may be said to represent pure spirit, and particularly in the music of the violin, the most ethereal of all instruments, the way to the nourishment which he craves (E 130).

At the outset his head was still filled with the mundane concerns which had preoccupied him as a traveling salesman: train connections, professional rivalry and envy, office politics (E 72–74, 79, 88 f.). After a time all such matters seem trivial and remote (E 122) and by the time of his death are supplanted by the nobler feeling of love for his family despite the fact that everyone in it, even to some extent his mother, has so egregiously and ungratefully deceived, betrayed, and physically maltreated him (E 136; 91, 92 f., 101–103,

117 f., 123, 133–136). A second metamorphosis has taken place. The first had only changed his body. The second has elevated his soul. No doubt this is the metamorphosis to which the title refers: for the title of a story should pertain to events which take place in it, not an event which precedes it.

To all of this it may be objected that Gregor at the end is swept up by the cleaning woman and discarded with the garbage (E 140 f.), unlike Gregorius, who after his spiritual purification is elevated to the highest office in Christendom. This argument confuses spiritual and material categories and is moreover irrelevant, for the story does not end with Gregor's death. Just as Pope Gregorius was able to grant absolution to both his parents (*Gregorius*, ll. 3831–3958), Gregor by his death brings relief and the prospect of a happy life to his family. He is symbolically reincarnated in Grete—hence the similarity of the names—as a token of his spiritual transfiguration. The fact that Kafka, who could easily have ended the story with the death of Gregor, nevertheless found it necessary to add a cheerful epilogue even though he—the most sensitive and self-critical of artists—knew it to be esthetically wrong[21] proves that it was central to his intention that the story end on a positive note of spiritual victory.[22]

It may be argued that Kafka even improved on his original. Hartmann inflicted as much degradation on his Gregorius as he could within the human framework. By leaving the limitations of the human realm and changing his Gregor into a verminous and malodorous insect, Kafka was able to carry degradation to its ultimate extreme and thereby begin the process of redemption at the very bottom of the scale. Hartmann has his hero find recompense for his sufferings—worldly glory—in this life, so that in the epic spiritual improvement is rewarded by material gain. This is as if Kafka had caused his Gregor, after the latter had suffered enough, to resume his human form and enjoy some sort of earthly reward. In that way he would have retained the incongruity inherent in the original. Instead, the theme being mortification of the flesh and salvation of the spirit, Kafka carried it to a logical conclusion which left body and spirit at their opposite poles. His Gregor dies even more ignominiously than he had lived but his spirit is set free. To devise an ending that would imply this while still being of a piece with the rest of the story was of course a difficult problem.

With respect to ready comprehensibility *Die Verwandlung* certainly falls short of *Gregorius*. Hartmann thoroughly motivates the punishment he visits upon his hero, who is both the child and the perpetrator of incest, and he motivates his salvation by causing his involvement to be involuntary; Hartmann's Gregorius is a "guoter sündaere." Kafka too meant his hero's sufferings to be understood as a punishment; in a letter to his publishers, the Kurt Wolff Verlag, he suggested that *Die Verwandlung* be published together with *Das Urteil* and *In der Strafkolonie* under the collective title *Strafen*.[23]

But for what transgression is Gregor Samsa punished? The problem is compounded, but its solution perhaps facilitated, by the fact that on an earlier occasion Kafka had proposed combining *Die Verwandlung* with *Der Heizer* (Chapter One of *Amerika*) and *Das Urteil* under the collective title *Söhne* (Br 115). A final clue is provided by Kafka's statement that if *Die Verwandlung* were to be published in conjunction with *Das Urteil* and *In der Strafkolonie* it should be placed second as a transition between them. Juxtaposing *Das Urteil* and *In der Strafkolonie* without *Die Verwandlung* as a bridge "hieße wirklich zwei fremde Köpfe mit Gewalt gegen einander schlagen" (Br 149).

The third of these clues would appear to be the most helpful, especially in conjunction with the other two. *Das Urteil* is simply autobiographical and was so perceived by Kafka himself (T 296 f.). *In der Strafkolonie*, by contrast, is not autobiographical but universal. It represents the world as a penal colony, all of whose human inhabitants are ipso facto guilty; it deals with the theme of original sin *sub specie aeternitatis*. In *Das Urteil* a son is punished; hence it is included in both *Strafen* and *Söhne*. In the case of *In der Strafkolonie* all men are punished; hence it is included in *Strafen* but not in *Söhne*. *Die Verwandlung* can serve as a bridge between *Das Urteil* and *In der Strafkolonie* because it is both universal and autobiographical. Whereas the name Gregor, as an allusion to Hartmann's epic, reflects the story's universal intention, the name Samsa, as a disguised form of Kafka, reflects its particular application.

Insofar as *Die Verwandlung* is a story of universal import like *In der Strafkolonie*, it may, like the latter, dispense with motivation; indeed, strictly speaking, it must. Simply to be human is to share in original sin, in other words in the innate human predisposition to evil. To some extent this consideration applies also to *Die Verwandlung* as an autobiographical document; for if all men are evil, then Franz Kafka is evil and merits punishment. However, by implication this reasoning subordinates the autobiographical to the universal aspect, in contrast to the story itself, which is very conspicuously autobiographical.

Die Verwandlung embodies more autobiographical allusions than any other work by Kafka. Samsa is obviously "a cryptogram for Kafka (s = k), even though in conversation with Janouch Kafka stressed that it would be wrong to equate the two, i.e., consider the character as merely autobiographical.[24] As Binder has revealed, the physical setting of the story agrees exactly with the floor plan of the apartment which the Kafka family occupied at the time at Niklasstrasse 36, with the arrangement of the doors between Franz Kafka's bedroom and the rest of the apartment, and even with the arrangement of the furniture in Franz Kafka's bedroom. As Binder also notes, the Kafka family, like the Samsas, had occupied their apartment for five years; the dietary preferences of Gregor Samsa prior to his metamorphosis had resembled Kafka's own; of Kafka's three sisters, Elli was married and living in her own home and

Valli was engaged, so that in a sense Kafka, like his Gregor, had only one sister (Ottla). Just as Gregor desired to finance Grete's study of music at the conservatory, Kafka later offered to finance Ottla's study of agronomy; and the overtones of incestuous attraction between Gregor and Grete are paralleled by such overtones in Kafka's relationship with Ottla.[25] A few additional similarities should be noted. The Kafka dwelling was on the top floor of their apartment house,[26] and so is the Samsa dwelling; for the top of the staircase is just outside their apartment (E 88). Moreover, the Samsa apartment seems to have the same number of stories beneath it as the Kafka apartment (E 91, 140). Like his fictional counterpart, Kafka was fond of dabbling in carpentry (E 80, 112; Br 14; T 547, 560). Like Gregor Samsa, who had begun work as a traveling salesman five years before the opening of the story (E 74, 101, 104), Franz Kafka began work with the Assicurazioni Generali in October 1907, five years before beginning work on the story, almost to the month.[27]

Seen from the autobiographical, in other words psychological, point of view, Franz Kafka's "guilt" as reflected in Gregor Samsa has to do with the author's relationship with his father; this is why Kafka included the story in a proposed collection to be called *Söhne*. Here a certain confusion arises. Gregor Samsa is not literally guilty of anything, not even, as has been alleged, of usurping his father's role as head of the family. Rather he is the embodiment of Kafka's illusion of guilt, and hence in this regard his "punishment" is no literal punishment but an attempted exorcism of Kafka's own phantom guilt. The origin of the latter was evidently a source of perplexity even to Kafka himself. In his "Brief an den Vater"[28] Kafka lays the blame for his irrational guilt complex at the door of his father. It is a moving and eloquent document but, as Kafka himself admitted, it is full of "advokatorische Kniffe";[29] in other words, it is purposely slanted to make a case against his father. Subtracting these artful "Kniffe," we are left with nothing but trivialities that do not explain anything. The actions he attributes to his father could have terrified only a child who was *already* timid and could at most have aggravated guilt feelings already present. All of this Kafka in effect concedes by calling his presentation slanted; yet his instinct correctly told him that the origin of his guilt complex somehow had to do with his father, and he even understood that it had to do with the *relationship* between him and his father rather than with his father per se. Moreover he seems to have suspected that his guilt complex ultimately went back to his discontent with his own puny body, which in the letter he contrasts with his father's impressive physique (H 168). Perhaps Kafka expressed this hatred of his own body by appearing in the story in the form of a repulsive insect. How much of this the naive reader could possibly understand from the story itself is hard to say. In any event the cruel and hostile father of *Die Verwandlung* is a phantom projection, not of Kafka's father as he really was, but of Kafka's perception of his father; and the "guilt" of Gregor Samsa, seen as an autobiographical figure, is a phantom projection of Kafka's phantom guilt.

The reader will be more easily able to comprehend *Die Verwandlung* as a universally applicable allegory. To do this he must see the story as a modernized version of Hartmann's *Gregorius* and furthermore he must understand that Hartmann's hero represents mankind as a whole, which like him is born with sin as its history and its fate. Such a reader will understand that both stories bring a message of hope but not of comfort: each man may liberate himself from the burden of sin but only at the price of great spiritual travail.

The two aspects of the story, its universal and autobiographical sides, converge by virtue of the fact that the message of Hartmann's *Gregorius* applies to both. Stripped of their fictional apparatus, both Hartmann's epic and Kafka's story convey the same meaning: withdrawal from the world, renunciation of physical comfort and pleasure, and devotion to solitary meditation can ennoble the spirit and liberate the soul. Kafka applied this message to himself as to all men, but for him it had a special application. To Kafka writing was a spiritual exercise, a "Form des Gebetes" (H 348) and required, ideally, total concentration made possible by a degree of isolation approaching Gregor Samsa's (F 250). As Gregor Samsa's soul was liberated by his bodily imprisonment, Kafka hoped to find liberation from his psychological guilt complex and from metaphysical guilt as well through literature.

NOTES

1. In Franz Kafka, *Erzählungen*, ed. Max Brod (New York: Schocken Books, 1946). Cited hereafter as E.

2. Stanley Corngold, *The Commentators' Despair: The Interpretation of Kafka's Metamorphosis* (Port Washington, N.Y.: Kennikat Press, 1973).

3. Idris F. Parry, "Kafka and Gogol," *German Life and Letters*, 6 (1953), 141–145.

4. Victor Erich, "Gogol and Kafka: Note on 'Realism' and 'Surrealism'," in *For Roman Jakobson: Essays on the Occasion of his Sixtieth Birthday*, ed. Morris Halle (The Hague: Mouton, 1956), pp. 101–08.

5. Mark Spilka, "Kafka's Sources for 'The Metamorphosis'," *Comparative Literature*, 11 (1959), 289–307.

6. Heinz Politzer, "Die Verwandlung des armen Spielmanns: Ein Grillparzer-Motiv bei Franz Kafka," *Jahrbuch der Grillparzer-Gesellschaft*, 3. Folge, 4 (1965), 55–64.

7. Evelyn T. Beck, "Kafkas 'Durchbruch': Der Einfluß des jiddischen Theaters auf sein Schaffen," *Basis*, 1 (1970), 204–223.

8. Klaus Wagenbach, *Franz Kafka: Eine Biographie seiner Jugend* (Bern: Francke Verlag, 1958), p. 100.

9. Heinz Politzer, *Franz Kafka: Parable and Paradox* (Ithaca, N.Y.: Cornell University Press, 1962), p. 77.

10. Kurt Weinberg, *Kafkas Dichtungen: Die Travestien des Mythos* (Bern & München: Francke Verlag, 1963), pp. 237–9.

11. Klaus Köhnke, "Kafkas guoter sündaere: Zu der Erzählung 'Die Verwandlung'," *Acta germanica*, 6 (1971), 114 f.

12. Edmund Edel, "Franz Kafka: 'Das Urteil'," *Wirkendes Wort*, 9 (1959), 216–225.

13. R. K. Angress, "Kafka and Sacher-Masoch: A Note on *The Metamorphosis*." *Modern Language Notes*, 85 (1970), 745–746.

14. Franz Kuna, *Franz Kafka: Literature as Corrective Punishment* (Bloomington & London: Indiana University Press, 1974), p. 37.

15. Hartmut Binder, *Kafka-Kommentar zu sämtlichen Erzählungen* (München: Winkler Verlag, 1975), p. 158.

16. Franz Kafka, *Briefe an Felice*, eds. Erich Heller & Jürgen Born (New York: Schocken Books, 1967), p. 102. Cited hereafter as F.

17. Simon Kuznets, *Seasonal Variations in Industry and Trade* (New York: National Bureau of Economic Research, 1933), p. 119.

18. *The Astronomical Almanac for the Year 1981* (Washington: U.S. Government Printing Office & London: Her Majesty's Stationery Office, 1980), p. A27. I wish to thank Mr. Donald Knapp, Director of the Planetarium of the Schenectady (N.Y.) Museum, for his assistance in the interpretation of the data in this almanac.

19. Hartmann von Aue, *Gregorius*, ed. Hermann Paul. Zehnte Auflage besorgt von Ludwig Wolff (Tübingen: Max Niemeyer Verlag, 1963).

20. Moss counts "almost one hundred references to the open or closed doors surrounding Gregor" in the story: Leonard Moss, "A Key to the Door Image in 'The Metamorphosis'," *Modern Fiction Studies*, 17 (1971), 37. To supplement Moss's statistical approach, it may be noted that the word "Zimmer," alone and in compounds, occurs 151 times, 68 of these with reference to Gregor's room.

21. Franz Kafka, *Tagebücher 1910–1923*, ed. Max Brod (New York: Schocken Books, 1948), p. 351. Referred to hereafter as T.

22. In the same vein Edel sees an optimistic symbolism in the fact that Gregor's death coincides with the dawn of a new day and the beginning of spring: Edmund Edel, "Franz Kafka: *Die Verwandlung*. Eine Auslegung," *Wirkendes Wort*, 8 (1957–58), 217–226.

23. Franz Kafka, *Briefe 1901–1914*, ed. Max Brod (New York: Schocken Books, 1958), p. 134. Referred to hereafter as Br.

24. Gustav Janouch, *Gespräche mit Kafka*. Erweiterte Ausgabe (Frankfurt am Main: S. Fischer Verlag, 1968), p. 55.

25. Binder, pp. 152–172.

26. Klaus Wagenbach, *Franz Kafka 1883–1924: Manuskripte, Erstdrucke, Dokumente, Photographien* (Berlin: Akademie der Künste, 1966), p. 60.

27. Wagenbach, *Biographie*, p. 142.

28. Franz Kafka, *Hochzeitsvorbereitungen auf dem Lande und andere Prosa aus dem Nachlass* (New York: Schocken Books, 1953), pp. 162–223. Referred to hereafter as H.

29. Franz Kafka, *Briefe an Milena*, ed. Willy Haas (New York: Schocken Books, 1952), p. 80.

J. BROOKS BOUSON

Insect Transformation
as a Narcissistic Metaphor
in Kafka's Metamorphosis

If Dostoevsky's ill-tempered Underground Man belligerently demands the notice of others, Franz Kafka's submissive human-insect, Gregor Samsa, who has lost the powers of speech, mutely signals his urgent desire for his family's attention. What we find openly expressed in the anti-hero's personality—the grandiose needs both to control others and be the center of attention—is repressed and thus expressed in a disguised way in the personality and behavior of Kafka's character. Like the Underground Man, Gregor suffers from a crumbling sense of self. But while the anti-hero only thinks of himself as subhuman, as an insect, Gregor Samsa, in contrast, *is* an insect. Thus to be empathically confirmed, for him, is not merely a way of sustaining his threatened self: it is literally a matter of life and death.

Provoked by the text, critic after critic has puzzled over the meaning of Gregor's transformation. Why is Kafka's character transformed into an insect? readers have long asked. Critical reactions to *The Metamorphosis*, which range from abstract philosophical and linguistic speculations to affective responses, reveal that the fantasies and defenses located in the text have been elicited from a number of its interpreters.[1] The defensive shields of fantasy, black humor, and narrative structure—*The Metamorphosis* is carefully organized around Gregor's repetitive enclosures and escapes—protect against but do not camouflage the horrors of Gregor's insect existence. And yet unconsciously responding to the

From *The Empathic Reader: A Study of the Narcissistic Character and the Drama of the Self*, pp. 51–63. © 1989 by The University of Massachusetts Press.

defensive stratagems of the text or attempting to fend off Gregor's fictional presence, a number of interpreters have likewise veered away from Gregor's situation, focusing attention instead on the sociological, political, philosophical, or religious implications of Kafka's narrative or on its linguistic puzzles or structural features. Other critics, reacting affectively to Gregor's plight, have reproduced in their criticism the angry substructures of this text which originated in Kafka's conflict with his family and his feelings of deep self-rejection. Such critics variously accuse Gregor, his family, or his exploitative economic system for his insect transformation. And still other critics have responded to Gregor's need for confirming attention and rescue. Engendering a potent reader-character transaction, *The Metamorphosis* re-presents and reactively defends against the narcissistic needs, anxieties, and vulnerabilities that inform it. What Kafka so poignantly captures in this story, as Kohut himself commented, is the experience of an individual "who finds himself in nonresponsive surroundings," whose family speaks of him coldly, in the "impersonal third pronoun," so that he becomes a "nonhuman monstrosity, even in his own eyes" ("The Psychoanalyst" 718; "Future" 680; *Restoration* 287). To depersonalize Gregor or turn him into a philosophic or linguistic abstraction, as some interpreters have done, is thus to reenact the narcissistic trauma presented in the text. In the critical conversation surrounding *The Metamorphosis*, we find an unwitting reperformance of key aspects of the text's hidden narcissistic script.

From the very first sentence of *The Metamorphosis* and throughout the narrative, Kafka focuses the reader's attention on the insect-Gregor. The narrator, located both within and without Gregor's subjectivity, acts as an objective reporter of his plight and as an extension of his consciousness. While essentially confined to Gregor's perspective and drawn into his inner world, the reader is also positioned at a slight remove from him, this partial detachment serving to ward off potential reader anxieties about being enmeshed in his claustrophobic insect's world. Encouraged to experience a wide variety of emotional responses, ranging from disgust and physical revulsion to pity and a desire to see Kafka's hapless anti-hero rescued, the reader, above all, is compelled to rivet attention on the insect-Gregor. Inscribed in *The Metamorphosis* is Gregor's protracted attempt to procure the notice of others so he can temporarily sustain his defective self.

The root trope of *The Metamorphosis*, Gregor's insect transformation, is a complex, overdetermined psychosymbol. A reification of his self-state, it reflects not only his inner feelings of worthlessness and powerlessness but also his repressed grandiosity, a grandiosity made distorted and grotesque because it has not been responded to empathically. Like the biblical Samson (the name "Samsa," as critics have noted, is an allusion both to Samson and Kafka),[2] he is at once enfeebled and imbued with secret, magical power. Both the suddenness of his metamorphosis and its magical, fantastic quality signal the eruption of the archaic grandiose substructure of the self and a surfacing of archaic feelings of omnipotence. Significantly, Gregor awakens as a "monstrous" insect (3) and he uses his "gigantic brown" body (36) to frighten others away. Although one of his initial worries, as he rocks himself out of bed, is that he will make a "loud crash" and thus perhaps cause his family "if not terror, at least anxiety" (8), unconsciously he wants to provoke just this response from those gathered outside his door. At the very outset of his ordeal, he, while disavowing his need for attention—he claims he wants to be left alone—listens to the discussion about him between the office manager and his parents, intent on not missing "a word of the conversation" (10). Later, when they stop talking, he imagines that they might be leaning against his door and listening to the noises he is making. Moreover, he is "eager" (12) to learn what they will say when they see him. As the office manager complains, Gregor is determined, albeit unconsciously, on exhibiting himself and "flaunting [his] strange whims" (11). Just as Gregor eavesdrops on his family and imagines his family listens in on him, so the reader is situated as an eavesdropper on the Samsa household. *The Metamorphosis* dramatizes, activates, and fulfills the regressive need for eavesdropping.

In the black comedy of his initial confrontation with the office manager and his family, Gregor satisfies his desire for attention and his grandiose wish to exert magical power over others. For when he makes his first appearance as an insect, his father clenches his fist as if to strike, then falters and begins to sob; his mother collapses; the loathed office manager, obeying Gregor's unconscious wish to get rid of him, slowly backs out of the room, then, his right hand outstretched, approaches the staircase "as if nothing less than an unearthly deliverance were awaiting him there" (17), and finally flees. But Gregor's exhibitionistic display is short-lived. His traumatic rejection at the very moment he shows himself points to a central cause of his self-disorder as it repeats and telescopes his experience of early parental rejection and the long series of similar rejections he has suffered throughout his life, these rejections pivotal in the formation of his distorted self-image.

Just as his family turns away from him, so the reader, while encouraged to sympathize with Gregor, is at the same time prompted to shun him as the text insistently focuses attention on his physically repulsive insect's body. And while we are meant, as one critic has observed, to "respond to the plight of the loathly son" in this scene, it is also true that "our compassion and our understanding seem mocked by the opposing image of a man shooing away a bug." In part, this scene reads like some sort of "grotesque joke" (Eggenschwiler, "The Metamorphosis" 206). Replicating the text's split perceptions of Gregor—that he is a repulsive bug and a dependent son in need of his family's support—critics are split on Gregor's nature. "When Gregor first appears before his family," writes Mark Spilka, "they are appalled by his condition, and their revulsion gives the full measure of his deformity" (*Dickens and Kafka* 77–78). While some critics claim that Gregor, as a vermin, remains "morally identical with his former self," which is "sweet, timid, and amiable" (Landsberg 130), others feel that his metamorphosis makes manifest his real parasitic nature (Greenberg 76) or that he "conceals" his "parasitical nature . . . beneath his solicitude" (Henel 154; translated by Corngold 135).

Punished for his self-assertiveness, Gregor is "pitilessly" (19) driven back into his room by his father and then made a prisoner. But Gregor's prison is also his refuge. Narcissistically damaged in each of his confrontations with the external world, he retreats to the protective isolation of both his room and his insect's shell. His public display rebuffed, he, from the refuge/prison of his room, attempts to defend his vulnerable self and become the center of his family's attention. Gregor's need for confirming attention is verified by the narrator. When Gregor, just after his metamorphosis, attempts to turn the key of his door, the office manager encourages him, "but," as the narrator comments, "everyone should have cheered him on. . . ." Gregor, in the false belief that they are "all following his efforts with suspense" (14), musters the necessary strength to complete his difficult task. Narcissistically defective, he needs external sources of approbation if he is to counteract feelings of helplessness and find the inner determination to act. In serving as an extension of Gregor's consciousness, the narrator makes Gregor the focal point of and dominant over the reader's perceptions and thus acts out, by proxy as it were, Gregor's repressed grandiose needs.

Two preoccupations which initially emerge in Gregor's sequestered, locked-room existence—a craving for food and for the eye glance—are narcissistic metaphors that express his desire for a nurturing, mirroring response. After his transformation, Grete, the only family member he feels close to, becomes his sole source of narcissistic supplies. When Gregor rejects the milk she brings him, he symbolically rejects his sickly, asthmatic mother who faints, that is, becomes nonresponsive, the first time he displays himself—this being a repetition of his early relationship with this emotionally unavailable and depleted woman. When his mother allows Grete to become his caretaker, she disclaims her responsibility for him and, in essence, abandons him. Disavowing his need to be noticed, Gregor determines he "would rather starve" than draw Grete's attention to his hunger. But he also feels "an enormous urge" to "throw himself at his sister's feet, and beg her for something good to eat" (23–24). When Grete first brings him food, he greedily devours the food that appeals to him. But the fact that what he eats is garbage does more than remind us of his repulsive insect state. It also suggests that his needs are not truly being met and thus serves to indict his family. In effect, he says through this behavior, "I know that this is all I'm worth to you. I'm garbage and so I'll eat garbage." Recognizing that his sister finds him repulsive, he hides under the sofa when she is in his room[3] and he fancies that she gives a thankful look when he covers with a sheet the small portion of his insect's body that protrudes from the sofa. In other words, he must efface and sequester himself—disavow his grandiose needs—to win approval and attention. Gregor's sensitivity to eye glances indicates his unmet, primitive need to be mirrored, to be the "gleam in the mother's eye" (see Kohut, *Analysis* 117–18). While Gregor craves attention, he also is ashamed to have others look at him, his shame a response to his exhibitionistic wishes and his distorted self. Emotionally abandoned by his mother, he finds a mother-surrogate figure in his sister. But tragically when Grete becomes his sole caretaker and thus becomes the center of Gregor's and her parents' attention, she begins to make narcissistic use of him as she asserts her own grandiose needs. Not only does she assume complete dominance over him, jealously guarding her caretaker's rights and flying into a rage when Mrs. Samsa cleans his room, an act that Grete interprets as a threat to her authority, she also begins to lose interest in him. As time passes, she comes to treat him more and more as an encumbering nuisance, an object.

Of perennial fascination to readers of *The Metamorphosis* is Gregor's initial reaction to his transformation. What shocks readers is passively, if not blandly, accepted by Gregor. Instead of reacting with open anxiety, Gregor thinks, at length, about his job and family; he becomes anxious about the passing time and preoccupied with his new bodily sensations and his strange aches and pains. In prolonging the narrative account of Gregor's initial discovery of his transformation, the text acts out what it depicts: Gregor's attempt to avoid confronting his diffuse, preverbal fears. Similarly, readers are shielded from full awareness of the anxieties subtending this scene. Despite this, the text discloses, in other ways, Gregor's sense of body–self estrangement and impending fragmentation: through his initial inability to control the chaotic movements of his insect legs and his later "senseless crawling around" his room (34); through his increasingly disorganized appearance, his growing lethargy and depression; and through his dissolving sense of clock time, an indicator of his loss of a sense of himself as a cohesive continuum in time. Suffering from a crumbling sense of self, he experiences what Kohut describes as the "fragmentation of" and "estrangement from" the mind–body self (*Restoration* 105). Gregor's metamorphosis gives experiential immediacy not only to what Kohut calls the "devastating emotional event" referred to as a "severe drop in self-esteem" ("Reflections" 503) but, more significantly, to the terrifying experience of the breakup of the self. As Gregor's fragile self falls apart, Kafka, as if unconsciously bent on aiding his vulnerable antihero, makes him more and more human in his needs and thus has prompted many readers to respond sympathetically to his character's growing helplessness and need for rescue.

When Gregor makes his second escape from his room, his mother faints and his sister, mirroring Mr. Samsa, responds first with open hostility and then by isolating Gregor, cutting him off from herself and his mother. Similarly, on both this occasion and the first time Gregor shows himself, his mother faints when she sees him, i.e., when he expresses his narcissistic needs and anger, and then he is rebuffed and attacked by his father and subsequently isolated by being locked in his room. Behind the manifest content of these repetitive incidents, which provide a mimetic recapitulation of infantile experiences of parental unavailability, rejection, and narcissistic injury, there lies an intricate cluster of archaic fantasies, fears, and defenses. The fainting mother, for example, suggests a telescoped memory of the nonresponsive mother and the anachronistic fantasy of the depleted mother who is harmed or destroyed through the infant's intense narcissistic neediness and rage. The hostile father and sister, moreover, simultaneously represent a telescoped memory of the angry father, warded-off aspects of the self—Gregor's enraged grandiosity—and a condensed image of the punishing oedipal father and the split-off "bad" mother who causes self-threatening, narcissistic injuries. Intrapsychically, all the authority figures in the novel depict both split-off aspects of Gregor's self and the omnipotent mother–father images. In a series of interlocking, peripheral incidents featuring authority figures, the three boarders assume power over the family only to be sent "hopping" off, insectlike; Gregor imagines telling his remote, godlike boss exactly what he thinks of him and thus making him fall off his desk; and he thinks that the office manager might wake up an insect one day (56, 4, 9–10). This repetitive thwarting of authority figures expresses Gregor's defensive devaluation of, projected rage against, and fantasied depletion or harming of the parental images as well as his abortive attempts to display his own sequestered grandiosity. Narcissistically fixated, Gregor exists in a strange, twilight world of resonating fears and fantasies. When he, in his current situation, reexperiences his primal traumas with his family members, his atrophied self slowly wastes away. Because he lacks a stable, cohesive self, he is deeply threatened by his own narcissistic needs and anger and by any behavior that he perceives as rejecting, neglectful, or hostile.

As Gregor's condition progressively worsens, he briefly succumbs to narcissistic rage, which is expressed as oral greediness. Angered at the "miserable" way he is being treated, he fantasies taking from the pantry the food that is rightfully his. He wants, in other words, to appropriate the narcissistic sustenance that he feels he is entitled to. But as his sister increasingly neglects him—twice a day she "hurriedly" shoves into his room "any old food" available (43)—he loses his appetite, begins to shun the scraps of food that she gives him, and thus slowly starves to death. When Grete becomes a mirror image of his neglectful, rejecting parents, he refuses the food she gives him just as he, at the outset of his ordeal, refused the mother's milk given him. Through his self-starvation, Gregor makes one last, desperate plea for attention as he masochistically complies with his sister's—and family's—wish to get rid of him. In mute protest, he sits in some particularly dirty corner when Grete comes in, attempting to "reproach" her for the filthiness of his room (43). But to no avail. Latent in Gregor's silent reproach is repressed rage which is later voiced by the middle boarder when he gives notice and considers taking some sort of legal action against the Samsas because of the "disgusting conditions prevailing" in the household and family (50). Instead of openly expressing his anger, Gregor responds in a seemingly accepting but really resentful way to his family's neglect when he observes how difficult it is for his "overworked and exhausted" family to find time to "worry" about him more than is "absolutely necessary" (42). Moreover, despite his mother's outrageous neglect of him, he defensively protects her against his anger through splitting: he keeps intact his conscious image of her as the unavailable (absent) but "good" mother and projects her "badness"—her rejecting, narcissistically injuring behavior—onto others. Hovering on the margins of the written text of *The Metamorphosis* is another more potent drama that is split off and evaded: that of the nonresponsive mother. A central cause of Gregor's blighted existence is his relationship with his absent, emotionally vacant mother.

In stark contrast to their neglect of Gregor, Grete and Mrs. Samsa do find the time to bother about, if not dote on, Mr. Samsa; moreover, the three boarders, who dominate the family, become the center of the Samsas' attention. Gregor watches while the family prepares lavish meals for the three boarders who then stuff themselves with food while he, abandoned, is starving to death. But though ignored by his family, he remains the focus of the reader's attention. Because he seems so much the passive victim, some critics have acted as his advocate and denounced his family members. Such critics, speaking for the mute, submissive insect and articulating his disowned hostility, verbally accuse his oppressors. One critic, for example, who describes "consideration" as Gregor's "basic impulse," condemns Grete for her "self-centered meanness" and Mr. Samsa for his "sheer animal hostility" (Rolleston 63). Another critic, who claims that the other characters in the story, especially the authority figures, are the "real vermin," comments that the "worst insect among the vermin in the story is . . . the parasitical father" (Spann 67).

When Gregor hears his sister playing the violin, he makes his final and fatal escape from his room. Although he is a hideous sight with his festering wound and filthy, deteriorating body, he feels no shame as he, in his desperate desire for human contact, advances over the clean living-room floor. At his most physically disgusting in this scene, he is also, to many readers, most touchingly human and thus most salvageable. Compelled because of what he thinks he hears in the music—authentic emotional expression—he wants Grete's eyes to meet his. He craves a confirming, healing gaze. Feeling as if the "way to the unknown nourishment" he longs for is "coming to light" (49), he wants to take Grete into his room and never let her out so long as he lives. His desire to exclusively possess Grete reveals his archaic needs. He wants to extract praise from her (he imagines she will be touched and admire him when he tells her how he had meant to send her to the conservatory); he wants to dominate over her (he disavows this need, imagining that she will stay with him of "her own free will" [49]); and he wants to merge with her power and strength. Not only does his plan miserably fail, he is both subject to the unempathic stares of the three boarders and made aware of how ashamed his family is of him when his father tries to prevent the boarders from viewing him.

At this point, Gregor, disappointed and weak from hunger, is verbally attacked. "I won't pronounce the name of my brother in front of this monster," his sister says to her parents as she pronounces judgment on him. "[A]nd so all I say is: we have to try to get rid of it. We've done everything humanly possible to take care of it and to put up with it; I don't think anyone can blame us in the least" (51). By refusing to recognize him as her brother, Grete invalidates him. Impaired, enfeebled, Gregor crawls back to his room, his "last glance" failing on his impassive mother who is "fast asleep" (53). Again, when he displays himself, his depleted mother becomes nonresponsive, he is punished, then locked in his room and, on this final occasion, left to die. Disavowing his anger and disappointment, Gregor, just before he dies, thinks of his family with "deep emotion and love" (54). Gregor's masochistic compliance and profound neediness have induced many readers to take his side and pass judgment on the family for their neglect of him. And the question which is asked when Gregor is drawn to Grete's violin playing—"Was he an animal, that music could move him so?" (49)—has prompted critic after critic to, in effect, rescue Gregor from his insect state by suggesting his newfound awareness of his aesthetic and/or spiritual needs.

When Gregor agrees with his sister's "conviction" that he must "disappear" (54), he expresses, on the family drama level, his feeling that his family is better off without him. This feeling is corroborated by the narrator's description of the family's cold, uncaring response to his death. "[N]ow we can thank God!" (55), Mr. Samsa pronounces when the family gathers around Gregor's emaciated body. "Stop brooding over the past," Mr. Samsa further insists (57). Abruptly, the family members leave off mourning and rejuvenate as they begin to celebrate their liberation from the insect-Gregor, their release from a shameful, secret family burden. In agreeing to "disappear," Gregor also acts out his deep self-rejection and masochistic desire to remedy his situation by effacing himself and thus nullifying his agonizing sense of worthlessness and defectiveness. Moreover, through his death he both punishes himself for his hidden aggression against the family and magically undoes his hidden crime against them. For as an invalid, he has passively exerted power over and devalued family members by obliging them to get jobs and thus assume with their employers the subordinate role he once was forced to play. His death, hence, revitalizes his family. In stark contrast to his sister's transformation— she has "blossomed into a good-looking, shapely girl" (58)—Gregor has been reduced to a thing, an "it." His "flat and dry" carcass (55) reifies his empty, depleted self. It is fitting that the cleaning woman, an embodiment of the neglectful, hostile aspects of the family, disposes of his body. Desperately seeking but never receiving the self-confirming attention, that "matrix of empathy" which Kohut feels the individual needs to form and sustain a cohesive sense of self, Gregor, in the end, is destroyed. His fragile self has been eroded, bit by bit, by the emotionally invalidating responses of his family and by his own sequestered anger. "The deepest horror man can experience," Kohut comments, "is that of feeling that he is exposed to circumstances in which he is no longer regarded as human by others, i.e., in a milieu that does not even respond with faulty or distorted empathy to his presence" (*Reflections* 486–87). In *The Metamorphosis* Kafka conveys, in exacting detail, the horror of such a situation.

Creating a compelling reader–character dyadic relationship, *The Metamorphosis*, which grew out of Kafka's quarrel with his family and with impersonal authority,[4] has incited endless quarreling among the critics. Ignored by his family, Gregor has been the center of a lively critical discussion as reader after reader has been seduced into explaining who is to blame for his condition. Some critics feel that Gregor is responsible. "[T]he final criticism," writes Edwin Honig, "seems not to be leveled against society so much as against Gregor, who sinks into his dilemma because he is unable to find his real self" (67). Franz Kuna, who views Gregor's metamorphosis as symbolic of his submission to the role of "economic man," blames Gregor for "allowing himself . . . to be forced into this subordinate and self-annihilating role" (51–52). Other critics blame the family for his plight. The family frequently has been condemned for their pettiness, their mindless cruelty, their parasitism on the preinsect Gregor, and their failure to love Gregor. Edmund Edel, for example, feels that after the metamorphosis Gregor needs his family's support but they fail "this chance of a humane existence for themselves" (trans. and summarized by Corngold 103). For Douglas Angus "the entire story is one long, varied and agonized appeal for love . . ." (70). Gregor's experience, in Carol Cantrell's view, "emerges as part of a coherent and destructive pattern of family life" (579).

A highly polemicized text, *The Metamorphosis* has provoked critics to make authoritative pronouncements on Gregor's plight—on who or what is to blame for his transformation—as well as on prior interpreters of the text. Stanley Corngold's description of how the "richness and subtlety and fidelity to the text" of a certain critic's commentary makes one "resent the intrusions and dislocations" of other interpreters (74) is not atypical of the irritable tone sometimes found in the criticism this text has engendered. Observing that the many interpretations of *The Metamorphosis* "hardly take account of each other" and "contradict one another in the crassest way," Benno Von Wiese, in an apparent desire to rescue the text from its interpreters, calls for "strict textual interpretation" of Kafka's work (trans. and summarized by Corngold 247–48). Meno Spann's anger against critics who denigrate Gregor is also revealing. Arguing that "the people surrounding the metamorphosed Gregor are the real vermin" (67), Spann denounces those critics who have denounced Gregor and who have, thus, missed the "paradox" which the "skilled reader" understands—namely that the actual vermin in the story are the "'normal' people" depicted in the text while Gregor "increasingly becomes a true human being in spite of his monstrous shape" (73).

And still other critics, acting out the needs to both ward off and rescue the hapless Gregor, have responded with interpretations which, as Benno Von Wiese aptly puts it, "liberate Gregor Samsa as rapidly as possible from his repulsive image and instead lend him a mysterious metaphysical status" (319; translated by Corngold 247). But some of these approaches, in depersonalizing Gregor, also repeat the central narcissistic trauma dramatized in the text. Wilhelm Emrich, for example, finds Gregor's insect state inexplicable. "The beetle is, and remains, something 'alien' that cannot be made to fit into the human ideational world. That alone is its meaning. It is 'The Other,' 'The Incomprehensible,' pure and simple, beyond the reach of any feeling or imagining. . . . It is interpretable only as that which is uninterpretable" (147). In Stanley Corngold's view, Gregor's insect transformation points to the author's "radical aesthetic intention" (9). "is it too odd an idea," asks Corngold, "to see this family drama as the conflict between ordinary language and a being having the character of an indecipherable word?" (11). Corngold conceives Gregor "as a mutilated metaphor, uprooted from familiar language" (12). He writes, "In organizing itself around a distortion of ordinary language, *The Metamorphosis* projects into its center a sign which absorbs its own significance . . ." (27–28). Is it too odd an idea to suggest that critics like Emrich and Corngold are responding to the reader's transient sharing of Gregor's intrapsychic world, a world that is frighteningly alien, distorted, and empty?

Kafka, in the words of Theodor Adorno, shakes the "contemplative relation between text and reader . . . to its very roots" (246). "A book for Kafka," writes Silvio Vietta, "should act as a blow on the head of the reader" (211). Temporarily implicated in the incognizable insect world depicted in *The Metamorphosis*, the reader palpably experiences Gregor's feelings of dislocation and self-unreality. No wonder some critics take refuge in the safer confines of abstract philosophic or linguistic constructs. That Kafka's narrative may also engender a wish in readers to escape from Gregor's proximity—a wish the closure acts out—is suggested in some observations made by Roy Pascal. Describing the "intense enclosedness of Kafka's stories," Pascal comments: "There is no escape from the spell they weave, scarcely an opportunity for reflexion, contemplation, for a relaxation of tension, until the spell is broken by the death of the narrator's chief medium, the chief character. And at that point the reader looks back in almost uncomprehending horror, cut off from this strange experience as the awakened sleeper is cut off from his nightmare" (57). While it is true that the narrative "completedness" of *The Metamorphosis* "forces" readers, in Pascal's words, to search out "the coherence of this apparent incoherence" (40), the fact that critics seem to feel strangely helpless before this text, which insistently demands and resists interpretation, suggests that the insect-Gregor's feelings of powerlessness may be induced in readers not only as they share Gregor's perceptions but also as they grapple with the resistant preverbal puzzles encoded in the narrative.

Creating in *The Metamorphosis* a character who is real and unreal, replete with meaning and empty of self, Kafka encourages the interpreter to fill in the deficit, the void that exists at the center of the insect-Gregor's self. Critics have long commented on the repetitive nature of Kafka's fiction. The "form" of Kafka's fiction, as one critic puts it, is "circular": the "basic situation" of a given narrative "emerges again and again like a trauma" (Anders 37). Reading *The Metamorphosis* through the lens of self psychology, we can gain significant insight into both the source of and our reaction to that central, narcissistic trauma.

Notes

1. For an overview of the critical response to *The Metamorphosis* up to 1971 see Stanley Corngold critical bibliography—*The Commentators' Despair*—which includes the work of American, English, Spanish, French, German, and Italian critics.

2. The Samson allusion has been noted, for example, by Norman Holland (148–49) and Jean Jofen (349). In a conversation with Kafka, Gustav Janouch commented that the name Samsa sounded "like a cryptogram for Kafka. Five letters in each word. The S in the word Samsa has the same position as the K in the word Kafka. The A...." To this, Kafka replied: "It is not a cryptogram. Samsa is not merely Kafka, and nothing else" (32).

3. Gregor's hiding under the couch recalls the behavior of one of the infants observed by Margaret Mahler and her collaborators. "[W]hen in distress," writes Mahler, "she would lie flat against the surface of the floor, or on the mattress on the floor, or would squeeze herself into a narrow space; it was as if she wanted to be enclosed (held together) in this way, which would afford her some of the sense of coherence and security that she was missing in the relationship with her mother" (94).

4. Essentially a family story, *The Metamorphosis* reflects, as many critics have noted, aspects of Kafka's life: his submissive relationship to his father, his alienation from his mother, his hidden anger and resentment, his hypochondria, depression, feelings of worthlessness, powerlessness, physical imperfection, loneliness, and isolation. Although

most discussions of the biographical elements of *The Metamorphosis* focus on Kafka's relationship to his insensitive, domineering father, which is well documented in Kafka's *Letter to His Father*. Margarete Mitscherlich-Nielsen, in her "Psychoanalytic Notes" on Kafka, offers an interesting speculation on his early relationship with his mother, pointing to a disturbance in the early mother–child relationship. "The early death of his [Kafka's] brothers and his mother's reaction to their loss—probably warding off emotion on the surface but deeply depressed beneath—," she writes, "must have had a profound effect on Kafka ..." (5). Equally suggestive are recent discussions of Kafka's narcissistic relationships with Milena (see Böhme) and Felice (see Bernheimer 152–61).

Kafka, in the words of biographer Ronald Hayman, used writing to "give him the illusion of inching his way towards his objective of being understood, of bringing the reader to know him as well as he knew himself" (198). In *The Metamorphosis*, Hayman comments, Kafka allegorized "his relationship with the family, building out from his sense of being a disappointment, a burden" (151). That Kafka was thinking of his own family situation when he wrote *The Metamorphosis* is revealed in the few recorded comments he made about the story. After its publication, he remarked to an acquaintance, "What do you have to say about the dreadful things happening in our house?" (Urzidil 18). In a conversation with Gustav Janouch, he described the story as an "indiscretion." "Is it perhaps delicate and discreet," he asked, "to talk about the bugs in one's own family?" When Janouch described the story as "a terrible dream, a terrible conception," Kafka responded, "The dream reveals the reality, which conception lags behind. That is the horror of life—the terror of art" (Janouch 32).

ALLEN THIHER

"The Judgment" and "The Metamorphosis"

Before turning to the two major stories of 1912, "The Judgment" and "The Metamorphosis," I should like to enlarge upon my discussion of Kafka's use of language to talk about language, or what is called metalanguage. This brief discussion should enhance an appreciation of these two stories as well as the rest of Kafka's work. To this end I shall consider a parable that Kafka wrote near the end of his life, in 1922 or 1923, and to which Max Brod gave the title "On Parables." The title reflects the fact that this is a parable on parables, or writing about writing, or more technically, a form of self-referential metalanguage. This parable about parables begins by noting that many complain of the uselessness of parables since, for example, when the writer or the sage tells us to "go over," he really has nothing precise in mind, and so a parable is of no use in practical life: "All these parables really set out to say merely that the incomprehensible is incomprehensible, and we know that already. But the cares we have to struggle with every day: that is a different matter" (457). But the parable goes on to say that a man once said that if we would only follow parables, then we would become parables and get rid of all our daily cares:

> Another said: I bet that is also a parable.
> The first said: You have won.

From *Franz Kafka: A Study of the Short Fiction*, pp. 33–50. © 1990 by G.K. Hall & Co.

The second said: But unfortunately only in parable.
The first said: No, in reality: in parable you have lost. (457)

This is one of the most teasing pieces in Kafka's *Nachlass*, and I have never been sure that I really understand it, but if the following explanation is approximately correct, then I think that this parable tells us a great deal about the struggle Kafka faced in undertaking his major writings.

As any logician knows, self-referential language—language referring to itself—is full of paradoxes, not the least of which is that a sentence can deny its own truth value (compare "This sentence lies."). How can language deny itself? For Kafka this property is not just a logical dilemma, but part of the dilemma of literature. For literature, in order to justify its claims, must speak about itself, and how can it do so without falling prey to the paradoxes of self-referential language?

In the parable "On Parables" the reader finds statements about the nature of literary language of which the statements themselves are primary examples. At the same time that they are statements about themselves they are also statements of a general nature about all parables or literary language. The mind has a bit of difficulty holding together the way that all of this functions: ordinary statements that at one and the same time are examples of metalanguage and are self-referential and are thus examples of the demonstration that the metalanguage would undertake. In a sense this is then a logical set that includes itself as a member. This is a statement about statements that is a statement, which has something of the same logical structure as imagining the set of all houses and saying that it is a house. We are pretty certain that the set that includes all elephants is not itself an elephant, so, how, we ask, can the set of all parables be included somehow in a parable? It appears that this set within a set is logically impossible, a contradiction, and yet we know that we must talk about language sets within language and with language.

In its modestly self-referential way the parable about parables seems to assume the necessity of logical contradiction in one of the two realms in which we can run our lives—in reality or in the realm of logical purity. The latter includes a realm of literature where language would function with a kind of logical necessity of which poetry can only dream. One can guess that a parable is only a parable, which means that, as Kafka puts it, one wins in the realm of reality; here one deciphers that his parable's self-referential language is merely an example of paradox. But with that stance one loses in parable that realm of logical purity that one might inhabit if one were able to listen to that language that would take one beyond mere paradox and bring us to the realm of necessary language, of law beyond contradiction and interpretation.

I am not sure that this interpretation eliminates the paradox of the parable on parables, or if it merely deepens it; in any case, this explanation should point to the kinds of reading difficulties and pleasures readers face when they turn to Kafka's major pieces of short fiction (including a good many pieces from the *Nachlass*). Kafka's fictions turn back on themselves, so to speak, in that they are forms of autorepresentation that use the kind of metalanguage and self-referentiality I have just elaborated. His stories ground themselves not primarily in some representation of external realities, but rather in that they are mirrors of their own functioning. Or perhaps one should say they reflect their own dysfunctional nature as logical paradoxes.

To paraphrase what many critics have said about Kafka, it may well be true that his works are reflections of an absurd world in which the emptiness left by the death of God, as Nietzsche put it, has been filled by the creation of a proliferating state bureaucracy, but the power of Kafka's work really lies in its power to sabotage the possibility of making any such clear statement about it. The works' power lies in their undermining any clear representational system or systems of reference that lies beyond the text itself. These stories refuse the referential grounding one needs in order to generate sense, as they designate, often in parodistically fragmented ways, how the fictions these stories contain can only mirror themselves as they attempt to represent a world. Mimesis in the sense of a symbolic representation is not excluded from Kafka's stories, but it is subordinated to a system of self-reference that points to the near impossibility of symbolic representation. And, as I suggested earlier with regard to the *Nachlass*, it is this sense of literature as a necessarily self-designating construct that marks the extent to which Kafka's work ushers in the era of postmodern literary sensibility.

With regard to the published work, it is with "The Judgment" that Kafka's narration first clearly begins to designate itself as incommensurate with any transcendent space of discourse that might allow the genesis of meaning to take place. "The Judgment" sets the pattern for which the parable on parables comes as a kind of ultimate—I hesitate to say—logical conclusion; Kafka's work closes in upon itself and becomes a self-referential interrogation about the text's relation to any other realm. In this respect the story comes to refuse the essential revelation that it seeks—the revelation that has been the goal of most modernist texts, as well as the scriptures. Kafka's work becomes a consistent demonstration of the impossibility of finding plenitude through language. And when he gives up on finding the Nature Theater of Oklahoma, his work presents perhaps the most radical example of a truly secular literature, for it marks the end of the modernist quest for salvation through literature.

I wish to stress this point, for one could well ask how many modernists, for example, the early modernist Flaubert who had such a strong influence on Kafka, could be said to have a religious side. But my point here is that the very structure of meaning in both realist and later modernist fiction of the early twentieth century is grounded in terms of a religious model: meaning is the making manifest of an absent discourse. Meaning is produced when the text is, in effect, read in terms of a logos, to use the biblical term, that would be its origin. Logos, I recall, is the term designating language's power to confer being. This originating logos, or discourse, exists outside the story. Realism in literature means that "reality" is a discourse that must be made present. And the proper reading of realist fiction means we read beyond the text and look for another text beyond it, which we call the "real" text or world (though, as "On Parables" suggests, it is not easy to win at that game). Realism means a story reveals some privileged essence in language that exists nonetheless outside of language, that is, in the realm of the real (and yet can exist only in the discourse that reveals that essence). In later modernists, such as Proust and Joyce, the desire to reveal essence, or "epiphanies" as Joyce, with a full sense of his religious mission, called them, offers us a comparable structure: the absent essence can be made present through the structure of language.

The goal of these modernist fictions is the disclosure of what is otherwise absent, invisible, unmanifest. In Kafka's work, on the other hand, the stories, seemingly laden with metaphors and symbols, may appear to aspire to this revelation of an absent discourse, a revelation of the transcendent discourse that would endow the narration with meaning and perhaps bring about salvation. But his fictions contain inscribed within themselves recurrent indices that show that this fictional language is to be read self-referentially. This self-reference stops the reader from making reference to a transcendent discourse. In Kafka language is fallen logos. His language is also metalanguage about that fall as it turns in upon itself in lamentation or, equally often, in parody of its aspirations to be that logos that the Bible places at the origins of what is.

"The Judgment" was written in one feverish sitting—late one night in the fall of 1912, after Kafka had been working for some time on the novel now known as *Amerika*. Kafka felt that this work was a breakthrough in his writing, though I have noted that he was not entirely aware of why this was so. I would propose that it was in this story that Kafka first found, perhaps intuitively, the narrative patterns that would increasingly predominate in the later stories. In this story the reader confronts a narration inscribed with signs of its own inadequacy, though in no systematic way. Systematic self-mirroring, as in André Gide's *The Counterfeiters*, can be a modernist technique that reflects a modernist's belief in language's capacity to double itself as a fullness, even if the novel is a tale of failure. In "The Judgment" the very fragmented and diffuse nature of the self-representation is part of a strategy to narrate a story that contains within itself a representation of its own radical incommensurability.

The third person narration in "The Judgment" seems to coincide with the restricted field of consciousness of the protagonist, Georg, a young businessman who works with his father. The story appears to present an objective narration in which the representation given to the reader by a neutral or absent narrator seems to coincide with Georg's own representation of his situation. (The narrator is absent in the sense that he, she, or it is never *in* the narration.) This narrative point of view is the one that promises, perhaps falsely, that the reader is entering an ordered realm of discourse in which meaning is generated according to well-known models. One of Kafka's favorite strategies is to exploit this kind of narration that, after a century of realist writers, had come to be codified as a form of discourse that guarantees the truth and stability of the represented world at the same time that it seems to offer a transparency through which the absent narrator promises to make present an absent but anticipated otherness. In Kafka's story, however, this use of a received narrative technique is the first step in ordering a fictional world that turns against its certain or transparent meaning in an ironic reversal.

Kafka begins the story by presenting an image of writing, for Georg sits mulling over the possibility of writing to a friend in Russia about Georg's forthcoming marriage or about his success in business. On one level this writing could be nothing more than the communication of a message, of information sent across a vast space. That space in a literal sense is the vast plains of Russia, though on reflection the reader may suspect that this is a space that, like the great expanse of China in later tales, no message could ever cross. Kafka starts the story, then, with a reference to the space of communication, or that space of infinite loss in which all messages go astray. Writing in this space of ironic reversals never really aims at an outer world, but only designates itself and the space within which it is enclosed. As the rest of the story makes clear, Georg's letter can never be mailed.

With this reference to writing at the story's beginning Kafka has inscribed within his text a double for what the reader takes to be a story's usual function. Like a letter, a story should transcend its own immanent space by performing referentially as a form of communication. This doubling is underscored when Georg, having finished the difficult task of writing the letter, continues to sit at the table: "With the letter in his hand, his face turned toward the window, Georg had remained seated at the table for a long time. As an acquaintance passed by and greeted him from the street, he had barely answered with an absent smile" (modified translation of p. 80). The image of the window here, as in the stories we have already discussed as well as in "The Metamorphosis" and *The Trial*, appears as an image of the desired transparency, of the opening onto the world that would allow the genesis of meaning and a communication opening out of the text. The constant play between inner and outer space in Kafka's settings often stands as an analogue for the relationship between the narrative space within language and an extratextual space beyond the closed labyrinth of the narration. Georg, the writer who has now completed his narration, seems to have trouble at this moment establishing a contact with some "exteriority" beyond the space that contains him. The passing acquaintance whom Georg scarcely acknowledges would, in this perspective, be another double in this network of doubles, in this case it would be a double for the friend in Russia to whom Georg's letter is addressed. And the absent smile is another sign of the absence that permeates this paradoxical text; it would be the ironic smile produced by the impossibility of making contact through the window that is often a barrier, not a source of illumination in Kafka's world.

The darkness of the narrative space becomes clear, to use a Kafkan reversal, when Georg enters his father's somber room for the first time in months. The representation of his situation that Georg made in his letter is somehow not adequate to account for the way the story suddenly portrays the remote inner space where the father sits in a corner hung with mementos of Georg's dead mother. The narrative movement is again doubled here by the image of reading. The father scans a newspaper that he holds to one side in order to overcome a defect in his vision. Not only does the father have trouble reading, but he also eats with little relish On the table stand the remains of the breakfast that the father has scarcely touched. Reading, especially reading newspapers, and eating or attempting to eat are recurrent motifs in Kafka's work, and their common presence in this first encounter with the father points to their doubling each other as emblems of sustenance. As a reader and as an eater the father initially seems inadequate. This impression undergoes an ironic reversal, for, if the father initially suffers from a weakness of vision, he can then claim superiority of insight when he imposes his interpretation of the family's situation on Georg.

In this first scene, however, the father is associated with the newspaper—an image of degraded language in Kafka's work—and with the sustenance he cannot ingest, with the food that the father, like Gregor Samsa or the later hunger artist, needs to stay alive. Deprived of meaningful discourse, incapable of nourishing himself, this sickly father is the first image of the interpreter of the law in Kafka's world.

Georg first confronts his father within the dark innerness of the house, which seems to double for the text's own enclosure. Here Georg learns that, according to his father's interpretation, Georg has completely misrepresented his situation to himself and to others. The paternal reversal begins when Georg tries to cover up the old man in bed—he wants to *zudecken*, and the verb here suggests that he might be attempting to conceal or to hide the father and hence the interpretation that condemns Georg's representations and writing. Suddenly the old man leaps up and, demonstrating his surprisingly superior strength as well as his interpretive skills, proclaims that Georg's marriage plans amount to no more than his being attracted to a whore. Denouncing the mendacity of Georg's writing, the father asserts that not only does he know Georg's friend in Russia, but also that he has been in communication with him and therefore knows that this supposed friend "crumples Georg's letters unopened" while he holds up the father's letters to read them through.

For the reader in search of certainty the friend in Russia, a faraway reader himself, now may seem to be no more than a projection of the father's fantasy. The friend is, as the father says, the son that the father had always wanted. Perhaps this claim lies behind the way in which the friend is curiously related to the father's newspapers, for he is described as being "yellow enough to throw away". All that seems certain here is that the friend is a distant reader about whom the son can never know if he has received his communication or not. And Georg thus finds himself, like the reader, trying to decipher a situation as unknown as the father's newspaper, that enigmatic text described as "An old newspaper whose name was quite unknown to Georg"—"mit einem Georg schon ganz unbekannten Namen" (Raabe, 31). Georg can now only imagine his friend—and double—lost and ruined in the remote stretches of Russia, separated by the impossible distance any letter would have to traverse before, much as in "An Imperial Message," a revelation might come to him who awaits a message from a privileged space beyond.

For having written his "lying little letter," and perhaps for usurping the powers of the father (it is significant that Georg is implicitly accused of wanting sexual potency as much as for his writing: the pen and the penis belong to the father), Georg is condemned to death by drowning. It is an incongruous sentence that is as grotesque as the judge who is now portrayed as an old comedian, prancing on his bed. This parody of justice and interpretation sets forth another of Kafka's basic configurations. If the protagonist can be condemned, then one inevitably supposes that this condemnation is the manifestation of a law and that the judge knows and can communicate the law. But if there is a law, if there ever were a law, it is known only by a clown father who divulges no more than the sentence the supposed law imposes. The law exists only as an absence. Kafka's fiction seems to ask readers to suppose they are witnessing the workings of a law, of a superior order, perhaps of a logos; but the decreeing of the judgment does not, any more than the existence of the narrated text itself, guarantee the existence of a transcendent discourse. All that one can say with certainty is that in this story Georg, the would-be writer, stands condemned for his misrepresentations—and this condemnation effects an ironic metacommentary on the story itself. This final bit of implied self-reference leaves the reader caught in a hopeless interpretive circle.

A dutiful son, Georg carries out the sentence. He rushes to the bridge to throw himself into the water; and as he arrives he grasps the railings "as a starving man clutches at food." Georg has now replaced the father as the one who is in need of sustenance. This need, here as in other stories by Kafka, can result only in death, withdrawal, and silence. Georg's literal fall from the bridge at the end of "The Judgment" is at once a death and a fall into silence, and perhaps the fall of discourse finally into silence.

There is something comic, however, in the way that Georg's fall is a performance. The charwoman covers her face as he rushes by her on the steps. And he performs his self-execution, as the narrator says, with the skill of the gymnast that, to his parents' pride, he once was. This idealized image of the son as an athlete provides another ironic measure for his fall. Another Kafkan pattern emerges here: the hero falls from corporal self-sufficiency to hunger and then to death and silence, as in "A Hunger Artist" or, as in "The Metamorphosis," the next story I shall consider.

In "The Metamorphosis" the protagonist's fall is perhaps more metaphorical than the fall in "The Judgment," since the hero does not literally dive down to his death. Rather, as several generations of bemused or horrified readers have tried to imagine with some difficulty, the main character, Gregor Samsa, awakens one morning and finds that he has been transformed into a vermin, an *Ungeziefer* of human proportions that may well stick in our mind as a big cockroach, especially since the *Ungeziefer* is an image of pollution and defilement. I recall that Karl Rossmann was also treated as a vermin at the stoker's derisive trial and that Kafka referred to himself as an *Ungeziefer* in his "Letter to His Father" to stress that Kafka was convinced at times that this image could best portray the fall from humanity into some state in which one's very existence was a profanation of the law.

The fall into verminhood very quickly becomes a fall from the language that might explain the fall. This fall is also ironically measured by the idealized image Gregor sees of himself when, scrambling to get ready for work as he learns to use his new legs, he looks from the inner space of his room, where he is isolated, into the outer family room or the room of community space: "The breakfast dishes stood in great number on the table, since for his father breakfast was the most important meal of the day, one he drew out for hours by reading various newspapers. Straight across on the opposing wall hung a photograph of Gregor, taken at the time of his military service, which showed how he, as a lieutenant, with his hand on his dagger, smiling in a carefree way, demanded respect for his carriage and his uniform" (modified translation of pp. 100–101). This idealized image of Gregor is also associated with elements that Kafka had associated with discourse and representation in "The Judgment." Gregor's father reads newspapers; he is a consumer of texts as well as of the nourishment that his big breakfast provides. In "The Metamorphosis" the father initially appears, like Georg's father, to be a weak figure—Gregor supports him and the family—but he is also the inhabitant of the unproblematic world where sustenance is available, in which the fallen discourse of newspapers fills time, and in which sons with military bearing can command respect. The utter antithesis of this kind of son is the son who exists as a profanation; and as such Gregor is excluded from the world of sustenance and language and becomes a being who wonders if garbage will satisfy him.

Kafka's story begins one morning when Gregor, a hard-working traveling salesman, awakens to stare down at his wiggling legs and wonder how he will get to work. Although he is a vermin who loses his capacity for language, he retains a human consciousness of his situation; and as in "The Judgment," much of the time the narrative point of view seems to espouse the character's perception. Kafka also broadens his narrative perspective at times to allow the reader to see Gregor as he is seen by those unfortunate enough to share his company. This strange and often comic dichotomy between Gregor's consciousness and his presence as a speechless vermin capable of making only "twittering squeaks" is heightened by the fact that neither Gregor nor his family ever ask how this metamorphosis could have occurred. It is as if he woke up with a very bad cold. Kafka is frustrating the doctor in every reader who wants to know the etiology of the sickness. Gregor is a monstrous presence that cries out for interpretation (which is a hyperbolic expression of Kafka's normal astonishment about the simple fact that things exist). Needless to say, interpretation has not been lacking.

In one perspective, for example, it seems true to say, as Wilhelm Emrich has put it, that Gregor "is interpretable only as the uninterpretable (*Uninterpretierbar*—which offers an appropriate Kafkan *Tier* or animal in the word itself). Or, from another perspective, as Stanley Corngold has expressed it, "One sense of Gregor's opaque body is thus to maintain him as a solitude without speech or intelligible gesture, in the solitude of an indecipherable sign. To put it another way, his body is the speech in which the impossibility of ordinary language expresses its own despair."

Kafka does, however, place interpreters of Gregor's actions within the story. His presence, acts, and intentions are interpreted, usually wrongly, by the story's characters, especially by the father. From this perspective it would appear that the characters again double the reader in hermeneutic inadequacy. The self-contained nature of "The Metamorphosis" also becomes clear when one sees, for example, that at the end of the first and the second part of the story the silent vermin is interpreted and judged by the father who, as an interpreter, stands as a comic double for the reader who attempts to decipher what Gregor's meaning might be. At the end of each of these parts the father's interpretations of Gregor's intentions result in violence that seems close to farce. In the first instance, when Gregor tries to return to his room, he has difficulty moving his new body, which lends itself to the worst of interpretations. And the judge-father gives the inexpert bug a good blow with a newspaper to drive him back into his own space. In the second instance the well-meaning beetle comes out of his room to try to help his sister, Grete, when his mother has fainted upon seeing her son. The father arrives in judgment again: "It was clear to Gregor that his father had taken the worst interpretation of Grete's all too brief statement and was assuming that Gregor had been guilty of some violent act" (120). The "worst interpretation" here results in the father's condemning Gregor, and so he bombards his scampering son with apples.

This strange judgment elicits the reader's interpretation. Apples recall the crime of original sin, but in this context I can hardly repress the feeling that Kafka is playing with Freudian notions about the relation of sons and fathers. The apples fly as if in some kind of farcical displacement of the castration fears that Freud ascribed to every son who would like to take the mother from the father. One should not, however, take Kafka's parodistic enactment of Freudian theory to mean that Kafka has written a Freudian allegory in which every event in Kafka's text illustrates some aspect of the way psychoanalytic theory describes the war between fathers and sons. On the contrary, Kafka's use of elements of Freudian theory—and this use seems quite self-conscious to me—is a way of disarming this interpretive tool before it can be applied.

In the scene in which the father drives the son before him with a spray of round objects the parody destroys the genesis of meaning even as it invites the reader to use a Freudian as well as a biblical framework for interpretation. At the end of the episode it is clearly a Freudian moment for Gregor when he sees his mother fall, half undressed, into the father's arms. Gregor decides not to witness the primal scene that, according to Freud, haunts all children; and so upon viewing this sexually charged scene with the disrobed mother, the vermin son loses consciousness. The loss of consciousness is like a censure that cancels out the erotic scene—though of course what is erased is always present as in an absence that reminds us that it is still there.

The two violent scenes of paternal judgment join the fragmented presentation of the kind of Oedipal indices described by Freud and become part of the parody of hermeneutics that underlies most of Kafka's later works. Kafka's inscribing in his text references to the hermeneutic quest is his paradoxical if oblique way of making manifest that revelation is impossible. He is using paradoxical metalanguage with a vengeance; these statements about statements declare the incomprehensibility of the very statements that refer to themselves. This configuration appears again in the third and final part of "The Metamorphosis." In the third part Gregor completes his itinerary; he has gone from a self-sufficient body to a withering away in silence. He is condemned to disappear, to die, and to become the rubbish that the sturdy charwoman can discard. As in most of Kafka's stories, the object of interpretation—the text's central enigma as it were—is never brought to any elucidation. It merely effaces itself, like a hunger artist starving away, before the incommensurate problems it has posed. The story's task has been to trace this itinerary, to present the way in which the hermeneutic quest runs up against death and silence, against an entropic passage to final disorder.

A contrast to Gregor's demise is the final image of "The Metamorphosis." Gregor's sister, Grete, also undergoes a transformation, though one that opposes Gregor's. She awakens to her body's sufficiency once Gregor has disappeared. Standing in contrast to a vermin's need for the kind of sustenance that art or literature might offer is the self-contained sensuality of the sister's body as she stretches out in anticipation of the joys of marriage. Kafka concludes his story with an ending that asks no questions:

> [I]t struck both Mr. and Mrs. Samsa, almost at the same moment, as they became aware of their daughter's increasing vivacity, that in spite of all the sorrow of recent times, which had made her cheeks pale, she had bloomed into a pretty girl with a good figure. They grew quieter and half unconsciously exchanged glances of complete agreement, having come to the conclusion that it would soon be time to find a good husband for her. And it was like a confirmation of their new dreams and excellent intentions that at the end of their journey their daughter sprang to her feet first and stretched her young body. (139)

Grete has become an animal whose sensually awakened body needs no language to express its fulfillment. The symmetry with Gregor is converse, for he has become the animal whose condition cries out for language to mediate it; and this symmetry invests the entire story. Kafka opens "The Metamorphosis" with a declaration that Gregor's fall was "no dream" whereas Grete's accession to self-sufficient sexuality is part of the family's "new dreams." Perhaps this is Kafka's final irony: nightmares express fallen human reality better than do dreams of animal satisfactions.

Any single reading of "The Metamorphosis" will be inadequate, and readers must go back to the beginning and follow Gregor's itinerary again in order to grasp the play of self-reflexive interpretive mirrors that Kafka has placed along the way. On repeated readings, using the principle of the self-frustrating quest as their guide, readers can experience a coherence and an emotional tonality that escape their baffled first reading. If the interpretive quest underlies the general structure of "The Metamorphosis," the story owes its affective specificity to the way that Kafka uses particular objects, images, and situations to mirror the quest and to force the reader to enter a diffuse hermeneutic labyrinth.

The presence of objects in "The Metamorphosis" would appear to be dictated by the code of realistic narration that Kafka respects even as he narrates a fantastic event (but only *one* fantastic event). Kafka puts objects on his narrative stage that one would expect to find in the apartment of a traveling salesman who works hard, but hardly lives well. The descriptions of objects, as in Dickens or Flaubert, would at first seem to vouchsafe a certain stability and veracity to Kafka's fictional world, for this world seems to rest on the same premises that make up our presumably stable world.

Of course the first effect of Gregor's metamorphosis, in spite of the presence of an alarm clock telling him to get up, is that it subverts the realistic code, for the realistic mode that promises stability and hence readability is juxtaposed with totally gratuitous instability. But the code of realistic narration is never fully destroyed in the story. The code continues to ground the fantastic in what is a very ordinary or quotidian reality, in what is a most banally and thus sociologically average world. The radical incongruity between the fantastic and the banally real is, I think, another expression of that sense of the impossibility of bearing the real which is found in the "Conversation with the Supplicant"; the fantastic and the real are essentially two ways of looking at the same world, what one sees is a matter of perspective, though rarely does one see both the fantastic *and* the real so clearly. This incongruity springing from the opposition between fantastic metamorphosis and the code of realist narration forces the reader to scrutinize those objects that, in Flaubert, once promised to reveal the essence of the real. For they now seem contaminated by the fantastic.

In "The Metamorphosis," for example, how is the reader to make sense of a woman's picture in a room in which an ordinary man can awaken to find himself transformed into an insect? "Above the table upon which an unpacked sample collection of drapery was spread out—Samsa was a traveling salesman—hung the picture that not long ago he had cut out of an illustrated magazine and had placed in a pretty, gilded frame. It showed a woman who, provided with a fur hat and a fur boa, sat upright and raised toward the viewer a thick fur muff in which her entire forearm had disappeared" (modified translation of p. 89). This strange, almost insulting image seems to acquire some meaning when, later, as Gregor's mother and sister begin to remove the furnishings from his room, Gregor tries to keep the picture in his room by pressing his vermin belly against it. The picture's own suggestive content plus the insect's comically sexual behavior obliges one to look for some kind of sexual theme here. Has Gregor's sexuality been projected onto or captured by some kind of fetishistic desire? Undoubtedly, but this reading—which one can hardly avoid—is short-circuited as soon as the reader realizes that the object on the wall is first of all an image, hence a form of representation, and as such, offers itself as another double for the story's representation of itself.

This way of reading the image through associations seems justified by the way that Kafka also associates the picture and its frame with newspapers, and newspapers are a recurrent emblem of a text's failure to have meaning or of inadequate language. The association occurs when, in the first part of the story, Gregor's mother explains to the irate chief clerk who has come to get Gregor for work how her dutiful son spends his time:

> The boy thinks about nothing but his work. It makes me almost cross the way he never goes out in the evenings; he's been here the last eight days and has stayed at home every single evening. He just sits there quietly at the table reading a newspaper or looking through railway timetables. The only amusement he gets is doing fretwork. For instance, he spent two or three evenings cutting out a little picture frame; you would be surprised to see how pretty it is; it's hanging in his room. . . . (95–96)

The chief clerk is indeed surprised when he views the room, though not for the same reasons as the reader who begins to grasp the way the textual elements tie together as self-referential signifiers.

Images can be associated with newspapers as forms of representation that fail to point beyond their status as doubles for the text itself. Newspapers in turn are associated with food, the sustenance that the story should give, but does not. After the metamorphosis Gregor's father apparently gives up reading newspapers aloud—perhaps a sign that he, too, is alienated from even this degraded form of logos?—and Gregor finds that his food is delivered to him on a newspaper by his sister after she finds that he no longer has a taste for the pure milk that he once liked:

> Gregor was wildly curious to know what she would bring instead, and made various speculations about it. Yet what she actually did next, in the goodness of her heart, he could never have guessed at. To find out what he liked she brought him a whole selection of food, all set out on an old newspaper. There were old, half-decayed vegetables, bones from last night's supper covered with a white sauce that had thickened; some raisins and almonds; a piece of cheese that Gregor would have called uneatable two days ago. . . . (107–8)

Rotten cheese on a newspaper, this is the food that Gregor "sucked greedily at."

For the fallen vermin, for our everyman in search of some sustenance commensurate to his situation, garbage is the only nourishment that is appropriate. And if the reader feels that Kafka is parodying both the reader's desire for spiritual substance and the text's capacity to give him or her any such nourishment, the reader is not entirely wrong. Old newspapers covered with offal seem to be all that remains of the Word that once offered tastier ts, an image that is at once derisive and plaintive in Kafka's world of comic anguish.

Not everyone is afflicted with such anguish, of course, such as the three lodgers whom the family takes in, briefly, in the third part of the story. They can eat great heaps of food before they turn to reading their newspapers: "They set themselves at the top end of the table where formerly Gregor and his father and mother had eaten their meals, unfolded their napkins, and took knife and fork in hand. At once his mother appeared in the other doorway with a dish of meat and close behind her his sister with a dish of potatoes piled high. The food steamed with a thick vapor" (128). The lodgers replace the family in a world where sustenance is a matter of course, where the vapor of a hearty meal seems to mask appearances, as does the smoke of their cigars when they turn to their newspaper: "The lodgers had already finished their supper, the one in the middle had brought out a newspaper and given the other two a page apiece, and now they were leaning back at ease reading and smoking" (129). The three with their full beards are related to those fathers in Kafka—fictional and real—for whom simple food is adequate and, by analogy, newspapers provide access to all that writing need reveal.

Kafka chooses precisely this moment when his three arrogant, self-complacent lodgers are ensconced in their chairs to make most clear the association between sustenance and art. Gregor's sister begins to play the violin. Having just said to himself (in vermin language, one supposes) that he is not hungry for the kind of food that the lodgers engorge with pleasure, Gregor is struck by the sound of music as if it were a call to some vestigial human part of himself. As Grete plays, Gregor comes out of his room: "Gregor crawled a little farther forward and lowered his head to the ground so that it might be possible for his eyes to meet hers. Was he an animal, that music had such an effect upon him? He felt as if the way were opening before him to the unknown nourishment he craved" (130–31). Kafka claimed to have no ear for music, which in a sense is all the more appropriate to this passage, for music is the promise of a sustenance that one cannot find, the promise of a revelation that does not occur as the notes unfold like so many foreshadowings of an annunciation. Gregor longs for a substance that nothing can grant him.

Objects—pictures, newspapers, food—function by representing within the text the inadequacy, if not the breakdown, of representation. This concern with representation also informs much of the way in which the Kafkan narrative unfolds; events, attitudes, suppositions in "The Metamorphosis" are largely grounded in misrepresentations. For example, after Gregor awakes at the story's beginning, he misrepresents his situation to himself. He struggles to get up and catch a train, wanting to believe that his newly acquired body is no more than a passing affliction, like a cold; and at the end of the story he still dreams at times of taking up his job again, of how with the next opening of the door he might "take the family's affairs in hand just as he used to do" (125). The reader also learns, after Gregor's awakening reflection on his situation, that he may have misrepresented his job security. As the head clerk storms about before Gregor's closed door, he yells that neither Gregor's security nor his reputation are as good as Gregor thinks. These are not Gregor's only delusions. It would appear that his family's situation, its capacity to get along without him and to fend for itself, has been misrepresented to Gregor. His father, it later appears, has some money set aside, and they are all capable of working diligently to make ends meet.

These misrepresentations are revealed in various ways, but especially by metamorphoses, as we see when Gregor, who is about to be judged by his father at the end of the second part, looks up from his vermin's point of view and sees the man looming above him in his new uniform. This sickly father, who, Gregor thought, was not capable of getting up in the evening, is suddenly a transformed man, or, as Gregor notes in astonishment, this was not the father he had imagined to himself. "Now, however, he stood quite straight up, wearing a tight, blue uniform with gold buttons, such as attendants in banks wear. Over the high stiff collar of his coat flowed his strong double chin. From under his bushy eyebrows pierced forward sharply and attentively the stare of his dark eyes. His usually disheveled white hair was combed down and parted in a meticulous and precise glistening hair-style" (modified translation of p. 121).

Like Georg in "The Judgment," Gregor has been guilty of misrepresentations, and perhaps it is this implicit guilt that underlies the hero's fall and transforms Gregor's father, like Georg's, into a judge, into a being of strength who can now march on the once dominant son. There is no stability in this tale of metamorphosis, however; none of the representations or misrepresentations are certain, and in the third part of the story the father appears to have lost much of his power. He again undergoes a metamorphosis as he sleeps evenings in his uniform, soiling his coat, and becomes another victim of the *Dreck* that covers everything. (Recall his appearance at the story's "happy end.")

In the third part of the story, however, the key and exemplary misrepresentation turns primarily on the sister. As a prelude to his disappearance, Gregor indulges in a final fantasy representation when he wants to bring his sister into his room. Having hungered after the sustenance her violin playing promises, longing for a spiritual nourishment that this parasite without language cannot name, Gregor imagines how he might give affectionate solace to his sister after her playing is rejected by the three boarders. This fantasy of solace, whose incestuous overtones continue a parody of sexual thematics, finds its counterpart in Grete's final interpretation of the vermin. As she tells her mother and father: "You must just try to get rid of the idea that this is Gregor. The fact that we've believed it for so long is the root of all our trouble. But how can it be Gregor? If this were Gregor, he would have realized long ago that human beings can't live with such a creature . . ." (134). Grete's interpretation is both true and false. Kafka is wreaking havoc on the law of identity with the dialectic of misrepresentation. By applying throughout the story the kind of dream logic that allows one to be and not to be the same thing, to be Gregor and to be non-Gregor the vermin, Kafka creates the possibility for paradoxical misrepresentation at every level in "The Metamorphosis." And one may well see in this suspension of the law of identity, if one wishes, a characterization of our contemporary plight.

I address the question of dream logic and the rhetoric of dream in some detail in the fifth chapter of this study. In conclusion, in "The Metamorphosis" dream logic is at work in the creation of a realistic world in which the fantastic can happen without changing the basic order of that world. Dream logic suspends ordinary logic, and in this respect dream logic collaborates with self-referentiality in the creation of paradox. As with Grete's interpretation of Gregor, as with Gregor's interpretation of his father, every assertion made from a seemingly objective point of view readily finds a counterstatement within the fiction itself. This is a basic Kafkan pattern in the later stories and the unfinished novels, *The Trial* and *The Castle*. This pattern in which representation is revealed to be misrepresentation or contradiction grounds the Kafkan fiction in its own series of deforming mirror images. Meaning is generated not by reference to exterior discourses that the fictions use only in order to cancel them out; it is generated by a constant play of reference from one element in the story to another and back again. And as these elements—objects, events, attitudes and interpretations—show themselves to be forms of metalanguage that deny their own validity, the final effect is the creation of a self-annulling reference system that is a demonstration of the infinite and therefore null possibilities of hermeneutics.

KEVIN W. SWEENEY

Competing Theories of Identity
in Kafka's The Metamorphosis

Although *The Metamorphosis* begins with Gregor Samsa finding "himself
changed in his bed into a monstrous vermin," the transformation is at this
stage psychologically incomplete, enabling Kafka to conduct a philosophical
exploration of the nature of self, personhood and identity. Given the nature of
the inquiry, it is significant that instead of providing a monologic commentary
with a consistent theoretical framework, Kafka offers a dialogical, polyphonic
work, an example of what Mikhail Bakhtin has called a "heteroglossia" of
opposed voices (262–64). Since Kafka does not privilege any one theoretical
perspective, the reader is encouraged to undertake what Gilles Deleuze and
Felix Guattari have called an "experimentation" (48–50), a process which
involves a recognition of the inadequacy of the respective opposed theories
and an acknowledgment of the unresolved nature of the debate.

Aiding the reader in this process of experimentation is the novella's
tripartite structure: in each section Gregor attempts to leave his bedroom
only to be driven back into it. Repetitive in this way, however, each section of
the work also advances a different and opposing philosophical theory about
the nature of the self and the maintenance of personal identity. The first
section presents a dualist conception of the person: Gregor is a consciousness
disembodied from his original body and locked into an alien organism. In
the second section, behaviorist and materialist views challenge the earlier

From *Mosaic* 23, vol. 4 (Fall 1990): 23–35. © 1990 by *Mosaic*.

theory. Finally, in the third section, both theories are countered by a social-constructionist theory of the self and personal identity.

* * *

In the history of Western, philosophical explorations of personal identity, John Locke's example of a prince's consciousness inhabiting the body of a cobbler is perhaps the most famous. At the outset of *The Metamorphosis*, Gregor Samsa seems to be a cross-species variation of Locke's prince-in-the-cobbler, with Kafka exploring a Lockean-Cartesian theory of self and personal identity. Like Descartes, Locke holds that a person (a self) is essentially a rational, unified consciousness. A person, says Locke, "is a thinking intelligent being, that has reason and reflection, and can consider itself, the same thinking thing, in different times and places.... For since consciousness always accompanies thinking, and it is that which makes every one to be what he calls *self* ... as far as this consciousness can be extended backwards to any past action or thought, so far reaches the identity of that person ..." (448–49). Thus to Locke, an individual is *personally identical* with someone at an earlier time, if the later individual can remember as his or her own the experiences of the earlier. Although he does not share the Cartesian ontological view that consciousness is a separate substance distinct from the body, Locke, as Anthony Quinton persuasively argues (396–97), agrees with Descartes's dualist view that the self could possibly exist independently of its original body.

According to Locke's memory test, the insect is certainly Gregor Samsa. Believing himself to be Gregor, he recognizes the bedroom, recalls Gregor's past experiences and worries about catching the morning train. A wide variety of mental phenomena (sensations, thoughts, intentions) are referred to, all seemingly connected to Gregor's psychological past. They support the conscious link to the past essential to the dualist theory of personal identity.

In keeping with the Lockean-Cartesian perspective, the first section of the novella highlights not only Gregor's consciousness but also his capacity for rational deliberation. For example, Gregor hesitates rocking his new body off the bed, thinking, "he had better not for the life of him lose consciousness ... [yet] the most rational thing was to make any sacrifice for even the smallest hope of freeing himself from the bed" (7). Sharing access to much of Gregor's interior conscious life, the reader sympathizes with Gregor's plight and tries to understand the rationale behind his behavior. In this narratively privileged position, the reader initially accepts the Lockean-Cartesian explanation for this bizarre catastrophe.

From this perspective, the reader sees Gregor as more than just spatially separated from his family. Outside his room, imploring Gregor to open the locked door, the family are excluded from sharing his trauma and only indirectly sense that something must be wrong. The locked room—"a regular human room" (3)—becomes a philosophical metonymy for Gregor's private mentality. His predicament symbolizes the philosophical problem of other minds: inferring the existence of a mind from physical events and external behavior.

In his *Discourse on Method*, Descartes discusses two criteria for distinguishing "men from brutes" (116–17), both of which play a role in the Samsa family's attempt to discover the truth about what is going on in Gregor's bedroom. First, only human beings *qua* persons have the linguistic ability to express thoughts. Secondly, while lower animals can do many things, some better than humans, they cannot act with rational deliberation but only react according to bodily predispositions. For Descartes, deliberate action and the rational use of language are the marks and test of a rational consciousness. Locke recognizes a similar test, although—citing the example of a talking parrot (446–47)—he is not as confident that only human beings can speak.

The Samsa family apply both of Descartes's criteria to interpret what is going on in the bedroom. On replying to his mother's questioning about not catching the early morning train, Gregor is "shocked to hear his own voice answering. . . . [It was] unmistakably his own voice, true, but . . . an insistent distressed chirping intruded, which left the clarity of his words intact only for a moment really, before so badly garbling them . . ." (5). These garbled sounds finally betray him when the office manager arrives, wanting an explanation for Gregor's missing the train. Startled by the manager's accusations, Gregor abandons caution and chirps out a long explanation. Family and manager are stunned at what they hear. "Did you understand a word? . . . That was the voice of an animal," says the manager (13). Realizing that his speech is now unintelligible to those outside his door, although it "had seemed clear enough to him," Gregor starts to lose confidence in his personal integrity. A metaphysical barrier now separates him from other people.

The family and office manager also doubt the rationality of Gregor's actions. Unable to understand why he continues to remain locked in his room, the manager calls to him through the door, "I thought I knew you to be a quiet, reasonable person, and now you suddenly seem to want to start strutting about, flaunting strange whims" (11). Clearly both family and manager find his behavior irrational and out of character. When he hears them call for a doctor and a locksmith, Gregor anticipates being "integrated into human society once again and hoped for marvelous, amazing feats from both the doctor and the locksmith, without really distinguishing sharply between them" (13). Gregor hopes that the locksmith will remove not only a spatial barrier but will reintroduce him into the human and personal realm. Spatial access and medical attention are seen as reaffirming what has come into question: Gregor's status as a person.

When Gregor does unlock the door and reveal himself, however, the family and manager are even more convinced of his irrational behavior. They draw back in horror at his insect epiphany and consider his entrance into the living room to be outrageous behavior. Wielding the manager's cane, stamping his foot and hissing, the father drives the loathsome insect back into the bedroom. Rational persuasion is deemed inappropriate. "No plea of Gregor's helped," the narrator observes, "no plea was even understood; however humbly he might turn his head, his father merely stamped his feet more forcefully" (18).

Faced with a being they believe to be incapable of linguistic comprehension and whom they see as acting irrationally, the family are in a moral and conceptual quandary. As the only being inside Gregor's locked bedroom who responds to their calls, the creature cannot be condemned simply as alien. Yet neither can it be accepted in its own right as a person. Their response is a compromise: they accept the creature as Gregor but take him to be suffering from a severe incapacitating illness. Adopting this attitude excuses his strange speech and behavior; they believe that he will be his *old self* again when he recovers. In the second section, both mother and father regularly ask their daughter whether Gregor has "perhaps shown a little improvement" (31). By believing Gregor to be ill, the family reconciles the opposing beliefs that Gregor still survives and that the monster in the bedroom is something less than a person.

The reader also comes to adopt a strategy of reconciliation, trying to bring together a dualist and a materialist theoretical context for the narrative. Although, as Harold Skulsky argues, it is implausible to interpret *The Metamorphosis* as a narrative of a "psychotic breakdown" (171–73), Gregor's mental states are so at odds with his transformed body that the reader gives some credence to Gregor's thought that he might be dreaming or imagining the whole situation. Lying in bed, Gregor muses that "in the past he had often felt some kind of slight pain, possibly caused by lying in an uncomfortable position, which, when he got up, turned out to be purely imaginary, and he was eager to see how today's fantasy would gradually fade away" (6). The vividness of his experience coupled with the doubt about its veracity suggests Franz Brentano's theory about the relation of mind to the world. From his attendance at lectures in philosophy at the university in Prague and his subsequent participation in a philosophical discussion group, Kafka, according to Ronald Hayman (35–36), was thoroughly familiar with Brentano's views as presented by Brentano's pupil, Anton Marty. For Brentano, mental phenomena exhibit *intentionality*: that is, all mental acts are aimed at objects which exist in the mind but for which no correlative object in the world might exist (i.e., one can think about or believe in the Fountain of Youth regardless of whether it actually exists).

The possibility that Gregor's predicament might be imaginary, even though the experience be vivid, challenges the reliability of his narrative point of view. By raising questions about the veracity of Gregor's self-conscious narration, the text makes room for an alternative conceptual explanation of Gregor's identity. Although the reader initially accepts the dualist perspective, Kafka gradually introduces an alternative to this original position, thereby raising doubts about whether the insect continues to be Gregor Samsa. As a result, the reader's attitude toward the underlying framework of the story begins to shift: while accepting the insect as Gregor, the reader comes to acknowledge evidence that undercuts this identity.

* * *

As Kafka initially presents it, the relation of Gregor's consciousness to his insect body is not a happy one. The carapace prevents him from acting as he chooses, not allowing him to get out of bed easily, unlock the door, or answer intelligibly his family's questions. He lacks that mental control over his new body that Descartes describes as being closer to one's body than a pilot to a ship. Gregor finds he has "numerous little legs, which were in every different kind of perpetual motion and which, besides, he could not control" (7). The new body also begins exhibiting a motivating character of its own, disrupting the integrity of Gregor's original character. A sign of this change occurs in the first section when Gregor enters the living room and involuntarily starts snapping his jaws at some coffee spilling from an overturned pot (18). The anxious reaction to his father's hissing is another example of insect behavior, one stressed later in the novella when Gregor himself hisses with rage (44).

In the second section, more indications of an insectile nature emerge. He feels a greater sense of well-being when his new body is allowed to behave in its own natural way rather than being forced to stand upright in a human posture. He also discovers the usefulness of his antennae, an ability to crawl up the bedroom walls and a penchant for hanging from the ceiling (19, 31–32). Insect patterns of sleep and waking develop: sleepy trances alternate with wakeful periods punctuated with hunger pangs (23). His taste in food changes. Milk, which had formerly been his favorite drink, is now repugnant to him, as are fresh foods. He prefers leftovers and rotten vegetables, delighting in a "piece of cheese, which two days before Gregor had declared inedible" (24). The range of his vision decreases—"from day to day he saw things even a short distance away less and less distinctly"—as does his sense of connection with the outside world (29). He also begins not to notice the passage of time (47).

His emotional reactions change, often in ways that he does not understand. He is anxious or frightened at things which formerly would not have affected him. He notices that "the empty high-ceilinged room in which he was forced to lie flat on the floor made him nervous without his being able to tell why ..." (23). This same uneasiness and fear are provoked by his sister's cleaning his room (30). Of course, a change of tastes and habits *per se* need not show the replacement of one person by another (or a person by an insect). Yet, increasingly in the novella, these changes take place outside the scope and limits of Gregor's awareness: he either does not understand why the shifts in attitude and preference have occurred, or he is only dimly aware of the new motivation. In the beginning of the second section, he crawls to the bedroom door: "Only after he got to the door did he notice what had really attracted him—the smell of something to eat" (21). Increasingly, Gregor acts from animal instinct rather than from self-conscious awareness. This invasion of his private self by a new motivating agency suggests the gradual replacement of his former personality.

In one of his rare moments of reflection, when gobbling down the "inedible" cheese, he ponders: "Have I become less sensitive?" (24). However, unlike the reader who starts to question this creature's identity, he resists an answer. He continues to act in ignorance, on occasion even concocting spurious reasons for his behavior. For example, he worries about not being able to support his parents and sister. "In order not to get involved in such thoughts," the narrator adds, "Gregor decided to keep moving and he crawled up and down the room" (22). An air of false consciousness pervades this "decision." Complicitously selective, the narrator withholds the full account of Gregor's motivations, providing only the rationale as Gregor perceives it. Instead of a conscious choice, a more likely motivation is that crawling up and down is an insect's instinctive response to a frightening situation. Gregor reacts in this same insect-like manner to other anxiety-producing incidents.

With the gradual encroachment of one character on another, the rational conscious self (on the Lockean-Cartesian model) loses its status as sole "pilot," and a new motivating agency exercises control. Gregor's individuality begins to unravel. When Grete (Gregor's sister) proposes to move some furniture out of Gregor's room in order to give him more crawling space, the mother protests: to her "the sight of the bare wall was heartbreaking, and why shouldn't Gregor have the same feeling." On hearing his mother's objection, Gregor realizes that in wanting the furniture removed he had been "on the verge of forgetting" his human past (33). If only for a moment, he perceives that his new attitudes and preferences are in conflict with his human past.

Gregor's awareness and understanding (mental activity identified with his humanity) clash with his new insectile character. In philosophical terms, the Lockean-Cartesian dualist account of Gregor-as-consciousness opposes a materialist-behaviorist account of his emerging instinctive character. From the latter perspective, the disposition to behave in insect-like ways is produced by the insect's physiology interacting with its environment. According to dualism, in contrast, Gregor's pre-transformational psyche or consciousness continues despite the physical changes that have taken place.

The clash between Gregor-as-insect and Gregor-as-consciousness can be seen in the following oppositions. First, the insect-states and behavior do not originate from Gregor's earlier human character: they are newly introduced and independent of Gregor's human past. Gregor's consciousness, however, is clearly related to his human past. Secondly, insect-character and human-character are unfused: no unified personality integrates both insect and human traits. Aside from a few acknowledgments of their existence, Gregor's new insectile attitudes and dispositions remain outside his consciousness. No sense of self-consciousness accompanies them. Although at times Gregor ponders their presence, he does not consciously claim them as his own. Thus, instead of a unified self, the transformed Gregor is fissured into two characters, clashing yet jointly existing in the same body.

Because of this unresolved theoretical clash, the novella does not provide an answer to the question of whether the insect is physiologically intact or composite. In their discussion of *The Metamorphosis*, both John Updike (121–33) and Vladimir Nabokov (250–83) see Gregor's physical indeterminateness as a necessary feature of the work. This biological indeterminacy is revealed in numerous anthropomorphic descriptions of the transformed Gregor (e.g., his "eyes streaming with tears of contentment" [24]). Leaving in doubt the exact nature of Gregor's physiological transformation more forcefully pits dualism against materialism. To assume that the insect has at least part of a human brain, allows the materialist/behaviorist a consistent explanation for both Gregor's human and insectile behavior.

* * *

Not only do dualist and materialist interpretations collide, but a third account of personal identity intrudes. Dominating the novella's final section, this third conception involves seeing a person as an individual constituted by certain social relationships. Personal identity is maintained by preserving the constituting social relationships. Failure to preserve them, even though an individual maintains psychological or material continuity, erodes personal identity.

Prefigured in Plato's *Republic*, social-constructionist theories of the self have a long and eminent history. Their most influential nineteenth-century advocates are Hegel ("Self-consciousness exists in itself and for itself, in that, and by the fact that it exists for another self-consciousness; that is to say, it is only by being acknowledged or 'recognized'" [229]) and Marx (400–02). In this century, George Herbert Mead's theory of the self as "social object" (136–44) and Louis Althusser's neo-Marxist account (127–86) are in that tradition. Recently, Erving Goffman has promoted a theory of the self as constituted by a nexus of social roles. Selves, he claims, are produced by particular forms of social interaction and do not exist independently of social contexts. For Goffman, the self "as a performed character, is not an organic thing that has a specific location, whose fundamental fate is to be born, to mature, and to die; it is a dramatic effect . . . [and] the means for producing and maintaining selves . . . are often bolted down in social establishments" (252–53).

Although most fully presented in the novella's final section, the social-constructionist theory of personal identity does appear in earlier sections. In the first section, the locked door, Gregor's chirping and his peculiar behavior are not the only obstacles to social reintegration and self-validation. The family's reaction to Gregor's new body also plays a role. "if they were shocked," the narrator comments, "then Gregor had no further responsibility and could be calm. But if they took everything calmly, then he too, had no reason to get excited . . ." (12). If the family accepts him, then his self (defined as provider, son, brother, household member, etc.) is maintained. If they reject him, these same self-constituting ties are severed and Gregor's identity begins to unravel.

In the second section, after the calamitous rejection by his family, Gregor seeks to reestablish his relationship with them. Wondering how best to lead his new life, he concludes "that for the time being he would have to lie low and, by being patient and showing his family every possible consideration, help them bear the inconvenience which he simply had to cause them in his present condition" (23). His passive resignation in favor of patience and consideration, however, does not actively fulfill his role as family member. It is undertaken more for his own convenience than to mend a ruptured social tie. Being locked in his bedroom by his family is actually reassuring: he feels gratified that there will be no frightening intrusions.

Instead of reintegrating him, Gregor's self-deceived commitment to patient resignation widens the separation between him and his family. The widening gap between them is also a verbal one. After his chirping explanation to the office manager and his subsequent supplication to his mother, he never attempts to communicate verbally with anyone. In turn, his family abandons the notion that he is able to understand their speech: "since the others could not understand what he said, it did not occur to any of them, not even to his sister, that he could understand what they said . . ." (25). He receives news of them only indirectly.

Nevertheless, his sister Grete does try to establish a new relationship with Gregor. Unfortunately, their relationship lacks reciprocity and she ends up creating only a new family role and identity for herself. Up until Gregor's transformation, Grete has been a child with few family responsibilities. By assuming the duty of feeding Gregor and cleaning his room, she takes on the role of an adult and with it an adult self. Gregor hears the family say "how much they appreciated his sister's work, whereas until now they had frequently been annoyed with her because she struck them as being a little useless" (31). Her childish indolence has given way to a more mature acceptance of responsibility. In her parents' eyes she has become an adult.

Although Grete maintains regular contact with Gregor, Grete and the family fail to reestablish a familial personal relationship with him. "If Gregor," the narrator says, "had only been able to speak to his sister and thank her for everything she had to do for him, he could have accepted her services more easily; as it was, they caused him pain" (29). Thus, for want of communication and a reciprocity of relations, Gregor's position in the family disintegrates and his sense of self erodes.

His insect-anxiety toward his sister increases until the watershed scene in which his sister and mother remove the furniture from his room. As the narrator notes, on hearing his mother's objections to moving the furniture, "Gregor realized that the monotony of family life, combined with the fact that not a soul had addressed a word directly to him, must have addled his brain in the course of the past two months, for he could not explain to himself in any other way how in all seriousness he could have been anxious to have his room cleared out." His decreasing contacts with his family have eroded his sense of being a person. Resolving to resist this gradual depersonalizing influence, he now wants "the beneficial influence of the furniture on his state of mind" (33).

The furniture comes to represent Gregor's past self-preserving relationship with his family, awakening him to the intrusion of his animal instincts. When he frightens his mother in an effort to halt their removing the furniture, Grete starts to shout at Gregor. "These were the first words," the narrator interjects, that "she had addressed directly to him since his metamorphosis." They awaken the hope that a family relationship might be reestablished. In the confusion of Grete's ministering to their mother, Gregor runs out of the bedroom, leaving the depersonalizing isolation of his bedroom for the public interactive space of the living room. Hearing that "Gregor's broken out," the father once again drives him back into the confinement of the bedroom, this time wounding him with a thrown apple (36). Patriarchal intervention has dashed Gregor's hopes of reintegrating himself into the family circle.

The third section, the section in which the implications of the social-constructionist theory are most fully explored, begins with the family's seemingly begrudging acceptance of Gregor as a family member. His wound "seemed to have reminded even his father that Gregor was a member of the family, in spite of his present pathetic and repulsive shape ... [and] it was the commandment of family duty to swallow their disgust and endure him, endure him and nothing else" (40). Yet this commitment to tolerance still allows Gregor no positive role in family matters. He eventually disregards both the open door, which the family leave ajar out of their awakened sense of duty, and his earlier resolution to be considerate of his family, especially in keeping himself clean (46). "It hardly surprised him," the reader learns, "that lately he was showing so little consideration for others; once such consideration had been his greatest pride" (48). Gregor is "hardly surprised" because much of his disregard for his family is motivated by his new instinctual character.

In keeping with this new character, Gregor now shows an interest in music. Unlike his sister who enjoys playing the violin, Gregor had earlier shown little interest in music. Nevertheless, in his role as provider and loving brother, he had planned to realize the "beautiful dream" of sending Grete to the conservatory to study her instrument (27). Hearing Grete playing her violin in the living room for three boarders whom the family have taken in to help meet expenses, Gregor once again leaves his bedroom, creeping through the inadvertently open doorway into the living room (48). Given his earlier complacency toward music, Gregor's attraction is likely produced by his insectile character. Although the Orphic myth of music charming the beast is the underlying theme here, the ambiguity of Gregor's action (the narrator does not specify whether Gregor's attraction is due to animal magnetism or deliberate choice) is sustained by his asking, and failing to answer, another of his self-reflecting questions: "Was he an animal, that music could move him so?" (49). In the reverie of the moment, Gregor starts to fantasize about bringing Grete back to his room and revealing his plan to send her to the conservatory. In his fantasy he attempts to reconstitute his relationship with his sister and reclaim his sense of self. Yet so remote is the likelihood of the fantasy becoming fact (i.e., Gregor's talking to Grete, and her being kissed by something she considers repulsive) that it highlights the absurdity of their reestablishing any personal relationship. A boarder's shriek at Gregor's dust-covered carapace abruptly ends his reverie. This latest outrage by Gregor prompts the family to discuss getting rid of "the monster" (51).

The social-constructionist theory of self underlies much of the family's discussion of what to do with the monster. "If he could understand us," the father bewails, "then maybe we could come to an agreement with him." To which Grete replies: "You just have to get rid of the idea that it's Gregor. Believing it for so long, that is our real misfortune. But how can it be Gregor? If it were Gregor, he would have realized long ago that it isn't possible for human beings to live with such a creature, and he would have gone away of his own free will. Then we wouldn't have a brother, but we'd be able to go on living and honor his memory" (52). Cut off from communicating with the creature, the family can neither reforge the familial bond with Gregor nor establish a new one. The sister's argument against the monster's being her brother does not appeal to the physical impossibility of his continued existence. To a great extent the family have accepted Gregor's physical transformation. Instead the appeal is social: given the widening disparity between their two life forms, there is no basis for a personal relationship. Not only has Gregor changed, but the family has changed as well, becoming now more resourceful and self-sufficient. All three of them have jobs.

Since the creature cannot maintain the former relationship of being a son and brother, it must not be Gregor. The sister, however, does allow the creature one *limit-position* in which to be a brother: the monster could disappear and by so doing show its consideration for the family. Such an act would be a *brotherly* act, fulfilling a role while at the same time dissolving it.

In the hope of resolving the metaphysical impasse, the reader might be inclined to interpret Gregor's death early the next morning as such an act of brotherly consideration. The undercutting of one theory of self by another, however, extends also to his death. The nature of Gregor's death and its causes are equally open to question by the respective theories. No one theory convincingly explains his end.

According to the dualist perspective, Gregor could be seen as consciously committing suicide because he realizes the hopelessness of his situation. After all, the family take his gestures of concern to be either threatening or irrational. No longer wishing to live separated from those he loves, he starves himself to death. Corroborating this view is the narrator's observation: "[Gregor] thought back on his family with deep emotion and love. His conviction that he would have to disappear was, if possible, even firmer than his sister's" (54). According to this account, his earlier refusal to eat leads up to this "conviction."

The limited and shifting focus of the narration, however, also allows for a materialist reading: the change in eating habits and the death indicate not conscious choices but the course of the insect's life cycle, exacerbated by the infected wound from the apple thrown by the father. Since not all of Gregor's personal reflections are to be trusted (e.g., his conscious rationalizations for his instinctively motivated behavior), events leading up to his death should not be seen as excluding a materialist interpretation. In the description of Gregor's death, there occurs a curious phrase about his lack of volition: "Then, *without his consent*, his head sank down to the floor, and from his nostrils streamed his last breath" (54; emphasis mine). The denial of "consent" calls into question Gregor's agency: death might be the result of an enfeebled condition rather than an intended starvation.

The social-constructionist theory can also provide an account of Gregor's death. Just before being drawn into the living room by his sister's violin playing,

Gregor listens to the boarders eating: "'I'm hungry enough,' Gregor said to himself, full of grief, 'but not for these things. Look how these roomers are gorging themselves, and I'm dying!'" (47). Hungry, "but not for these things," Gregor yearns for nourishment other than food, for an emotional sustenance derived from an active involvement with his family. With the dissolution of the family bond, he emotionally and socially starves to death.

Gregor's fantasy of announcing to Grete his intention to send her to the conservatory also supports a social-constructionist interpretation of his later demise. Even if his death is something he consciously contemplated, his passive and fantasized past behavior renders suspicious Gregor's "conviction that he would have to disappear ..." (54). The narrator is unreliable about Gregor's passive "contributions" to his family: Gregor's patient hiding in his room is instinctively motivated rather than consciously intended. Thus, the reader should be suspicious of crediting Gregor with actively bringing about his own end. On the social-constructionist view, only within the bounds of the family relationship can Gregor act positively and have a sense of personal agency. Despite the sister's claim that Gregor would disappear if he were her brother, the family does not recognize his death as an act of consideration. In fact, they react to it as good fortune.

Thus, by maintaining an ambivalence among the dualist, materialist and social-constructionist explanations for Gregor's death, Kafka preserves the tension and opposition among all three of Gregor's "identities:" a self-consciousness, an instinctual organism and a social persona—a "shadow being" trying fantastically to maintain itself in a disintegrating family relationship.

* * *

The sustained opposition and tension among the three positions cloud not only the nature of Gregor's death but the extent of the family's moral responsibility toward him. Each of the three theories undercuts the other two positions; this mutual undermining leaves unresolved questions about the limits of responsibility toward those whose personhood is in doubt, just as it leaves unresolved questions about the basis for moral relationships in the face of instinctual behavior and the extent to which social ties create moral responsibilities.

In contrast to the moral debate of the third section, the novella's epilogue introduces a false sense of closure. It drowns out the debate by depicting the family as reunified, smug in their togetherness, having weathered the catastrophe of Gregor's final appearance and death. The epilogue thus obscures an ethical issue that the reader must still confront: whether, prior to his death, Gregor stops being a person who deserves the moral support of his family. The epilogue, especially what Stanley Corngold has called "the falseness and banality of the tone of the ending" (174), cuts off this moral questioning. It closes the work by resolving its moral ambiguity, covering up its thematic antagonisms and destroying what Joseph Margolis (27–42) sees as the philosophical tensions of the work.

In his *Diaries*, Kafka himself expressed displeasure at the novella's "unreadable ending" (12). For a writer who registered repeated disapproval of his writing, this castigation may be no more than the carping of a perpetually unsatisfied artist unwilling to acknowledge that the writing has ended. Yet, it may also register his adoption of the stance of the reader and a call for the type of "experimental" reading process I have described. Indeed, as Camus has noticed, "The whole art of Kafka consists in forcing the reader to reread. His endings, or his absence of endings, suggest explanations which, however, are not revealed in clear language but, before they seem justified, require that the story be reread from another point of view" (92). Rather than arriving at a "justified" closure, one is more apt on rereading the novella to sense the clash and mutual undercutting of philosophical theories. Perhaps Kafka's displeasure at the epilogue thus reveals not artistic dissatisfaction but rather a desire not to obscure the competing ethical and philosophical issues that the work raises.

In the twentieth century more than any other century, human beings have faced perplexing questions about the nature of their identities as persons. From our educational heritage, we have developed as rational consciousnesses, while at the same time we have increasingly come to understand the biological (i.e., material) determinants of our characters. The rapid social changes of the recent past have made us realize both the role that social organization plays in the constitution of who we are and our dependence on a stable social context for maintaining our identities. These ways of thinking about ourselves (as conscious, biological or social beings) are far from compatible conceptual schemas. Kafka's novella makes this incompatibility all too clear.

Works Cited

Althusser, Louis. "Ideology and Ideological State Apparatuses." *Lenin and Philosophy*. Trans. Ben Brewster. New York: Monthly Review, 1971. 127–86.

Bakhtin, Mikhail M. *The Dialogic Imagination: Four Essays*. Ed. Michael Holquist. Trans. Caryl Emerson and Michael Holquist. Austin: U of Texas P, 1981.

Camus, Albert. "Hope and The Absurd in The Works of Franz Kafka." *The Myth of Sisyphus*. 1942. Trans. Justin O'Brien. New York: Vintage, 1955. 92–102.

Corngold, Stanley. *The Fate of the Self: German Writers and French Theory*. New York: Columbia UP, 1986.

Deleuze, Gilles, and Felix Guattari. *Kafka: Towards a Minor Literature*. Trans. Dana Polan. Minneapolis: U of Minnesota P, 1986.

Descartes, René. *Discourse on Method*. 1637. *The Philosophical Works of Descartes*. Vol. I. Trans. E.S. Haldane and G.R.T. Ross. Cambridge: Cambridge UP, 1911. 79–130.

Goffman, Erving. *The Presentation of Self in Everyday Life*. Garden City, NY: Doubleday, 1959.

Hayman, Ronald. *Kafka: A Biography*. New York: Oxford UP, 1982.

Hegel, G.W.F. *The Phenomenology of Mind*. 1807. Trans. J.B. Baillie. New York: Harper, 1967.

Kafka, Franz. *The Diaries of Franz Kafka, 1914–1932*. Trans. Martin Greenberg and Hannah Arendt. New York: Schocken, 1949.

———. *The Metamorphosis*. 1915. Ed. and trans. Stanley Corngold. New York: Bantam, 1972.

Locke, John. "Of Identity and Diversity." *An Essay Concerning Human Understanding*. 1694. Vol. I. Ed. A.C. Fraser. New York: Dover, 1959. 439–70.

Margolis, Joseph. "Kafka vs. Eudaimonia and Duty." *Philosophy and Phenomenological Research* 19 (1958): 27–42.

Marx, Karl. "Theses On Feuerbach." 1845. *Writings of the Young Mars on Philosophy and Society*. Ed. and trans. L.D. Easton and K.H. Guddat. Garden City, NY: Doubleday. 1967. 400–02.

Mead, George Herbert. *Mind, Self, and Society*. Chicago: U of Chicago P, 1934.

Nabokov, Vladimir. *Lectures on Literature*. New York: Harcourt, 1980.

Quinton, Anthony. "The Soul." *The Journal of Philosophy* 59 (1962): 393–403.

Skulsky, Harold. *Metamorphosis: The Mind in Exile*. Cambridge, MA: Harvard UP, 1981.

Updike, John. "Reflections: Kafka's Short Stories." *The New Yorker* (9 May 1983): 121–33.

MARK M. ANDERSON

Sliding Down the Evolutionary Ladder?
Aesthetic Autonomy in The Metamorphosis

Was he an animal that music moved him so?

(*The Metamorphosis*)

I

A few years ago an art gallery in New York created a mild sensation by
dousing a number of human models, clothes and bodies, in green paint and
hanging them on its bare white walls. Although the models adopted various
poses, they made no attempt to deny their living status, and interacted freely
with the bemused public. Somewhat at a loss to describe the artwork, which
apparently was not for sale, the media spoke of 'Dada', 'performance', and
'action' art. Franz Kafka's literary masterpiece of 1912, *The Metamorphosis*,
enacts essentially the same scenario when its human-sized bug hero climbs
the wall of his bedroom and usurps the aesthetic space occupied by a gilt-
framed photograph, hugging his flat body against the glass until it 'completely
covers' the picture. When his mother, less blasé than a New York audience of
the 1980s, enters the room, her senses are overwhelmed. She perceives only a
huge brownish spot against the flowered wallpaper and, crying out 'Oh God!
Oh God!', falls into a dead faint. No avant-garde artist of the modern period
could ask for a more satisfying public response.

From *Kafka's Clothes: Ornament and Aestheticism in the Habsburg Fin de Siècle*, pp. 123–144.
© 1992 by Mark M. Anderson.

Since the story's initial publication in 1915, few if any readers of *The Metamorphosis* have wished to recognize Gregor Samsa's metamorphosed body as an aesthetic form. For Kafka's early public the bug was simply too repulsive, and was explained away with allegorical notions like 'alienated labor' or 'unconscious self-loathing.'[1] Further, although Günther Anders in an early and quite perceptive essay interpreted Gregor Samsa as a *Luftmensch* and 'artist' figure,[2] and although subsequent critics have seen a parallel between Gregor's isolated condition and Franz Kafka's monk-like dedication to his writing,[3] readers have been hard put to reconcile this aesthetic dimension with the specificity of Gregor's outward form. In fact, close scrutiny of the story has led critics to deny that the bug has any reliable visual specificity at all: actual descriptive details are scant and contradictory, and since the story is narrated largely from Gregor's perspective, his own body tends to disappear from the reader's view. The opening designation of Gregor as an 'ungeheure Ungeziefer' or 'giant vermin' is notoriously ambiguous, for *Ungeziefer* refers to a broad range of animal parasites rather than a single type, *ungeheuer* ('monstrous') is by definition vague, and the 'un-' prefixes in both words double the term's lack of specificity into a kind of negative infinity. Significantly, when the cleaning lady calls to Gregor with the precise term *Mistkäfer* (dung beetle), he refuses to respond. Thus abstractly or negatively defined, the bug would seem to have no discernible form, and to the reader at least it remains a visual cipher.

This critical tendency to de-emphasize the bug's status as a visual object of representation reached its most extreme and brilliant limit in Stanley Corngold's influential essay 'The Metamorphosis of the Metaphor'.[4] Drawing on Anders's insight that Kafka often literalizes metaphors as the basis for his central images and plot lines, Corngold interprets Gregor's form as primarily linguistic and rhetorical rather than visual. Because the text circumvents the dialectical relationship of metaphor, insisting that Gregor is a bug but without denying him specifically human traits, the monstrous vermin form functions as a 'mutilated metaphor, uprooted from familiar language' (59), an 'opaque sign' (56). Anything disturbing about his appearance arises primarily from a disturbing use of rhetorical structure, an 'unclean' mixing of the metaphor's human tenor and its material vehicle:

> It appears, then, that the metamorphosis in the Samsa household of man into vermin is unsettling not only because vermin are disturbing, or because the vivid representation of a human 'louse' is disturbing, but because the indeterminate, fluid crossing of a human tenor and a material vehicle is in itself unsettling. (56)

Such interpretations have an indisputable hold on Kafka's story and, I suspect, are ultimately correct. Kafka knew that his story was a kind of literary tease, that it depended on the reader's imagination to visualize what is only suggested by the text. When confronted with his editor's plan to illustrate the bug for the cover of the first edition, his response was unambiguous: 'The insect itself cannot be depicted' (letter of 25 October 1915). He proposed instead the image of a half-opened door with only darkness behind it—the bug itself remains unseen and the reader must perform the same act of imagination that is required by the text in the passage from linguistic sign to mental image. Kafka's suggestion was in fact taken up, and a black-and-white illustration by Ottomar Starke adorned the story's first edition in Kurt Wolf's series *Die weißen Blätter*.

Nonetheless, one cannot help feeling that such critical and authorial strictures have something of a magician's legerdemain—Now you see him, now you don't—and hide as much as they reveal. Although the text is a verbal artefact which expertly subverts the metaphorical function of language, it also requires the reader to make a sustained effort to visualize the bug within a minutely described environment. Moreover, such strictures obscure the fact that the text repeatedly displays Gregor's body as a visual object of unusual power—a scandalous, grotesque object difficult to behold, yes, but one that is attributed with an undeniable aesthetic function, as in the scene when Gregor hangs himself on the wall in front of his mother and sister. Indeed, the basic movement of all three sections of the novella consists in covering and uncovering Gregor's body, like a monster at a fair or a sacred icon.

Accordingly, this chapter will attempt to describe Gregor's form in visual and aesthetic terms, even when the text itself leaves these terms vague or obscures their reference. Two avenues of interpretation will be followed: a historical, deliberately digressive approach that compares Kafka's use of the vermin image to contemporary developments in science and literature; and a textual reading in terms of the problematic of *Verkehr*, clothing, and corporeal gymnastics that I have delineated in the preceding chapters and on which *The Metamorphosis*, perhaps more crucially than any of Kafka's other writings, depends.

II

Kafka's most famous text has been with us so long that it is easy to forget the audacity of using a human-sized cockroach as the main figure in a literary text. Nothing in the classical literature of animal fables or even in the Romantic literature of the uncanny or the grotesque is quite like *The Metamorphosis*, with its mixing of the monstrous and the everyday, the repulsive and the beautiful.[5] And yet there is precedent for Kafka's modernist masterpiece in the scientific and aesthetic discourses of the *fin de siècle*. *His* story is about a metamorphosis from human to animal form, and like all his animal narratives it arises from—

and in reaction to—the ubiquitous presence of Darwin's theory of evolution.[6] The idea of 'metamorphosis' was in the air. Goethe's *Metamorphosis of Plants* and the *Metamorphosis of Animals* were held in high regard in scientific circles as Romantic harbingers of Darwin's own writings. German scientists like Ernst Haeckel and Wilhelm Bölsche propagated Darwin's teachings in Germany, not only in their research but in popular lecture series and *Volksausgaben* for a broad audience; Haeckel held an influential lecture on the evolutionary theories of Goethe, Lamarck, and Darwin in 1882, a year before Kafka's birth. Largely because of Haeckel's efforts, Darwin's evolutionary monism gained increasing currency in German-speaking countries, as all life forms were understood to be united in a great chain of being stretching from single-celled plasma to the highest primates.

Such theorizations found their equivalent in art and literature of the period. The *Jugendstil*, with its proliferation of swirling plant, mineral, and animal forms, espoused a monistic philosophy of an all-permeating life force, of organic change and becoming. Not infrequently, *Jugendstil* artists drew inspiration from contemporary scientific representations, which increasingly emphasized unusual, unknown, exotic, or otherwise bizarre forms of the natural world. Haeckel's *Kunstformen der Natur* (*Art Forms of Nature*, 1899–1903), which included 100 colour illustrations of protozoa, ocean sponges, medusas, coral, tropical birds, flowers, and exotic insects, served as a veritable handbook for the *Jugendstil* movement.[7] In his foreword he notes that the higher forms of plants and vertebrate animals that had dominated scholarly and artistic attention until the nineteenth century have given way to 'strange and marvellous forms'.[8] Addressing himself explicitly to contemporary artists, he promises that his book will bring these hidden treasures to light, thereby providing them with a 'rich supply of new and beautiful motifs'.[9]

Haeckel's work had a twofold importance for literary and visual artists at the turn of the century. First, it offered them spectacular new material—vivid colors, flowing lines, translucent textures, grotesque and fantastic creatures from another realm of experience—that could be used in representations of organic and inorganic forms. It thus helped to enlarge the canon of aesthetically valid subjects, treating what might have been dismissed as ugly, overly stylized, bizarre, or lowly organisms as beautiful aesthetic forms in their own right. On a theoretical level, Haeckel promoted the notion of an originary *Kunsttrieb* or artistic impulse that could be found in all of nature. Attempting to explain the remarkable sensuous beauty, symmetry, and variety of even the most primitive organisms, he posited a 'soul' within each cell that constantly struggled for 'plastic' definition and self-realization: 'One can describe the artistic impulses of protists as "plastic cellular instincts", for they stand on the same rung of the soul's activity as the well-known instincts of higher, multiple-celled animals and plants' (12). The will to art not merely as a democratic possibility but as a biological necessity arising from the depths of every living organism—here was a philosophy for turn-of-the-century reformists and educators.

Kafka's first encounter with these ideas came in the Gymnasium. Under the influence of his science teacher Adolf Gottwald, a convinced Darwinist, he read the author of *On the Origin of Species* at age 16. And according to his classmate Hugo Bergmann, he read Haeckel's *Welträtsel* (*The Riddle of the Universe*, 1899) with 'unusual enthusiasm' in the same period.[10] A few years later he would find similar ideas in the literary writings of Hugo von Hofmannsthal and his friend Max Brod. The ornamental exoticism that one finds in their early work, as indeed that of the entire *fin-de-siècle* and *Jugendstil* generation, is sustained and legitimized by their naturalist curiosity in contemporary evolutionary theories linking plant, animal, and human intelligence.[11] Brod's early novellas abound in vegetable and animal exotica whose *correspondance* with the human soul he attempts to convey by an abundance of synaesthetic tropes. The following description from his 'Carina Island' (in which he portrays Kafka as a detached, melancholy aesthete) gives us a typical sampling:

> It was a forest full of passion through which we strode. In the deep tranquillity and solitude, magnificent magnolia trees put forth their blossoms like large, violet bowls of porcelain. Humming-birds flashed through fragrant symphonies of scarlet and snow-white oceans of flowers, through palagonitic bushes and lilies and begonias. Giant silk-like moths spread their shimmering wings, butterflies showed off their violet and emerald-blue shades of colour. Giant beetles, which looked like precious jewels or like foliage, crept their way through the oily, red soil.[12]

Hofmannsthal also echoes Haeckel's monistic exoticism in his early *Jugendstil* story 'Fairytale of the 672nd Night' (1895), when the main protagonist recognizes in the ornaments of his plush, *fin-de-siècle* furniture 'a magic image of the intertwined wonders of the world'. In these carved ornaments he sees 'the forms of animals and the forms of flowers and the merging of flowers with animals; the dolphins, lions, tulips, pearls and acanthus . . . It was a great heritage, the divine work of all generations and species.'[13] In his Lord Chandos 'Letter' written seven years later, the emphasis on ornamental flora and fauna shifts to less exotic, indeed 'insignificant' creatures; but Haeckel's influence is still evident in the fluid, evanescent passage between them and the protagonist's human consciousness. The text, which Kafka knew and valued, is particularly relevant to *The Metamorphosis*:

In these moments an insignificant creature—a dog, a rat, a beetle, a crippled appletree, a lane winding over the hill, a moss-covered stone—mean more to me than the most beautiful, abandoned mistress of the happiest night.... [Such creatures] can become the vehicle of a divine revelation ... of my flowing over into these creatures, or my feeling that a fluid of life and death, dream and waking, flowed into them for an instant—but from where?[14]

Kafka's story is another matter, of course. His beetle does not crawl through the earth of Brod's exotic tropical island but through the drab, petty bourgeois apartment of a European city. And unlike Hofmannsthal, who keeps Chandos's mystical revelation within a human framework, Kafka reverses the camera angle, forcing us to see not so much the insect as the world of higher primates from the insect's perspective. Moreover, Gregor's metamorphosed body does not cater to contemporary aesthetic taste for stylized exotica. Like the cockroach that Kafka mentions in the 'Letter to His Father', the vermin form in *The Metamorphosis* is meant to sting and bite its audience, to upset traditional aesthetic notions with a scandalous, 'inhuman' otherness. Frau Samsa's reaction—her appeal to 'God' as well as her fainting—is again exemplary.

As an assault on conventional bourgeois taste, the novella thus definitely belongs within the canon of Expressionist and avant-garde modernism, rather than in *fin-de-siècle* 'decadence' or the *Jugendstil*. Its closest visual counterpart is to be found in the early drawings of Kafka's Prague contemporary and acquaintance Alfred Kubin, whose allegorical symbolism often relies on a similar grotesque crossing of human and abstract insect-like figures. But like Kubin's zoological fantasies, Kafka's story draws on the visual forms promoted by *fin-de-siècle* scientific and literary discourse, on 'strange and marvellous forms' from a radically other realm of experience. More crucially, it insists on what one might well call the animal's 'humanness', which emerges most poignantly in his relation to art. Just as Haeckel recognized in single-celled protozoa a human 'soul' and a primal *Kunsttrieb*, so does *The Metamorphosis* endow a lowly, potentially repulsive form with a human consciousness and a will toward art. However grotesque and 'other' the *Ungeziefer* may appear to the Samsa family, the text's true subject (as in Kafka's other animal stories) is the condition of being caught between human and animal forms, caught in the fluid of an evolutionary life force. That Gregor slides down the evolutionary ladder in his quest for artistic self-realization is only one of the ironies behind his bizarre transformation.

III

To describe Gregor's animal form as it manifests itself in the narrative, one can best begin by noting what it is not: clothing. In Kafka's novel fragment of

1907, *Wedding Preparations in the Country*, we find an anticipation of Gregor Samsa's transformation. There Eduard Raban imagines himself split into two distinct selves: a giant beetle who stays in bed while his 'clothed' human body is sent into the *Verkehr* of the world, 'travelling' to the country to get married:

> I don't even need to go to the country myself, it isn't necessary. I'll send my *clothed body* . . . For I myself am meanwhile lying in my bed, smoothly covered over with the yellow-brown blanket . . . As I lie in bed I assume the shape of a big beetle, a stag beetle or a cockchafer, I think. (*CS* 55–6, my emphasis)

What is surprising here is that Raban's grotesque form as a beetle connotes protection and warmth. He feels no horror, surprise, or shame at his metamorphosis, but rather an odd kind of satisfaction, as if his hard beetle shell were simply one additional layer of protection from whatever menaces him in the outside world. On the other hand his 'clothed body' is sent like a messenger to take part in the 'traffic of clothes', travelling to the country where he will perform the social rituals necessary for his impending marriage. This clothed body is clearly the unessential self: it 'staggers out of the door', a movement that indicates not the body's fear but 'its nothingness' (*CS* 55). And if it is not certain, as Walter Sokel maintains, that what remains behind in bed is Raban's 'essential', 'naked' self (protected by blanket, beetle shell, and the fetal position of his legs, Raban is everything but naked), it has been removed from the *Verkehr* of society. Raban's beetle self is unclothed and yet covered—'naked' in the sense than an animal is considered naked.

The fiction of *The Metamorphosis*, of course, is to turn Raban's dream into reality. 'It was no dream', a disembodied narrative voice announces at the text's beginning. Here, too, clothing and *Verkehr* are intertwined. Previously Gregor worked as a travelling salesman, selling 'cloth samples' for a large company; his collection of clothing lies open, like a suitcase, ready to be packed up for another day's journey. His metamorphosis signals first of all a break with this order of reality, with the order of work, travel, clothing, and mortality, as is made clear in Gregor's first extended monologue:

> Oh God, he thought, what an exhausting job I've picked on! Traveling about day in, day out. It's much more irritating work than doing the actual business in the office, and on top of that there's the trouble of constant traveling, of worrying about train connections, the bad and irregular meals, casual acquaintances that are always new and never become intimate friends [*ein immer wechselnder, nie andauernder, nie herzlich werdender menschlicher Verkehr*]. (*CS* 89–90)

Gregor's lament is directed not against work but against the 'travelling' nature of his work, the movement that prevents him from realizing a truly 'affectionate' relation to society, a 'human' *Verkehr*. The irony of this phrase is the rhetorical reversal underlying the entire story, that of an 'animal' who is more human than his human co-protagonists. 'The devil take it all!', Gregor exclaims in a Faustian invocation, and immediately he senses the strangeness of his reptile body—an 'itching up on his belly' which is now covered with small white spots, 'the nature of which he could not understand' (*CS* 90). This 'pact' with the devil seals Gregor's break with his human past, removes him from the 'traffic of clothes', and prepares him for his existence as a radically singular, 'animal' being, whose foreign body he must first learn to master.

The most striking counterexample to Gregor's grotesque form is the photograph that hangs in the Samsas' living room, depicting him during his military service as 'a lieutenant, hand on sword, a carefree smile on his face, inviting one to respect his uniform and military bearing' (*CS* 101). This image of military authority, virility, and happiness depends on the effacement of individual singularity. Gregor wears the uniform that literally and symbolically establishes his participation in a social order whose identity is maintained by a common form of clothing. The 'uniformity' of his military appearance coincides with the nature of his employment as a salesman who shows cloth 'samples' (*Muster*) to his clients. Critics have often taken this word as a pun on *Musterknabe*, as if the text meant to say that Gregor was a 'model child'. He was, but only in the sense of being without any particular identity that would set him above or apart from the others—equivalent and interchangeable, like the cloth samples in his travelling kit. (Or, in an image whose uncanniness gives us a measure of Kafka's ambivalence toward the effacement of individual difference, like the three unnamed, indistinguishable men who later take lodging in the Samsa household.)

Kafka develops further the notion of the uniformization of work and social *Verkehr* through the father, who is forced to take a position as a bank messenger for which he wears a uniform with gold buttons and monogrammed cap. Herr Samsa thus enters the world of commerce as the transmitter of financial messages, a scarcely human vehicle in the circulation of commercial meanings. His uniform secures his identifiability in this network at the same time that it marks him as a prisoner and underling who has sacrificed his personal identity to an abstract order. Branded with the bank's monogram and uniform, Herr Samsa's body functions only as a sign, a bearer of information in the *Verkehr* of the world's meaning; he even eats and sleeps in his uniform, 'as if he were ready for service at any moment and even here only at the beck and call of his superior' (*CS* 123). As always in Kafka, this traffic signifies something irremediably base and unclean: 'his uniform, which was not brand-new to start with, began to look dirty, despite all the loving care of the mother and sister to keep it clean, and Gregor often spent whole evenings gazing at the many greasy spots on the garment.'

Mother and sister also enter the world of *Verkehr*. Grete takes a job as a salesgirl and is learning shorthand to work as a secretary, thus serving as the transmitter of money, letters, information—a 'vehicle' in social and economic traffic. Frau Samsa helps out by sewing 'elegant underwear' for a fashion boutique, working late into the night (*CS* 123). With this covert reference to the fancy goods sold in his father's shop, Kafka depicts Gregor's mother as an unwitting madam *à distance*, mediating the *Verkehr* of elegant clothing, social ritual, and sexual couplings. At the end of the text the notion of traffic is literalized when the Samsas ride a streetcar to the country and envision their daughter's entrance into the sexual *Verkehr* of marriage: 'It struck both Mr. and Mrs. Samsa [that their daughter] had bloomed into a pretty girl with a good figure. They grew quieter and half unconsciously exchanged glances of complete agreement, having come to the conclusion that it would soon be time to find a good husband for her' (*CS* 139).[15]

IV

Gregor's metamorphosis, then, makes a cut in his life, isolating him from the paternal and social order of work, clothing, business, 'traffic'. It defines him negatively: against the family's names he is nameless; against its human uniforms he has his singular animal covering; against its participation in the circulation of social or economic meaning, he remains cloistered in his room, cut off from human discourse. And yet the narrative does not limit itself to a merely negative definition of Gregor's identity. In opposition to this family 'traffic' of clothing, it delineates an alternative, Utopian space of play, distraction, and childlike innocence that is curiously consistent with late nineteenth-century definitions of aesthetic experience. In fact, Gregor's metamorphosis fulfils the dream of every serious *fin-de-siècle* aesthete: to become not just an artist, but the artwork, the visual icon, itself.

The second paragraph of *The Metamorphosis*, immediately following the account of Gregor's transformation, describes a picture of a lady dressed in fur that, hanging on the wall opposite him, seems to mirror his newly transformed, animal self:

> Above the table . . . hung the picture which he had recently cut out of an illustrated magazine and put into a pretty gilt frame. It showed a lady, with a fur cap on and a fur stole, sitting upright and holding out to the spectator a huge fur muff into which the whole of her forearm had vanished! (*CS* 89)

The picture clearly constitutes an aesthetic moment within the Samsa's petty bourgeois world. As we learn later, Gregor has himself fashioned the 'pretty gilt frame' with his fretwork, a pastime or 'amusement' that is explicitly contrasted with his work as a travelling salesman. 'The boy thinks about nothing but his work', Frau Samsa explains to the chief clerk. 'He just sits there quietly at the table reading a newspaper or looking through railway timetables. The only amusement he gets is doing fretwork. For instance, he spent two or three evenings cutting out a little picture frame; you would be surprised to see how pretty it is; it's hanging in his room' (*CS* 95–6). Here the mortality of *Verkehr*, evoked through the railway timetables and newspapers (*Zeitungen*), is contrasted with Gregor's 'amusement' or distraction (*Zerstreuung*) in making the picture; alienated labour is contrasted with a form of play that results in art, a framed image that is 'beautiful' (*schön*).

Of course, one should be wary of idealizing what is after all a kind of pin-up—an erotic photograph cut out of a magazine that a lonely salesman hangs in his room. And what about the woman's fur clothing? Isn't it part of the same *Verkehr* of clothing, social intercourse, and mortality that defines the Samsa household? Fur was after all the clothing that Adam and Eve put on after being expelled from the Garden, as Kafka noted when he copied this passage from Genesis into his diary.[16] In fact, these furs function as emblems not so much of wealth and social status as of animality, which in this story symbolizes a liberation from specifically human problems of sin, guilt, mortality, even from pain and self-consciousness. This is the basic narrative movement to *The Metamorphosis*: after his initial transformation, Gregor will attempt to realize the promise implicit in this photograph, to merge with his mirror-image, to descend the evolutionary ladder into an animal state, to become the animal-artwork.

As several studies have pointed out, Kafka borrowed the image of the fur-clad lady as well as the basic plot structure for his story from a classic novel of *fin-de-siècle* eroticism, Leopold von Sacher-Masoch's *Venus in Furs* (1880).[17] The picture Gregor has cut out of a magazine thus functions as a coded reference to Kafka's own appropriation of Sacher-Masoch's narrative. This is not the place to rehearse the numerous and surprising similarities between the two texts, which include not only the fur clothing, but also uniforms, the name Gregor, and analogous 'punishment fantasies', which, in Sacher-Masoch's text, turn the protagonist metaphorically into a 'dog' or 'worm' grovelling at his mistress' feet. Two points of contact between these texts are however worth stressing. The first is that in both works fur functions as a metonymy for sexual desire, either in the Freudian sense as a fetish recalling the mother's genitalia and pubic hair, or in the popular sense of 'animal' passion and corporeality.[18] Secondly, in both texts desire is a product of images—paintings, sculptures, photographs, staged erotic encounters—in other words, art. One paradigmatic moment in *Venus in Furs* describes for instance the narrator's desire for a white marble copy of the Venus de Milo, which is draped in fur. The novel also opens with the description of a painting of Venus to which it returns in the closing scene.

From Sacher-Masoch's novel one may hypothesize that masochistic desire is dependent on images because by definition the images preclude fulfilment. In between the opening and closing description of the painting, we witness the main protagonist orchestrate his desire in the guise of masochistic self-abasement, dressing his female partner in a variety of fur costumes, engaging her to act out pre-established scenarios of punishment and humiliation with him and other men, while all the time setting up formal obstacles to the consummation of his desire. In effect, the masochist turns his mistress into an actress, himself into her public. He 'frames' her as art, establishing an inviolable line between his reality and material bondage on the one hand and her aesthetic freedom and power over him on the other. The image is merely a more radical form of this same inviolability, its inaccessibility as image guaranteeing the frustration of desire. The frame is so to speak the masochist's rope and chains.

This same dialectic of image, power, and desire is implicit in Gregor Samsa's unspoken relationship with his 'pretty' picture. Unlike, say, Georg Bendemann in 'The Judgment', Gregor has no mistress or fiancee, only the photograph, which through his own efforts he has inscribed as art, framing it and putting it behind glass. Already 'only' an image, the woman is thus raised to the level of art, put into an ideal space that Gregor can aspire to, but never truly enter. And this seems to be the source of its attraction and power. In the story's second section, Gregor's identity is threatened when his sister and mother begin cleaning out his room. He asks himself which object he should choose to rescue, considers (but rejects) his desk, then settles on the image of the woman in fur hanging on the wall. The encounter with art is explicitly erotic, the 'cool' glass which separates Gregor from the image providing the actual 'comfort':

> [H]e was struck by the picture of the lady muffled in so much fur and quickly crawled up to it and pressed himself to the glass, which was a good surface to hold on to and comforted his hot belly. This picture at least, which was entirely hidden beneath him, was going to be removed by nobody. (*CS* 118)

What is unusual about Kafka's text and distinguishes it from Sacher-Masoch's racier but ultimately more conventional narrative, is that the movement toward 'animality' and masochistic desire does not result in sin and guilt, but in a cleansing of these 'human' remnants from Gregor's past. The animal is innocent. Thus his metamorphosis is akin to a rebirth, to a childlike awakening, to self-absorbed games and play. We are told for instance that Gregor's insect legs 'dance . . . as if set free', that he learns to get out of bed by rocking himself to and fro—'the new method was more a game [*Spiel*] than an effort' (94)—and that, despite his grotesque form, he shows no hesitation in offering himself for public viewing. 'He was eager to find out what the others, after all their insistence, would say at the sight of him' (98).[19] The sentiment voiced here is more than a comic device: Gregor is in the process of losing his capacity for self-judgement through the eyes of the world, of becoming an unselfconscious child-animal.

This reacquisition of an originary freedom and innocence coincides with Gregor's *Kunsttrieb*, his impulse toward art and self-display. Two moments stand out in this process. The first is the delightful interlude of unselfconscious play that takes place in the novella's second section. Despite the damage inflicted to his body by his father, Gregor enjoys a beatific state of distraction (*Zerstreuung*), innocent of memory, swinging like a gymnast from the ceiling, walking the walls, defying the material constraint of gravity much like the trapeze artists, circus riders, and floating dogs figured in Kafka's other writings. High above the furniture in his room, Gregor can breathe more 'freely':

> He especially enjoyed hanging suspended from the ceiling; it was much better than lying on the floor; one could breathe more freely; one's body swung and rocked lightly; and in the almost blissful absorption induced by this suspension it could happen to his own surprise that he let go and fell plump on the floor. Yet he now had his body much better under control than formerly, and even such a big fall did him no harm. (*CS* 115)

A happy state of distraction, easy breathing, the almost musical rhythm rocking his body—these are all privileged terms in Kafka's vocabulary. Capable of 'falling' from a great height without harming himself, Gregor has achieved a state of innocent grace untroubled by his father's *Schulden*, the financial 'debts' that are also, in German, the result of moral transgressions. But this 'immortality' is achieved by the 'artist' who has made his body into the vehicle of his art, a vehicle which performs, in these moments of unselfconscious play, as gracefully as the marionettes in Kleist's essay 'Über das Marionettentheater.' If *Luftmensch*, as Günther Anders points out, connotes in German the artist who has no solid footing beneath his feet, Gregor is the *Lufttier*, much like the floating dogs in the later story 'Investigations of a Dog' who are animated by an uncanny, silent music, or the Japanese tumblers Kafka drew in his diary as an image of artistic freedom (*DI* 12). Gregor literally floats above the traffic of human time, his consciousness absorbed by his dancing, though hardly *Jugendstilian*, body.

The second moment occurs in the third section of the novella and brings out the musical implications of Gregor's artistic self-realization. Gregor's sister Grete begins playing the violin for her parents and the lodgers while Gregor lies in his dirty, dark room. Animated by a corporeal *Kunsttrieb* or will to art, oblivious to the material consequences of his action, he creeps toward his sister or rather her 'playing', her *Spiel*:

> Gregor's sister began to play; the father and mother, from either side, intently watched the movements of her hands. Gregor, attracted by the playing, ventured to move forward a little until his head was actually inside the living room.... [I]n spite of his condition, no shame deterred him from advancing a little over the spotless floor ... Gregor crawled a little farther forward and lowered his head to the ground so that it might be possible for his eyes to meet hers. Was he an animal, that music moved him so? He felt as if the way were opening before him to the unknown nourishment he craved. (*CS* 130–1)

Again Kafka's text insists on the ludic, innocent character of this encounter. Despite his animal condition, the filth that his body has accumulated, or even the evidently incestuous nature of his attraction to his sister, 'no shame deter[s] him' on his path toward the 'unknown nourishment' evoked by the music. We should note too the text's insistence on a lived, corporeal experience of the music: the boarders who read the musical notes over Grete's shoulder rather than experience music physically like Gregor are clearly portrayed as philistines. Gregor, the innocent 'child-animal' who wants to 'play' with his sister, has access to the secret of art because his body is itself striving for a weightless, ethereal, musical condition. And this artistic impulse results, for the third and last time, in the body's self-display in a context of aesthetic performance.

Even the process of dying has an aesthetic, spiritual dimension. Like the initial rejection of clothing, cloth 'samples', and the *Verkehr* of his employment, Gregor's progressive rejection of organic nourishment initiates a movement back to the innocence of childhood or, in biblical terms, to the moment in Eden before the eating of the apple. (The apple that Gregor's father throws at him interrupts this movement and ultimately seems responsible for the son's Christ-like death. But the apple originates with the father, not the innocent child, and as such represents the violent intrusion of the 'traffic' of Gregor's previous life into his aesthetic paradise.) As the memory of his human past fades away, Gregor begins to 'play' with his food like an infant, eventually renouncing it altogether for the pleasures of his home gymnastics: 'he was fast losing any interest he had ever taken in food, so that for mere recreation he had formed the habit of crawling crisscross over the walls and ceiling' (*CS* 115). This fasting flattens and lightens Gregor's form, removing it from the circulation of human, organic life, 'spiritualizing' it until it is completely empty. Grete, who shows a particular fascination for the corpse, remarks: "'Just see how thin he was. It's such a long time since he's eaten anything. The food came out again just as it went in." Indeed, Gregor's body was completely flat and dry' (*CS* 136–7).

The Christian overtones of this death are clear and support the basic narrative of conflict between father and son. Herr Samsa makes the sign of the cross, for example, and Gregor is described as being 'festgenagelt', 'nailed fast' to the floor by the paternal apple bombardment. Yet Gregor is not only a fasting Christ or monk who has withdrawn from the world, but first of all the *fin-de-siècle* aesthete who 'hungers' for music, the highest of the arts in Romantic and Symbolist poetics.[20] Within the corpus of Kafka's own writings, Gregor bears an unmistakable affinity with other artist figures. One thinks for instance of Georg Bendemann in 'The Judgment' who performs his gymnastic 'turn' over the bridge but then hangs to the railing 'as a starving man clutches for food'. Or of the famished musical dogs in 'Investigations of a Dog', or the disappearing artist figures of the last stories, 'A Hunger Artist' and 'Josephine the Singer'. But Gregor's metamorphosis into a dancing musical bug is the most astonishing of all Kafka's self-referential literary figures. Emptied of all organic substance, perfectly isolated from the paternal 'traffic of clothes', he dies as a two-dimensional object, as 'flat' and 'dry' as the pages of printed characters on which he is now immortalized.

V

In the above remarks I have deliberately read Kafka's text against the majority of its critical interpretations, which see in Gregor's metamorphosis a tragedy visited upon an unsuspecting victim that ends with the 'liberation' of the family through his ritualistic sacrifice. On the contrary, I see the family as enslaved and deindividualized by its re-entrance into the *Verkehr* of work, sexuality, and commerce (the realm of 'Clothing'), whereas Gregor carries out the project of self-definition, individual autonomy, and freedom implicit in his transformation into to a 'giant vermin'. He takes off the 'clothes of the world', to put it in the terms of this study, not to reveal an 'essential self' or to retreat into religious seclusion, but, in line with the *fin-de-siècle* substitution of aesthetics for religion, to put on the grotesque mask of art, to retreat into the self-enclosed world of aesthetic play and freedom symbolized by his animal shell. Whether self-willed or not, a consciously Faustian transgression of human limits or a sudden eruption of repressed desire, Gregor's behaviour in his new form is sustained by a constant *Kunsttrieb*, an unconscious artistic will that prevents him from ever questioning the necessity of his metamorphosis or attempting to reverse it. Indeed, this consistent volition to *display* himself goes hand in hand with his 'monstrosity' (etymologically related to *monstrare*, 'to show'), which chases the chief clerk from the scene, puts the formerly parasitic Samsas to work, and dislodges the boarders, allowing Gregor to devote himself to narcissistic play, distraction, and innocent desire. Whatever the cause of his transformation, its implicit, unspoken *telos* is finally aesthetic: to turn the clothed, human body into a pure, autonomous artwork.

This is the place to stress Peter Cersowsky's insightful remark in his study of Kafka's relations to literary decadence that Gregor's metamorphosis into an animal can be seen as part of the traditional 'melancholic disposition' and thereby linked to the melancholy of the *fin-de-siècle* decadent aesthete. Noting that Bourget had already defined the decadent as the isolated individual 'unfit for the common labor of society', Cersowsky rightly stresses the parallel with Gregor's exclusion from family and society as an 'unproductive' bug. In this sense Gregor is a decadent 'type' like Kafka's other bachelor figures— isolated, self-absorbed, ill adapted to work, melancholy, sexually impotent by definition (as the single example of his 'species'), and therefore the endpoint of the Samsa family line. In essence Gregor's metamorphosis establishes the same opposition between aesthete self and bourgeois family, that characterizes Thomas Mann's early novellas (which Kafka greatly admired), with all their connotations of health and vitality on one side, parasitism, decadence and death on the other. Gregor represents the bizarre end of his 'race', the tired, melancholy decadent who willingly departs from this life to make way for his 'healthy' family.[21]

What this interpretation leaves out, however, is the positive, even aggressive countertendency in Kafka's text that insists on Gregor's form as the autonomous artwork. *The Metamorphosis* displays none of Mann's nostalgia for blond and blue-eyed *Bürgerlichkeit*. Indeed, the petty bourgeois environment of the Samsa household—dirty, constricted, animated by a mean will for profit and social conformity—finally provokes the reader's disgust, perhaps the very disgust initially associated with the grotesque bug but which fades away as the story progresses and Gregor's 'humanity' comes to the fore. As we have seen, the text's positive affirmations concern Gregor's form: its childlike aptitude for games, dance, music, and spiritual nourishment. And whereas Gregor's consciousness lags behind the radicality of his aesthetic form (even in death he seems tolerant and forgiving of his family), the body itself proclaims all the aggressive, even jubilant qualities of the avant-garde or modernist artwork: Art as an attack on Life, not just its impotent and nostalgic opponent; Art as the grotesque, abstract, ultimately incomprehensible object that has removed itself from the bourgeois social order.

But not outside the biological order of decay and death. Gregor's blissful state of 'free breathing' and self-absorbed *Zerstreuung* while hanging from the ceiling in his room lasts only a brief while, eventually giving way to a melancholy yearning for an 'unknown nourishment' he has never tasted. And the very refusal of organic nourishment that excludes him from the human, social realm and that augments his ethereal, *Lufttier* nature ultimately leads to his death and disappearance. The animal-artwork is not granted an unnatural physical permanence, but is effaced by the same cycle of life forces that is presumably responsible for its original transformation. On 9 December 1912, two days after finishing what would become his most famous story, Kafka sent Felice Bauer a postcard of Strindberg asking her if she knew his story 'Alone', thus secretly revealing the meaning and aestheticist origins of his own text. 'That is finally what it means to be alone', Strindberg says at the end of his autobiographical narrative in reference to his isolation as an artist. 'To spin oneself into the silk of one's own soul, to mask oneself in one's own cocoon, and wait for the metamorphosis, which never fails to come about.' Kafka spun himself into his own literary cocoon and waited. Yet the metamorphosis that took place in Prague in November 1912 did not produce the strange, beautiful butterfly of Strindberg's *fin-de-siècle* imagination, but a grotesque, primitive ornament of modernity: the 'monstrous vermin'.

Notes

1. For an overview of the secondary literature on The *Metamorphosis*, see S. Corngold's *The Commentators' Despair: The Interpretation of Kafka's 'Metamorphosis'* (Port Washington: Kennikat Press, 1973) and P. Beicken's *Franz Kafka: Eine kritische Einfürhrung in die Forschung* (Frankfurt: Fischer Taschenbuch, 1974), 261–72. One of the earliest interpretations of the story in psychoanalytic terms was by H. Kaiser, whose 'Franz Kafkas Inferno: eine psychologische Deutung seiner Strafphantasie' appeared in the official psychoanalytic journal *Imago* in 1931. A large number of critics have taken over Kaisers notion of a 'punishment fantasy' including H. Tauber, H. D. Luke, C. Neider, W. Sokel. For Marxist readings of the story, see K. Hughes (ed.), *Franz Kafka: an Anthology of Marxist Criticism* (Concord: University Press of New England, 1981).

2. 'Because Gregor Samsa wishes to live as an artist (i.e. "free as air" (*wie ein Luftmensch*), he is considered in the eyes of the respectable, down-to-earth world, to be a "bit of an insect"; thus, in *The Metamorphosis*, he wakes up as a beetle, whose idea of happiness is to be clinging to the ceiling.' Franz *Kafka*, trans. A. Steter and A. K. Thorlby (London: Bowes & Bowes, 1960), 43. See also the historical meaning of Luftmensch discussed in Ch. 3.

3. Corngold offers the suggestive hypothesis that Kafka's experience of writing 'The Judgment' in September 1912, the story which 'came out of (him) like a real birth, covered with filth and slime' (*DI* 278), is the implicit biographical meaning of *The Metamorphosis*. See the expanded version of his essay 'The Metamorphosis of the Metaphor', in *Franz Kafka: The Necessity of Form* (Ithaca, NY: Cornell University Press, 1988). P. Cersowsky

notes interestingly the tradition of metamorphosis into an animal as 'an extreme image of the melancholy disposition', thereby linking Gregor to the melancholy 'decadent type'. See *'Mein ganzes Wesen ist auf Literatur gerichtet'* (Würzburg: Künigshausen & Neumann, 1983), p. 76.

4. First published in 1970, the essay was reprinted in an expanded version in *The Necessity of Form*, which is the edition quoted here.

5. In his *Introduction à la littérature fantastique* (Paris: Éditions du Seuil, 1970), Todorov rejects an affiliation with the fantastic, noting that Kafka's text proceeds in an opposite movement: 'Le récit fantastique partait d'une situation parfaitement naturelle pour aboutir au surnaturel, *la Métamorphose* part de l'événement surnaturel pour lui donner, en cours de récit, un air de plus en plus naturel; et la fin de l'histoire est la plus éloignée qui soft du surnaturel' (179).

6. See Margot Norris's discussion of Darwin and Nietzsche in relation to Kafka in *Beasts of the Modern Imagination* (Baltimore: Johns Hopkins University Press, 1985).

7. See Jörg Mathes, introduction to *Theorie des literarischen Jugendstils* (Stuttgart: Reclam, 1984), 32.

8. Foreword to 1st edn., *Kunstformen der Natur* (Leipzig: Bibliographisches Institut, 1899).

9. As it turned out, Haeckel was richly rewarded for his efforts. In his 1913 introduction to *Die Natur als Künstlerin* (*Nature as Artist*) (Berlin: Vita), he remarks that since the publication of his earlier work he has received numerous pieces of furniture, dishes, cups, and pillows, all 'tastefully embellished with the charming forms of the above-mentioned protists' (12).

10. As quoted by K. Wagenbach, *Franz Kafka: Eine Biographie seiner Jugend* (Berne: Francke, 1958), 60.

11. Maurice Maeterlinck, whose writings played a key role in Symbolist and *fin-de-siècle* literary movements, was an amateur zoologist and botanist who dedicated several works to minute descriptions of ants, bees, and the *intelligence des fleurs*; he felt that their activity revealed a sense of order and beauty, an innate 'artistic instinct'. Other writers, notably Jens Peter Jacobsen (a trained botanist who translated Darwin into Danish), Joris-Karl Huysmans, and Octave Mirbeau in France, developed similar ideas about natural evolution in their works.

12. 'Die Insel Carina', in *Experimente* (Berlin: Axel Juncker, 1907), 46.

13. 'Das Märchen der 672. Nacht', in J. Mathes (ed.), *Prosa des Jugendstils* (Stuttgart: Reclam, 1982), 41–2.

14. 'Ein Brief', as reprinted in U. Karthaus (ed.), *Imprestionismus, Symbolismus und Jugendstil* (Stuttgart: Reclam, 1977), 148–50, my translation. The above quotations appear in three separate passages but all refer to the same mystical, unutterable experience.

15. Kafka's depiction of the counter-metamorphosis that takes hold of the Samsa family reveals the extent of his ambivalence not only toward bourgeois sexuality and marriage but also toward the bourgeois notion of work. Since the Enlightenment, work in the public sphere had been seen as the key to individual self-definition, for liberal and Marxist philosophers alike, personal autonomy and freedom are guaranteed by one's profession or trade, through which individuals realize their identities and participate in the social collectivity. Kafka is closer to Max Stirner and other anarchist philosophers who see work and any participation in the *Verkehr* of the socio-economic sphere as a threat to individual identity. See especially the chapter entitled 'Mein Verkehr' in Stirner's *Der Einzige und sein Eigentum* (1843), in which he emphasizes the individual's need to withdraw from the 'traffic' of familial responsibilities.

16. 'And the Lord God made for Adam and for his wife garments of skins [*Röcke von Fellen*], and clothed them.' (Diary entry for 19 June 1916.)

17. Sacher-Masoch's book has recently been reprinted in English with an extensive introduction by Gilles Deleuze (New York: Zone Books, 1989). On the relationship between Sacher-Masoch and Kafka see Ruth Angress, 'Kafka and Sacher-Masoch: A Note on *The Metamorphosis*', *Modern Language Notes* 85 (1970), 745–6; F. Kuna, 'Art as Direct Vision: Kafka and Sacher-Masoch', *Journal of European Studies* (1972), 237–46; and my own 'Kafka and Sacher-Masoch'. *Journal of the Kafka Society of America*, 2 (Dec. 1983), 4–19 (repr. in Harold Bloom (ed.), *Franz Kafka's the Metamorphosis*, Modern Critical Interpretations (New York: Chelsea House, 1988)).

18. Freud writes: 'fur and velvet—as has long been suspected—are a fixation of the sight of the pubic hair, which should have been followed by the longed-for sight of the female member.' Cf. 'Fetishism' (1927), in *The Standard Edition of the Complete Psychological Works of Sigmund Freud* (London: The Hogarth Press, 1961), xxi. 147–58. The fetish allows the subject to maintain his fantasy of a female penis, thus sidestepping the threat of castration. This interpretation seems to have validity for Sacher-Masoch's hero, who frequently fantasizes that the furs enclose some hard, erect object (such as a marble statue of Venus) or a source of violent energy. Masoch's emphasis on electricity, his image of the woman in furs as an 'augmented electric battery', seems to suggest that the impersonality of the punishment is a key element in the masochistic experience of pleasure. (The apples that the father bombards Gregor with at the end of the second section roll about as if 'electrisiert'; the machine in 'In the Penal Colony' runs on electric power.) The image of the woman's forearm and fist in the fur muff also corresponds to Freud's notion of the (male) child's fantasy of the female member.

19. This itinerary is essentially the opposite of that travelled by Red Peter in Kafka's later story 'A Report to an Academy', an ape living in blissfully unselfconscious freedom on the 'Gold Coast' who is captured and introduced into the *Verkehr* of human society: he learns to talk, wear trousers, drink schnapps, and fornicate with a trained (i.e. half-human) chimpanzee. By contrast *The Metamorphosis* describes Gregor's progressive acquisition of the freedom in his animal body, thereby returning to the 'Gold Coast' of a childlike, prelapsarian innocence.

20. Walter Pater's claim in *The Renaissance* that all the arts strive for the 'condition of music' best sums up this tradition. Knut Hamsun's novel *Hunger* (1890) established the connection between fasting and the dedication to writing for an entire generation of German writers at the turn of the century, including Thomas Mann and Kafka. Mann used the trope in his early story 'Die Hungernden', Kafka most notably in 'A Hunger Artist' and 'Investigations of a Dog', where it is also related to music.

21. See Cersowsky, 'Mein ganzes Wesen', 74–6.

ROBERT WENINGER

Sounding Out the Silence of Gregor Samsa: Kafka's Rhetoric of Dys-Communication

By struggling to sound out the depths of their respective languages, poets like Hölderlin, Rimbaud, Mallarmé, Trakl, or Celan—to name only a few— have pursued their art to the limits of their medium. Their goal was, among other things, to listen in to the silence behind words. By doing so, many came close to silencing themselves. In various forms of "chosen silence" (Steiner 47), some actually did; Hölderlin's retreat into madness, Kleist's suicide, Novalis' early mortal illness, Rimbaud's flight from the choking influence of Verlaine into the heart of Africa, Trakl's self-dispensed overdose of drugs. All their reactions might be viewed, if not literally then symbolically, as different symptoms of one and the same cause, a condition in which they felt their language to have ceased to communicate persuasively between poetic aspiration and life's sometimes sordid realities, between *Begeisterung* (a term popular among Hölderlin's and Hegel's generation) and melancholy (a term popularized in 19th century literature), between the outside and the inside. "This election of silence by the most articulate is," according to George Steiner, "historically recent" (46). In a similar vein, Susan Sontag has pointed out that:

> the exemplary modern artist's choice of silence is rarely carried
> to this point of final simplification, so that he becomes literally

From *Studies in Twentieth Century Literature* 17, no. 2 (Summer 1993): pp. 263–286. © 1993 by Kansas State University.

silent. More typically, he continues speaking, but in a manner that his audience can't hear. Most valuable art in our time has been experienced by audiences as a move into silence (or unintelligibility or invisibility or inaudibility). (184)

Thus the poet who ends in silence stands opposed to the poet who uses silence as an end. Taking my cue from Steiner's and Sontag's remarks on poets and silence, I would like to focus attention on an author whom we might consider the "classic" *prose* writer of the same existential condition that was outlined above, a condition that is based upon the salient, yet often perfidious, relationship between language and life. If any, it is Franz Kafka's oeuvre that may be called in fictional terms a metaphor of silence.[1]

I

Walter Sokel once remarked: "Kafka's goal was 'truth,' *i.e.* the perfect *adaequatio* between word and feeling, between linguistic sign and inner being.... This 'poetics' presupposes two distinct entities—the inner self or inner world, which is to be expressed, and the medium of expression—language. If perfect correspondence between the two is achieved, writing becomes the true vehicle of being" ("Kafka's Poetics" 8). Yet Kafka hardly ever reached that point of satisfaction—or so he believed; his diaries, notebooks, and letters testify to his ordeal with his inability to communicate his inner world in linguistic terms. Kafka complains time and again of this lack of a language with which to surmount the inner divide suggested by Sokel. In his third octavo notebook he once jotted down: "There is no such thing as observation of the inner works, as there is of the outer world.... The inner world can only be experienced, not described" (*Wedding Preparations* 72). In his diaries he commented: "It is certain that everything I have conceived in advance, even when I was in a good mood, whether word for word or just casually, but in specific words, appears dry, wrong, inflexible, embarrassing to everybody around me [an imperfect rendering of 'der ganzen Umgebung hinderlich'], timid, but above all incomplete when I try to write it down at my desk, although I have forgotten nothing of the original conception" (*The Diaries* 151).

Of course, Kafka's unique modernist narrative originates not only from his stringent artistic credo, from his perfectionistic—if often vain—quest for the adequate word.[2] It is nurtured, too, as is well known, by the intellectual crisis brought about by a stifling family history and the corrosive relationship with his father. For obvious reasons this relationship has been the focus of many studies on Kafka's literary achievement—and it recently inspired Alan Rennet to produce his wonderfully knowledgeable burlesque, *Kafka's Dick*.[3] The father–

son conflict remains one of the central extra-literary avenues to the psychological aspects of Kafka's narrative universe; the Oedipus-theme underlies more or less transparently many interpretive approaches reaching from Max Brod's religious exegesis through psychoanalytic analyses to autobiographical or socio-historical ones that stress, amongst other things, the role of authoritarian socialization in turn-of-the-century Prague. But, as Bennet hints, had it not been for that most famous (or should I say infamous) letter of world literature, Kafka's "Letter to his Father" (which was written but never sent), we would most probably have little more to say about Kafka's relationship to his father than about any other author's. And yet, in spite of all that has been written about the "Letter" and Kafka's fictionalization of this Relationship (with a capital 'R'), I would like to come back to it one more time.

The reading of Kafka's "Metamorphosis" that I propose on the following pages is based on two assumptions that are derived from widely divergent approaches to Kafka's writings. The first is the offspring of psychological interpretation and recognizes that homologous unconscious strategies are operative in the "Letter to his Father" and Kafka's tale.[4] Josef Rattner, writing about the *Ur-Situationen*, the "primal situations" that Kafka experienced as a child and which produced in him his most basic psychological attitudes (Rattner calls them *Grundhaltungen*), concludes: "Kafka's life is an incessant attempt to cope with his father-experience. His father is at the base of his anxiety of life and his crippling hypochondria.... Sadism and masochism are distinctive features of Kafka's works."[5] The second, brought to the fore by recent scholarly examinations of the institutional reception of Kafka's texts by, and their effect on, academic and non-academic readers alike, recognizes that equally homologous strategies underlie both Kafka's "Metamorphosis" and our critical readerly reactions to the text. Thus Allen Thiher remarked only recently that "if the interpretive quest underlies the general structure of 'The Metamorphosis,' the story owes its affective specificity to the way that Kafka uses particular objects, images, and situations to mirror the quest and to force the reader to enter a diffuse hermeneutic labyrinth" (45). For precisely this reason Horst Steinmetz has called—not in the abstract Barthesian sense but on more pragmatic grounds—for a moratorium in Kafka-interpretation. In his essay, Steinmetz presents a graphic picture of the dilemma of Kafka-interpreters like himself who, on the one hand, hardly wish to abandon the quest for more precise readings of Kafka's texts, but who feel, on the other hand, so severely inhibited by the overabundance of scholarship, which is being produced at an ever increasing rate, that he would rather call a halt to it all. Steinmetz concludes: "Kafka-scholarship reflects in its structure, in its basic attitude, [*in ihrer fundamentalen Grundeinstellung*] the structure and basic attitude of Kafka's writing, it forms a mirror-image of the central structural principles of Kafka's fiction" (159).[6]

Surprisingly, both Steinmetz' and Rattner's methods, however large the distance may be between them, display a common notion of what Kafka's basic attitudes, his *Grundhaltungen* or *Grundeinstellungen*, may have been. What Rattner (and like-minded psychological interpreters) and Steinmetz (along with like-minded reception-oriented critics) have in common is their view that they are dealing with a homology of some sort where one half of the equation is Kafka's texts; in the one instance it affects the writer's (un)conscious and his fiction, while in the other there is a palpable correlation between Kafka's narrative world and its interpreters' plight (abbreviated by Steinmetz into yet another level of receptive *Grundeinstellung*). In the tripartite structure that is formed by author, text, and reader, each method is content to elaborate on one of the binary oppositions to the exclusion of the other. The more traditional kinds of psychological interpretation will focus on the author–text relationship to the exclusion of the reader, while reader-oriented studies tend to disregard, or devalue, the authorial component of the equation.[7] The resulting readings co-exist as alternative interpretations of the same text. They may illuminate one another, more often they clash, but rarely do they interact in any methodical way. But obviously, if both assertions are right, then it should be possible to reveal behind Kafka's (un)conscious authorial design, his textual universe, and its interpreters' hermeneutical dilemma, a unified triangular correspondence rather than two divaricating mirrorings.

It is this possibility that I would like to explore by providing against the background of "The Letter to his Father" and our divergent responses to "The Metamorphosis," as documented by Stanley Corngold's *The Commentator's Despair*, yet another close (but by no means closed) reading of Gregor Samsa's case and, in particular, of his *vocal silence* (the oxymoron is intended and will be explained in the course of this essay). Rather than investigate—as has been done before—how the approaches outlined above work to multiply textual readings without their ever bearing on one another, or how they might succeed in cancelling each other out, my aim is to combine their disparate (if not conflicting) axiomatic claims into an integrated reading of Kafka's text that runs seamlessly from the authorial unconscious through the text and its tale to the reader's predicament.

Many individual points that need to be made in the course of my argument will be known, of course; other details will, hopefully, come to be seen in a new light. For example, most if not all readers accept Gregor's loss of language as a fact; oftentimes it is taken for granted that he had the power to communicate before his transmogrification, which caused him to lose this human faculty. If not literally, then no doubt figuratively it might be argued, however, that Gregor Samsa never really possessed the capacity to speak and had, in effect, neither been able to communicate his subdued feelings of anger, isolation, and frustration, nor that he ever was in a position to express his opinion outright—

don't we all agree that this is what finally causes him to metamorphose into an insect? As such this insight may not be original, but if we extend this line of reasoning to focus anew on the dialogue and the structure of communication that reigns in the Samsa family we come to discern next to that insidious emotional *silence* that looms unsettlingly behind their *Familienroman*—as Freud would have put it—a latent palimpsestical story of inverted, rather than (as is commonly assumed) aborted, communication. Communication, it seems, can hardly cease for Gregor because it never really began (or, to put it minimally, it stopped many years before that decisive morning). Whatever the case, we shall see in the following analysis that Gregor *does* eventually succeed in expressing himself, but in a very unexpected way. And, ironically, it is his metamorphosis with its concomitant loss of speech that will allow his voice to become heard. Indeed, one of the most striking features of this story is how it allows the disquieting contortions of communication displayed on the various levels of its action to reflect simultaneously its author's biographical circumstances and psychological bearing (as the first method represented above suggests) as well as to inflect the reader's puzzlement at its indeterminacy (a notion that must govern any reader-oriented approach). That is to say, with regard to how communication comes about or is delayed or averted or even inverted in this tale, its components converge in one common rhetorical strategy, that of dys-communication. As we shall see through an initial analysis of Kafka's "Letter to his Father" and a more detailed reading of the story itself, dys-communication accounts for the text's production as well as for what it produces.

II

As has often been remarked, Kafka's "Letter to his Father" is located switchboard-like between his biographical circumstances and his literary oeuvre. As autobiographical discourse, the "Letter" is akin to both spheres of fiction and life. In it Franz Kafka set down *eine Geschichte* (the German term suggests simultaneously a story and a history) of his relationship to his father. This relationship was not only an encompassing emotional and physical presence governing all his day-to-day decision making; it was simultaneously a past historical fad of his childhood experiences that had inscribed itself as rule (in its double sense) into Kafka's mental existence.

Tellingly, the "Letter to his Father" begins with the sentence: "Dearest Father, you asked me recently why I maintain I am afraid of you [1]. As usual, I was unable to think of any answer to your question [2], partly for the very reason that I am afraid of you [3], and partly because an explanation of the grounds for this fear would mean going into far more details [4] than I could even approximately keep in mind while talking [5]" (157).[8] Clearly, this is a prime example of a vicious circle. And the remark is revealing in more than one respect: first, Kafka knows the answer but will not admit it [3 & 4]; second, he cannot utter the reason because his brain refuses to operate when thinking of the cause [2 & 5];[9] third, pronouncing the word "Furcht" 'fear' does not suffice to explain the cause—Kafka feels he must elaborate [4]; and finally, by indicating that the father has no notion why his son should be afraid he cautiously suggests that father and son do not communicate well spiritually [1]. This initial sentence is, moreover, profoundly ambiguous; transferred from its subjunctive form in indirect speech back into direct speech, Kafka's father would have asked: "Warum behauptest du, daß du Furcht vor mir hast?" 'Why do you claim to be afraid of me?', thereby dismissing Kafka's fear as unjustified from the very start. Yet another remarkable component of this complex statement might pass unnoticed (to demonstrate this I did not highlight it in my initial citation): two words testify to the full import of Kafka's opening words and the disillusionment on which they hinge, namely "wie gewöhnlich" 'as usual.' He is, of course, hinting at the frustration incurred by the perpetuated experience of violated communication—or the *scandalon* of utter dys-communication between father and son. It is this withholding of speech that makes Kafka's situation within the family so precarious, a situation that remains essentially unchanged throughout his life. Dys-communication is thus the pattern that pervades Kafka's memories of childhood no less than his present situation within the family and his relationship with Felice at the time when he began to write "The Metamorphosis."[10] And, as we shall see, dys-communication is a forceful narrative pattern in Kafka's literary oeuvre.

Whether he complains of the "extraordinary terror" he once experienced and the "inner harm" (162) that he suffered from being left outdoors on the balcony during the night, or whether he relives the "disgrace of showing myself in public" (164), in many of the incidents described retrospectively in the "Letter," Kafka analyzes, emphasizes, and conveys to the narratee of the document not only his complaint about the breakdown of communication but also about the repetitive nature of this terrifying experience. Words and phrases suggestive of this abound: "This, your usual way of representing it" (158); "your unceasing reproaches" (158); "That then was only a small beginning" (162); "I am not here speaking of any sublime thoughts, but of every little enterprise in childhood" (165); "The point was, rather, that you could not help always and on principle causing the child such disappointments, by virtue of your antagonistic nature" (165); "But that was what your whole method of upbringing was like" (166). If we take Kafka's words at face value—although for good reason we should be cautious about doing so—his father's education was the direst of drills, while the rules of the drill eluded the child. Or, to put it differently, the child was taught to observe (i.e. to study *and* to follow) orders, i.e. manifestations of a language, whose grammar he could not put together in a consistent way, as in that famous and illustrative passage of the "Letter" where Kafka ridicules the father's rites (and rights) at the dinner table (a passage which, if the subject were not so serious—Heinz Politzer once referred to it as "a kind of middle-class inferno" (169)—one might envision being enacted as a farce).

The result of this kind of education—if it actually took place in this manner—is utterly predictable: the child would be required to internalize rules whose individual enunciations appear inconsistent, opaque or, worse still, contradictory, he was to adhere to laws which the authority himself breaks at his whim; no communication takes place between father and son as to the import or meaning of these directives.[11] Consequently, the grammar that the child is eventually led to assimilate—since some grammar must eventually take hold—will reflect by content not those rules originally imposed on him through parental pressure, but rather their transformed semblance. Is it not obvious that one and the same rule may take on quite different functions within a grammar of command and within a grammar of submission? Whether the father was insensitive to his son's plight or whether the son was merely hyper-sensitive and hyper-critical of his father's personality, the transformed set of rules will produce in either case in the child a disjunction of word and meaning and of prescription and action. Thus, two levels of dys-communication originate: one in which words don't match the meaning, in which *language* has become detached, incomprehensible, and ambiguous; and one in which actions occur without reasonable cause or against all laws of probability, in which (narrative) *logic* therefore has become detached, incomprehensible, and ambiguous. As hardly need be pointed out, these two forms of dys-communication are two of the most potent ingredients informing Kafka's literary poetics.

And yet another consequence emerges in respect to the child's daily behavior, a reaction that Kafka describes in detail:

> The impossibility of getting on calmly together had one more result, actually a very natural one: I lost the capacity to talk I dare say I should never have been a very eloquent person in any case, but I should after all have had the usual fluency of human language at my command. But at a very early stage you forbade me to talk. Your threat: "Not a word of contradiction!" and the raised hand that accompanied it have gone with me ever since. What I got from you—and you are, as soon as it is a matter of your own affairs, an excellent talker—was a hesitant, stammering mode of speech, and even that was still too much for you, and finally I kept silence, at first perhaps from defiance, and then because I couldn't either think or speak in your presence. And because you were the person who really brought me up, this has had its repercussions throughout my life. (170)

The grammar of childhood, i.e. the glaring contradictions he experienced at home, the unwarranted maltreatment of servants, employees and family members that he observed, the danger he sensed at revealing his thoughts and the incapacity to do so (with the consequent silence he observed when confronted by his father), and the tendency to conceal himself before the man—all this surfaces anew in a poetics of silence, repressed speech, and dys-communication that informs, as we shall see in the following analysis, as much the groundwork of Kafka's "Letter to his Father" as the grammar of his narrative "The Metamorphosis."[12]

III

One morning, Gregor Samsa awakes after troubled dreams to find himself transformed into a gigantic insect.[13] Although the title of Kafka's tale refers prima facie to this change in physique and Gregor's delayed mental adaptation to his novel condition—which led Günther Anders to speak of an "anti-sensationalism of tone"—the story of his metamorphosis parallels the metamorphosis of *all* family members, i.e. his father, his mother, and his sister Grete.[14] By the very next day, the inability of Gregor, previously the family's sole financial provider, to continue to support his relations has been established. Within two months his mother and sister have taken on menial work; his father, too—who previously had been a sluggish and progressively fossilizing veteran—appears revitalized, now dressed in the uniform of, as Gregor speculates, some local banking institution. Gregor's story ends, of course, only three months after his metamorphosis with his untimely death and with the family's deliverance from the socially stifling circumstance of having to put up with a giant beetle living in their apartment. Outwardly, the cause of Gregor's premature death is that gradually decaying apple, that "Andenken im Fleisch" 'visible reminder' (110), which his father had thrust into his back in unwarranted defence of the mother; this is the physical aspect of his passing. Yet the apple's decay in Gregor's body is an index, too, of an analogous spiritual decay taking place between Gregor and his relations; it symbolizes, as we shall soon see in more detail, the final deterioration of communication that conclusively brings about Gregor's demise.

By virtue of his altered nature, Gregor is speechless from the outset. Understandably, his new insect-like body cannot form human sounds, at best he can produce senseless brutish screeches. It is, surprisingly, this factor that confounds Gregor most: for the first time this morning he reveals genuine astonishment at his incapacity to communicate with his family, especially because, intellectually, he feels as active as ever:

"Gregor," said a voice—it was his mother's—"it's a quarter to seven. Hadn't you a train to catch?" That gentle voice! Gregor had a shock as he heard his own voice answering hers, unmistakably his own voice, it was true, but with a persistent horrible twittering squeak behind it like an undertone, that left the words in their clear shape only for the first moment and then rose up reverberating round them to destroy their sense, so that one could not be sure one had heard them rightly. Gregor wanted to answer at length and explain everything, but in the circumstances he confined himself to saying: "Yes, yes, thank you, Mother, I'm getting up now." (70)

No one can understand him now that he has turned into a beetle. Like at the opening of the story, we should expect Gregor to fall prey to an attack of panic. Any reasonable person would. But again the reader is surprised. The stunning fact that even now Gregor remains composed and demonstrates little awareness of the urgency of his condition makes us more alert to various seemingly detached facets of his present situation as well as of his occupational and familial pre-history. We come to note, for example, that Gregor has often imagined giving notice to his chief and, moreover, giving him a piece of his mind, but he has been constrained by his father's debts to the company. We notice further how the family reacts to Gregor's futile attempt to communicate his normality:

The wooden door between them must have kept the change in his voice from being noticeable outside, for his mother contented herself with this statement and shuffled away. Yet this brief exchange of words had made the other members of the family aware that Gregor was still in the house, as they had not expected, and at one of the side doors his father was already knocking, gently, yet with his fist "Gregor, Gregor," he called, "what's the matter with you?" And after a little while he called again in a deeper voice: "Gregor! Gregor!" At the other side door his sister was saying in a low, plaintive tone: "Gregor? Aren't you well? Are you needing anything?" He answered them both at once: "I'm just ready," and did his best to make his voice sound as normal as possible by enunciating the words very clearly and leaving long pauses between them. So his father went back to breakfast, but his sister whispered: "Gregor, open the door, do." (71)

Obviously, none of them can really make out a word of what he is saying, and we might expect them to show some sign of alarm. Yet only his sister's conduct evidences any apparent concern for Gregor's bestial noises and his atypical tardiness. It soon becomes clear that neither his father nor his mother take any interest in their son's spiritual well-being, that is, as long as he lives up to his role as provider for the family. Thus by now it should be fairly well-established that Gregor Samsa, by means of his metamorphosis, has reversed a humiliating situation that has prevailed for the last five years, namely the parasitic exploitation by his family. But if we look more closely, we can also notice that the basic structure of relationship has actually remained unchanged, except that the figures in the play have exchanged roles. For Gregor, his mutation can hardly be called upsetting, since in regard to the family's disinterestedness toward their son and brother nothing much has changed. And as we shall see, even Gregor's massive corporeal intervention does little to improve the interpersonal constellation. Indeed, from Gregor's perspective, the fact that his relatives and the chief clerk, who was dispatched to criticize him for his absence from work, can communicate with him, but not he with them, can hardly be called a new situation at all. Their reactions merely sustain, or even reinforce, the speechlessness and the formulaic behavior that had prevailed in and outside the family prior to his metamorphosis. Accordingly, following his mutilated dialogue with the chief clerk, who sermonizes in the name of the Trinity of mother, father, and chief, Gregor at last recognizes that "The words he uttered were no longer understandable . . . although they seemed clear enough to him, even clearer than before" (79–80).[15] This sentence is revealing: Gregor's language seems clearer than ever, but neither now nor previously was anyone seriously interested in what he felt and what he had to say.

In view of his being wedged firmly and uncomfortably between family and profession, of the constraints that grew out the family's financial default (a plight that the father was continually exaggerating), and of the neglect of Gregor's physical, spiritual, and emotional needs, his sister Grete must appear as the only consolation and bright spot in his bleak life.[16] It is she who whispers to him a warning of the chief clerk's rapid appearance; it is she who places the basin with fresh milk (before his metamorphosis, Gregor's favorite beverage) with little sops of white bread in his room; it is she who takes note of his repugnance and replaces the milk with a selection of food reaching from dry bread to delicious half-decayed vegetables. Grete is from the outset the family member who cares most for Gregor. She alone retains the umbilical cord between him and his family. Yet even with her, of whom Gregor thinks so highly, communication does not hold for long. Her conduct soon establishes for herself a new and more powerful function within the family, one of authority even:

> For the first fortnight his parents could not bring themselves to
> the point of entering his room, and he often heard them expressing

their appreciation of his sister's activities, whereas formerly they had frequently scolded her for being as they thought a somewhat useless daughter. But now, both of them often waited outside the door, his father and his mother, while his sister tidied his room, and as soon as she came out she had to tell them exactly how things were in the room, what Gregor had eaten, how he had conducted himself this time and whether there was not perhaps some slight improvement in his condition. (99–100)

She is the "expert" (103); her advice is followed, and her arguments prevail when, for example, mother and daughter discuss whether to leave Gregor's room untouched in remembrance of things past, or, as Grete urges, to empty the room of furniture to accommodate Gregor's newly acquired natural habit of roaming over walls and ceiling.

Of course, her decisions display her self-interest in that they serve to amplify her power: "Another factor might have been also the enthusiastic temperament of an adolescent girl, which seeks to indulge itself on every opportunity and which now tempted Grete to exaggerate the horror of her brother's circumstances in order that she might do all the more for him. In a room where Gregor lorded it all alone over empty walls no one save herself was likely ever to set foot" (103). Thus her management of Gregor's affairs is deceptive. Maybe she is motivated at the beginning by remnants of affection for her brother, maybe she *does* feel that she has a more intimate understanding of her brother's needs but as the story unfolds her care is progressively downgraded to a mere call of duty. Increasingly she handles his affairs with detachment, and her actions assert ever more strongly her control over Gregor's standing in the family. Her willingness to communicate with Gregor and to manage his needs immediately following his metamorphosis allows her, later in the story, to disregard his existential desires all the more energetically.[17]

Moreover (and hardly noticeable to Gregor himself, who remains throughout the story a virtuoso of self-deception), Grete manages his life while gradually fusing with the father-figure. This culminates on that fatal day, the focal point of the story, when his sister has set her mind on rearranging his quarters by removing all his furniture. The brutality of the scene manifests itself in the extreme dys-communication that obtains between brother and sister, man and woman, insect and human. Her superficially sincere desire to create a more appropriate habitat for his bestial life-style only veils her ultimate attempt to dehumanize and evict the brother. Her maneuver is counterpoised by Gregor's haunting sense of helplessness and speechlessness. Gregor, who is not at all enthusiastic about his sister's scheme to deprive him of these last exterior rudiments of his humanity, envisages losing, too, the romantic portrait of the lady with the muff and, in his alarm, to save her he places his insectile body squarely on her portrait. The following scene ensues:

> They had not allowed themselves much of a rest and were already coming; Grete had twined her arm round her mother and was almost supporting her. "Well, what shall we take now?" said Grete, looking round. Her eyes met Gregor's from the wall. She kept her composure, presumably because of her mother, bent her head down to her mother, to keep her from looking up, and said, although in a fluttering, unpremeditated voice: "Come, hadn't we better go back to the living room for a moment?" Her intentions were clear enough to Gregor, she wanted to bestow her mother in safety and then chase him down from the wall. Well, just let her try it! He clung to his picture and would not give it up. He would rather fly in Grete's face.
>
> But Grete's words had succeeded in disquieting her mother, who took a step to one side, caught sight of the huge brown mass on the flowered wallpaper, and before she was really conscious that what she saw was Gregor screamed in a loud, hoarse voice: "Oh God, oh God!" fell with outspread arms over the sofa as if giving up and did not move. "Gregor!" cried his sister, shaking her fist and glaring at him. This was the first time she had directly addressed him since his metamorphosis. (105–06)

This episode is crucial for two reasons in particular. Not only—as most critics have pointed out—do the sexual implications of Gregor's metamorphosis surface by way of his flagrant conjugation with the flamed lady (we are told that the glass of the picture "comforted his hot belly") and his clearly fecal appearance; we also experience a sister who at last drops her mask and openly substitutes for the father. Now it is she who, in the absence of the father, defends the mother. She urges her to leave the room of shame, thus driving a wedge between mother and son as if she were her father's oedipal counterpart; she chides the brother for his insolence. Moreover, by raising her fist and her voice, she momentarily metamorphoses into the father figure of the opening paragraphs of the story.

Gregor, we now hear, is once and for all "cut off from his mother" (106). The ties to his sister, too, are severed by his radical effort to undermine her objective. And, as if to ratify the breach between Gregor and the family, the father, who returns only moments after the ordeal in Gregor's den, misinterprets both Grete's words and Gregor's appeasing behavior:

"Ah!" he cried as soon as he appeared, in a tone which sounded at once angry and exultant. Gregor drew his head back from the door and lifted it to look at his father. Truly, this was not the father he had imagined to himself; admittedly he had been too absorbed of late in his new recreation of crawling over the ceiling to take the same interest as before in what was happening elsewhere in the flat, and he ought really to be prepared for some changes. And yet, and yet, could that be his father? (107–08)

The father chases his son around the table and bombards him with apples, one of which finally enters Gregor's back. Its decay will eventually lead to his death. So, with the father's strength, ire, and hatred redoubled, with Gregor's separation from his mother, and with his sister's emotional withdrawal, all remaining bridges between the human beetle and his relations have been destroyed. Communication, before Gregor's metamorphosis only a shroud covering familial vacuity, during his recreated presence as beetle a lifeline upheld with sheer condescension, may now emerge in its true and aboriginal nature.

But for a short while, Gregor's increasing debility changes the family's attitude toward him:

The serious injury done to Gregor, which disabled him for more than a month—the apple went on sticking in his body as a visible reminder, since no one ventured to remove it—seemed to have made even his father recollect that Gregor was a member of the family, despite his present unfortunate and repulsive shape, and ought not to be treated as an enemy, that, on the contrary, family duty required suppression of disgust and the exercise of patience, nothing but patience. (110)

The translation would be misleading if we were not to mention that in German the word "patience" is expressed by the term "dulden"; more than patience, this verb means to endure, to tolerate, and to suffer. These words circumscribe accurately the emotions Gregor must have gone through in the period preceding his metamorphosis. The injurious action taken by the father has, of course, forced the family unwittingly into Gregor's previous position. They now cannot blame *him alone* for his invalidity. The "Andenken im Fleisch," rendered by Willa and Edwin Muir as "a visible reminder," obliges them to recognize at last the fact that they themselves are ultimately one cause of Gregor's deterioration. And it produces, as with Gregor in his prime, a sense of guilt, even if only for a short while. From his vantage-point, Gregor has succeeded, maybe more effectively than if he had been outspoken, but also more effectively than he had hoped for, in demonstrating to his family what his situation must have been like before his metamorphosis.

While Gregor's metamorphosis has enforced a reversal of dependence, it perpetuates the basic structure of dys-communication. And Gregor has added to that domestic state of predictable dys-communication the fact that this new family structure is irreversible. This of course makes Gregor's story so immensely disturbing for the reader. We sense that beyond the physical appearance of the family members—Gregor's beetle-like constitution, the father's new attire, the mother's and sister's new occupations—very little has changed.[18] (If a change takes place at all besides Gregor's corporeal metamorphosis, it seems to be located at the end of the story rather than at the beginning.) And we feel from the beginning and throughout the story as it evolves that there is so much to be said between father and son, mother and son, and even sister and brother, that remains uncommunicated. Gregor's metamorphosis not only originates from a deficit, it nurtures rather than corrects this familial shortcoming. Familial dys-communication is a paralyzing force. Yet the reader, who intuits the dilemma and pins his or her hopes on some sign of rapprochement, remains disappointed to the end. With the feeling of desolation and demotion that now proliferates in the family, Gregor's situation is bound to grow worse. Adding to his mortal injury, Gregor soon experiences an increasingly humiliating treatment by his family members. No one has time for him, no one cares for his well-being, no one ever tries to communicate with him, with the exception of the maid who treats him with spite. Even his sister has completely emancipated herself from the brother; her behavior has become utterly devoid of affection:

> His sister no longer took thought to bring him what might especially please him, but in the morning and at noon before she went to business hurriedly pushed into his room with her foot any food that was available, and in the evening cleared it out again with one sweep of the broom, heedless of whether it had been merely tasted, or—as most frequently happened—left untouched. The cleaning of his room, which she now did always in the evenings, could not have been more hastily done. (114)[19]

The emotional silence that prevails in the family comes to the fore when parents and daughter argue over the duties each of them should perform. Even Gregor cannot refrain from "hiss[ing] loudly with rage because not one of them thought of shutting the door to spare him such a spectacle and so much noise" (115). Here the relationship among the family members is portrayed in its true light—and Gregor, too, shows himself a true son of the family!

The appearance of those three obscure boarders toward the end of the story only serves to corroborate this reading. One evening after dinner, Grete plays her violin in the kitchen. Soon the boarders ask her to play for them in the living room. Gregor is attracted by his sister's playing, and he ventures further into the room than usual. As soon as Mr. Samsa discovers Gregor's presence, he tries to shepherd the three boarders into their room to prevent their noticing the vermin. But they react as Gregor should have reacted many months earlier:

> The old man seemed once more to be so possessed by his mulish self-assertiveness that he was forgetting all the respect he should show to his lodgers. He kept driving them on and driving them on until in the very door of the bedroom the middle lodger stamped his foot loudly on the floor and so brought him to a halt. "I beg to announce," said the lodger, lifting one hand and looking also at Gregor's mother and sister, "that because of the disgusting conditions prevailing in this family and household"—here he spat on the floor with emphatic brevity—"I give you notice on the spot." (123)

Their outspokenness is balanced against Gregor's reticence; they verbalize what he has suppressed. And not only do *they*, by proxy for Gregor, give notice to the family; the family, having endured for the short span of a couple of weeks what Gregor suffered for close to five years, reciprocally gives notice to Gregor. After the boarders have retreated, his sister declares to father and mother: "things can't go on like this . . . we must try to get rid of it. We've tried to look after it and to put up with it as far as is humanly possible . . . it will be the death of both of you, I can see that coming. When one has to work as hard as we do, all of us, one can't stand this continual torment at home on top of it. At least I can't stand it any longer" (124).

Clearly, Grete is expressing what Gregor has felt all along. Through his metamorphosis, Gregor, who was incapable beforehand of communicating his quandary and now has no control over human speech, has forced everyone else, from family members to boarders, to express in words precisely what he had felt plaguing him for years. His speechlessness has marvelously compelled others to speak in his name. His silence has become his form of speech. Or, as Stanley Corngold once described Gregor's predicament: "his body is the speech in which the impossibility of ordinary language expresses its own despair" (13). Nevertheless, it enters no one's mind that their grievance against him should mirror Gregor's own (albeit unuttered) complaint about them. However fitting their words may be to Gregor's circumstances before his metamorphosis, neither father, mother, nor sister suspects any connection between their present and his past predicament. This attests once more to the inveteracy of dys-communication in the Samsa family.

IV

As we have seen, Gregor's obtrusive presence in his family is grounded in the mutual inability to communicate with even the closest of fellow beings. Maybe his situation *was* a cul-de-sac in human and emotional terms and suggested to him no other solution than physical transformation. He could have tried to speak, of course—but that would have been another story, a more contemporary one perhaps, and certainly not Kafka's. But, more probably, even if he had used words, understanding would hardly have come about—does not the "Letter to his Father" bear testimony to this fact? And other texts and other protagonists tell the same story. We are dealing throughout Kafka's oeuvre with a grammar of communication that is partially derived from his childhood experiences, a grammar that was imprinted by his father on the susceptible child as a pronounced, but hardly pronounceable, second nature. His father's core of regimentations translated for Franz into a grammar of dys-communication. This begat his quintessential doubt, which "in me turned into mistrust of myself and into perpetual anxiety in relation to everything else" (*Wedding Preparations* 191).

Similarly, analysis of "The Metamorphosis" reveals that beneath the surface structure of the text, beneath its manifest appearance, we find on Gregor's part—next to his need for self-expression—a desperate strategy of avoidance or circumvention of verbal confrontation A fitting metaphor for this strategy is, of course, the form he has taken through his transformation, his shell or "Panzer." Most critics of the story point out correctly that with his physical transformation Gregor succeeds in turning the tables on his family, less attention has been given to the fact that this does not apply to the use of language and the vocalization of sentiment. For many years prior to his metamorphosis, Gregor lived in a state of virtual silence and hardly, if ever, did he dare to express his opinion of his employer, his job, his father or mother or sister. Not so his family, his employer, or the three boarders once they are put in his position: sooner or later they all articulate their grievances and vocalize their complaints. They speak out and verbalize the problems he is causing, thereby giving him (or those who symbolically take his place) a piece of their mind. At the outset of the story the chief clerk addresses Gregor with the words: "You amaze me, you amaze me. I thought you were a quiet, dependable person, and now all at once you seem bent on making a disgraceful exhibition of yourself. . . . But now I see how incredibly obstinate you are, I no longer have the slightest desire to take your part at all" (77). Like with his family's and the boarders' statements, the chief cleric's words echo Gregor's most secret thoughts.

That through his transmogrification Gregor is enabled to ventriloquize his voice onto other speakers is indicated by the text itself when Gregor's first aborted attempts to communicate are described: "Gregor had a shock," we read, "as he heard his own voice, it was true, but with a persistent horrible twittering squeak behind it like an undertone, that left the words in their clear shape only for the first moment and then rose up reverberating round them to destroy their sense, so that one could not be sure one had heard them rightly" (70). His speech is uttered from below: "wie von unten her," from inside his body. This need not imply, as Sokel suggests from a psychological vantage-point, that it issues from his unconscious; we might as well read it literally as referring to the physical strain of trying to produce words through the belly—which would be quite appropriate for an animal that lacks human organs of speech. So while through his transformation Gregor inscribes his silence into his body, he (unnoticeably for all involved) eventually succeeds in relegating his subdued voice to his counterparts, thereby forcing them to speak his mind. To be sure, his shell symbolizes his withdrawal, his isolation, and his alienation, but it also forces others to pronounce his unspeakable thoughts, to make his motives known for those who wish to hear. Through ventriloquy, Gregor compensates for his loss of language. We see him regain his language in form of a palimpsest which, by doubling on speech, makes his repressed thoughts known without others knowing. Ironically, this flawed reversal works to increase our discomfort as readers of the story's conclusion: although Gregor has found a means to overcome his silence, unfortunately neither he nor any of the actors recognize how their words tend to echo the suppressed feelings of his former self. Again, the father's last words in the story are telling: "Let bygones be bygones," he says, "and you might have some consideration for me" (132). They would have befitted his son. In a way, we as readers sense that the family is reacting (or will react) as he should have done long before the story began, namely by changing jobs, leaving home, and taking a new apartment (and, possibly even, by taking a wife, as his sister is predestined to take a husband).

Gregor's "ventriloquist method" thus clearly mirrors Kafka's own: narrated silence (in German we might use a similar oxymoron, "erzählte Sprachlosigkeit") is a paradox; it is a form of speech that allows language to resist meaning and yet be meaningful. We all know how, in Kafka's tales, events can be vague and actions unpredictable while the language of the teller displays unusual clarity and stunning precision. We, as much as the characters, come upon places that are perplexingly inaccessible, in spite of personal perseverance. Meetings cannot take place because people who seem so close at hand are suddenly worlds apart. Others find themselves banished and dislodged for no recognizable reason at all. Time and again their behavior is misinterpreted, their language turns out ambiguities, their words are taken amiss. By and large, men fail to communicate. In Kafka's universe these are "alltägliche Verwirnungen," 'everyday misapprehensions.'[20] And no one is immune from them.

In turning back to our initial reading of Kafka's "Letter to his Father," we notice not that the past torments of his childhood, but rather their structure re-emerges time and again as the ingrained mold of his narratives. By dint of repetition, Kafka's father produced in his son a sense of the world and its language as dys-communication, one where the meaning of an enunciation is not determined by plain words—there is, of course, no such thing for Kafka—and palpable social law, but rather by an incomprehensible, unpredictable, and unbearable logic of authority. The father's and the son's difference is one of language: while the father is an eloquent speaker, the child is prone to stutter. Stuttering is a repetition of sound, in itself linguistically meaningless, but psychologically all the more eloquent. Stuttering is sounding silence, meaning deferred yet fraught with emotion.

The correspondence between the grammar of the *author's* childhood experiences and the famed illogicity of his *textual* world (we recall that first interpretive approach that assumes a mirroring of Kafka's unconscious processes in his fiction) can demonstrably be carried over to the third level of *readers'* responses (and the second interpretive approach that recognizes an homology between the opacity of Kafka's textual universe and the continually aborted quest of critics and readers for sense and interpretive closure). Thus, technically, Kafka's mature narrative point of view reproduces for us as readers a form of stuttering and deferred meaning, much as Gregor's transformed body does for his family. That is, Kafka performs through the language of his narrative on us what his father did to him In this way, we as exegetes of Kafka's texts, the Samsa family as readers of Gregor's "Panzer," and Kafka as interpreter of his father's speeches take on analogous roles. The silence of the child brings out the voice of the writer, the silence of Gregor brings out his voice in the family, the silence of the text brings out the voice of the critic. And none of us recognize the rule. Like his father's table talk, Kafka's prose is replete with words, but is lacking in definite meaning and logic for the reader—as so many critics have acutely observed.[21] The configuration of his stories does not match the rules we are accustomed to. So our reaction is much like Kafka's reaction: to cope with the menacing void he produced text upon text; we procure from the texts palimpsest upon palimpsest of meaning. But in the multitude of meanings that our readings engender we fail, like Kafka in his childhood, to make out the grammar that governs them all. So, finally, while he has become the eloquent speaker, we are now prone to stutter. Through the rhetoric of dye-communication, Kafka has, in the end, become the Father for us.

Notes

1. Maurice Blanchot once referred to Kafka's works as "fundamentally silent works" (11).

2. Some critics have opposed Sokel's view that Kafka's writings are representative of a modern "Sprachkrise" or "Sprachskepsis" ("Kafka's Poetics" 7). In the context of the story "The Metamorphosis," Ingeborg Henel has argued for example: "Das Bild von dem zum Insekt gewordenen Menschen, der die Sprache verloren hat, hat nichts mit verhindertem Schriftstellertum zu tun und auch nichts mit Sprachskepsis. Es war nicht Sprachskepsis, sondern sein Perfektionismus, ähnlich dem Flauberts, der Kafka, abgesehen von äußeren Umständen, Schwierigkeit beim Schreiben verursachte und Zweifel in ihm aufkommen ließ, Zweifel nicht an den Möglichkeiten der Sprache, sondern an seiner eigenen Kraft" (80).

3. For a sampling of essays and books cf. Frederick Hoffmann, Heinz Politzer, Josef Rattner, Heinz Hillmann, Gilles Deleuze and Felix Guattari listed below.

4. For reasons that will become apparent, this approach is restricted here to psychological criticism. As Stanley Corngold has pointed out, this form of criticism can more generally be subsumed under approaches that rest on the belief that there is a "residue of real meaning" in Kafka's tale, that it is "an essentially realistic tale of humiliation and neurosis [that] reflects Kafka's tortured personality. Innumerable attempts have been made," he continues, "to explain Gregor's debasement in terms of the ways in which a man can be humiliated. The Marxist critic Helmut Richter, for example, alludes to the deformed products of a mechanical work process, to Gregor the alienated salesman; Sokel, as a psychologist, stresses Gregor's intent to punish through his repulsiveness the family that had enslaved him. Kaiser views the metamorphosis as retribution for an Oedipal rebellion; the pathologist Wilfredo Dalmau Castañón sees it as the symptomatology of tuberculosis" (*The Commentator's Despair* 17–18).

5. "Kafkas Leben ist der unaufhörliche Versuch, mit seinem Vater-Erlebnis fertig zu werden. Dem Vater verdankt er seine Lebensangst und seine lähmende Schwermut.... Sadismus und Masochismus sind Grundzüge des Kafkaschen Werkes" (*Kafka und das Vater-Problem* 47).

6. "Die Kafka-Interpretation bildet in ihrer Struktur, in ihrer fundamentalen Grundeinstellung die Kafkasche Struktur und Grundeinstellung ab, sie ist zum Spiegel des strukturellen Zentralprozesses des von Kafka Erzählten geworden" (my translation).

7. More recent psychological interpretations tend to move away from this exclusive bias for the author–text relationship to include readerly reactions; one instance is an excellent Freudian reading of "The Metamorphosis" by David Eggenschwiler.

8. All references to the "Letter to his Father" are to *Wedding Preparations in the Country*.

9. Incidentally, the subsequent sentence of the "Letter" relates that "the magnitude of the subject goes far beyond the scope of my memory and power of reasoning."

10. In Chapter 3 of his book *Kafka. De Schafensprozeß*, which traces both the extra-literary sources for and the biographical background of Kafka's creative process, Hartmut Binder describes the Samsa family's relationships as "ein Spiegelbild sowohl der gegenwärtigen als auch der Verhältnisse in der Kindheit Kafkas" 'a true image of both Kafka's present and his childhood circumstances' (175). With regard to "The Metamorphosis," Binder stresses in particular the "lebensgeschichtlichen Strukturen" 'biographical structures' at the close of 1912, i.e. the argument about the factory, Kafka's disappointment about his sister Ottla taking sides with his parents on this issue (which almost brought about a suicide attempt),

and the crisis with Felice. He goes on to say that it is very likely that Kafka himself would have been conscious of the homology between his present situation around 1912 and his experiences of early childhood: "Es ist zu vermuten, da diese Ereignisse ihm in bestürzender Weise zum Bewußtsein brachten, wie abhängig er eigentlich von seinen Eltern war, da dadurch Emotionen freigesetzt wurden, die Kindheitserinnerungen zum Durchbruch verhalfen und ihm verdeutlichten, da die Gesetzlichkeiten seines gegenwärtigen Lebens vielfach deckungsgleich mit längst überwunden geglaubten Kindheitsmustern war" (173; for more details cf. 136–90).

11. Josef Rattner put it thus: "Die strafenden Eltern erscheinen dem Kinde als unberechenbare Tyrannen, denen man auf Gnade oder Ungnade ausgeliefert ist. Das lähmende Gefühl der Ohnmacht ist die Folge solcher Episoden" (21).

12. Kafka remarks: "I became completely dumb, cringed away from you, hid from you, and only dared to stir when I was so far away from you that your power could no longer reach me, at any rate directly" (171).

13. All references are to the text of "The Metamorphosis" in *The Penal Colony. Stories and Short Pieces*.

14. Anders wrote: "Nicht die Gegenstände und Ereignisse als solche sind bei Kafka beunruhigend, sondern die Tatsache, daß seine Wesen auf sie wie auf normale Gegenstände oder Ereignisse—also unerregt—reagieren. Nicht da Gregor Samsa am Morgen als Käfer aufwacht, sondern daß er darin nichts Staunenswertes sieht, diese Alltäglichkeit des Grotesken macht die Lektüre so entsetzenerregend" (*Kafka. Pro und Contra* 13).

15. The Trinitarian connotation is contained quite overtly in the chief clerk's statement: "I am speaking here in the name of your parents and of your chief" (77).

16. Gregor describes his situation with the phrase: "Ich bin in der Klemme" which is rendered into English less forcefully and less ambiguously as "I'm in great difficulties" (83).

17. In a letter to Grete Bloch Kafka writes: "Incidentally, the heroine's name is Grete and she doesn't discredit you at all, at least not in the first section. Later on, though, when the agony becomes too great, she withdraws, embarks on a life of her own, and leaves the one who needs her" (*Letters to Felice* 394–95).

18. This impression coincides with Erich Heller's claim that "the most oppressive quality of Kafka's work is the unshakable stability of its central situation. It takes place in a world that knows of no motion, no change, no metamorphosis" (*The Disinherited Mind* 220).

19. Hartmut Binder relates Grete's reversal of behavior to two autobiographical incidents involving Kafka's sister Ottla and Felice Bauer. In respect to the former Binder concludes: "Denn nicht nur vollzieht Grete einen Ottlas Stellungnahme vergleichbaren Positionswechsel, sondern Gregor verliert auch wie sein reales Vorbild jede weitere Lebensmöglichkeit. Kafka hat, so könnte man sagen, die lebensverneinenden Folgerungen, die sich für ihn aus der Sache ergaben, an Gregor Samsa delegiert" (*Kafka* 144; for more details cf. also 183).

20. The story referred to here, "An Everyday Occurrence," is an entry in Kafka's third octavo notebook. It relates, in a quasi post-Einsteinian setting, character A's thwarted attempt to meet his business partner B.

21. To my knowledge, the first to analyse this in a methodical way was Ulrich Gaier.

Works Cited

Anders, Günther. *Kafka. Pro und Contra*. München: C.H. Beck, 1951.
Binder, Hartmut. *Kafka. Der Schaffensprozeß*. Frankfurt: Suhrkamp, 1983.

Blanchot, Maurice. "Reading Kafka." *Twentieth Century Interpretations of The Trial. A Collection of Critical Essays.* Ed. James Rolleston. Englewood Cliffs: Prentice Hall, 1976. 11–20.

Corngold, Stanley. *The Commentator's Despair. The Interpretation of Kafka's Metamorphosis.* Port Washington and London: Kennikat, 1973.

Deleuze, Gilles, and Felix Guattari. *Kafka. Pour une littérature mineure.* Paris: Les Éditions de Minuit, 1975.

Eggenschwiler, David. "'The Metamorphosis,' Freud, and the Chains of Odysseus." *Franz Kafka. Modern Critical Views.* Ed. Harold Bloom. New York: Chelsea House, 1986. 199–219.

Gerier, Ulrich. "'Chorus of Lies'—On Interpreting Kafka." *German Life and Letters* 22 (1969): 283–96.

Heller, Erich. *The Disinherited Mind. Essays in Modern German Literature and Thought.* New York and London: Harcourt-Brace-Jovanovich, 1975.

Henel, Ingeborg. "Die Grenzen der Deutbarkeit von Kafkas Werken: Die Verwandlung." *Journal of English and Germanic Philology* 83 (1984): 67–85.

Hillmann, Heinz. *Franz Kafka. Dichtungstheorie und Dichtungsgestalt.* Bonn: Bouvier, 1973.

Hofmann, Frederick. "Escape from Father." *The Kafka-Problem.* Ed. Angel Flores. New York: New Directions, 1946. 214–46.

Kafka, Franz. *The Diaries of Franz Kafka 1910–1913.* Ed. Max Brod. Trans. Joseph Kresh. New York: Schocken Books, 1948.

———. Letters to Felice. Ed. Erich Heller and Jürgen Born. Trans. James Stern and Elisabeth Duckworth. New York: Schocken Books, 1973.

———. *The Penal Colony. Stories and Short Pieces.* Trans. Willa and Edwin Muir. New York: Schocken Books, 1948.

———. *Wedding Preparations in the Country and Other Posthumous Prate Writings.* Trans. Ernst Kaiser and Eithne Wilkins. London: Secker and Warburg, 1954.

Politzer, Heinz. "Franz Kafka's Letter To His Father." *Germanic Review* 28 (1953): 165–79.

Rattner, Josef. *Kafka und das Vater-Problem. Ein Beitrag zum tiefenpsychologischen Problem der Kinder-Erziehung. Interpretation von Kafkas "Brief an den Vater".* Munich-Basel: Ernst Reinhardt Verlag, 1964.

Sokel, Walter H. "Kafkas 'Verwandlung': Auflehnung und Bestrafung." *Monatshefte* 48 (1956): 203–14. Rpt. in *Franz Kafka.* Ed. Heinz Politzer. Darmstadt: Wissenschaftliche Buchgesellschaft (= Wege der Forschung, 322), 1973. 267–85.

———. "Kafka's Poetics of the Inner Self." *From Kafka and Dada to Brecht and Beyond.* Ed. Reinhold Grimm, Peter Spycher and Richard Zipser. Madison: University of Wisconsin Press, 1982. 7–21.

Sontag, Susan. "The Aesthetics of Silence." *A Susan Sontag Reader.* Intro. Elizabeth Hardwick. New York: Farrar-Strauss-Giroux, 1982. 181–204.

Steiner, George. *Language and Silence. Essays on Language, Literature, and the Inhuman.* New York: Atheneum, 1972.

Steinmetz, Horst. "Negation als Spiegel und Appell. Zur Wirkungsbedingung Kafkascher Texte." *Was Bleibt von Franz Kafka? Positionsbestimmung—Kafka-Symposium Wien 1983.* (Schriftenreihe der Franz-Kafka-Gesellschaft, Vol. 1). Ed. Wendelin Schmidt-Dengler. Vienna: Braumüller, 1983. 155–64.

Thiher, Allen. *Franz Kafka. A Study of the Short Fiction.* Boston: Twayne, 1990.

MICHAEL G. LEVINE

The Sense of an Unding: *Kafka, Ovid, and the Misfits of Metamorphosis*

> Is impossibility, then, a stone wall?
>
> Dostoevsky, *Notes from Underground*

In a letter to his friend Max Brod, written in June 1921, Franz Kafka placed his literary production under the sign of a fourfold impossibility: "the impossibility of not writing, the impossibility of writing German, the impossibility of writing differently," and finally even "the impossibility of writing" itself.[1] As other parts of the letter make clear, the sense of impossibility that is intoned with a kind of percussive insistence in these lines conveys more than a feeling of frustration. For while the writer may indeed be confronted by obstacles at every turn, the impossibilities mentioned here are by no means mere impediments; they are instead, as we shall see, the very twists, turns, and interlocking holds of an ineluctible double bind. Each mention of a particular "impossibility" is nothing more or less than an attempt to seize an inextricable knot by one of its constituent threads, an attempt to display an overdetermined and ever-mutating problem in a number of its determinate permutations.

This problem, it should be stressed, is not primarily psychological in nature—at least not in this case and certainly not in the more restricted, personal, intrapsychic sense of the term. Indeed, Kafka's enumeration of the manifold impossibilities of writing is prompted by reflections on the current state of German Jewish *linguistic* relations and, more specifically, on a particular

From *Writing Through Repression: Literature, Censorship, Psychoanalysis*, pp. 149–177. © 1994 by The Johns Hopkins University Press.

mode of linguistic performance known as *mauscheln*. "This *mauscheln*," he says, "taken in the broadest sense, the only sense in which it should be taken, consists in a bumptious, tacit, or painfully self-critical appropriation of another's property, even though there is no evidence of a single solecism. . . . It is an organic compound of bookish German and pantomime."[2]

Throughout the letter, Kafka is exercised by the question of why Jewish writers should be "so irresistibly drawn" to the German language. Gradually, he is led to formulate a response that comes close enough to Freudian theories of generational conflict to elicit a defensive gesture on his part.

> Psychoanalysis lays stress on the father-complex and many find the concept intellectually fruitful. In this case I prefer another version, where the issue revolves around the fathers Jewishness. Most young Jews who began to write German wanted to leave Jewishness behind them, and their fathers approved of this, but vaguely (this vagueness was what was outrageous to them). But with their hind legs they were still glued [*klebten sie noch*: they still adhered] to the father's Jewishness and with their waving front legs they found no new ground. The ensuing despair became their inspiration.

In this magnificent image of generational conflict, the Jewish sons are captured rearing their front legs, suspended in the very gesture of revolt. And while this prolonged suspension perhaps potentiates the uprising movement of rebellion, it also conveys a sense of flailing filial impotence. Such gestures, I would suggest, define Kafka's own four-legged writing and its inspiration born of despair. "An inspiration," Kafka continues,

> as honorable as any other, but on closer examination showing certain sad peculiarities. First of all, the product of [the sons'] despair could not be German literature, though outwardly it seemed to be so. They existed among three impossibilities, which I just happen to call linguistic impossibilities. It is simplest to call them that. But they might also be called something entirely different. These are: The impossibility of not writing, the impossibility of writing German, the impossibility of writing differently. One might also add a fourth impossibility, the impossibility of writing.

With the enumeration of these impossibilities, Kafka's letter ceases to move forward in a progressive, linear fashion. Instead, as was suggested earlier, it appears to falter at every step as though mired in the very sense of despair and futile necessity it speaks about. In such circumstances the only possible step to be taken, the only way to gain time and room to maneuver, the only way to negotiate the double binds articulated here is, paradoxically, to write. Thus, he adds a comment that, it seems, could only have been advanced in the suspension of a parenthetical aside: "(since the despair could not be assuaged by writing, is an enemy both of life *and* of writing, writing is here only a moratorium [*ein Provisorium*], as for someone who is writing his will shortly before he hangs himself—a moratorium that may well last a whole life)" (trans. mod.).

Like Kafka's own last-minute proviso appended to the preceding list of linguistic impossibilities, "writing" here functions as the very spacing—the indispensable temporizing movement—of deferral.

Getting One's Bearings: Benjamin on Kafka

While it is doubtful that Walter Benjamin ever had access to this letter, his essay "Franz Kafka: On the Tenth Anniversary of His Death" focuses on just this connection between writing, dying, and dilatory expedients. To do justice to the complexity of Benjamin's essay would obviously require a separate chapter.[3] In what follows I propose merely to treat those aspects of his text that bear on the issues mentioned above. Such an approach, however, is complicated by the fact that Benjamin's essay is an "interpretation" of Kafka in both the hermeneutic and performative senses of the term. His essay must be read both as a theoretical discourse, whose primary aim is to elucidate and unfold the complexities of the texts it treats, and also as a transferential repetition and creative displacement of the stresses and gestures of those texts.

Benjamin himself alludes to the necessity of such an approach when speaking about the "unfolding [*Entfaltung*] of the parable" in Kafka. "It is the reader's pleasure," he says, "to smooth it out so that he has the meaning on the palm of his hand [*so daß ihre Bedeutung auf der flachen Hand liegt*]" (112).[4] Benjamin's own pleasure, by contrast, lies elsewhere: not on the palm of the hand, where differences are ironed out and everything appears, as it were, as clear as day (*auf der Hand*), but rather in the indelible creases of the palm, whose mysteries are reserved for the skilled chiromancer. In reading the flat of the hand, Benjamin suggests, it is necessary not only to trace the furrowed lines of the palm but also and above all to follow the silent writing—the *gestural movements*—of the hands themselves. This mute language is compared in his essay to Chinese theater, "one of the most significant functions" of which, he says, "is to dissolve happenings into their gestic components" (120). As though to emphasize the gestural twists and turns of this graphic art—whose adverse effects are legible in the very squirming of those written upon—Benjamin links it in section 3 of his essay to a kind of ornamental *writing on the back* (such as one finds in "The Penal Colony") rather than to more traditional modes of handwriting. If, as he says of this writing, "it is thus the back on which it lies, the back on which everything depends [*Es ist also der Rücken, dem es aufliegt*] and it was always this way with Kafka [*Und ihm liegt es bei Kafka seit jeher auf*]" (133), the stress here lies not only on the back but also on the verb *aufliegen*. In other words, to say that everything lies on the back rather than on the palm of the hand, as clear as day, is to turn the seemingly self-evident gesture of meaningful presentation back on itself, reposing it as a question and interrogating the very gesture by which meaning presents itself as the smoothing out of a complication, the elucidation of an enigma, or the parabolic illustration of a truth. Implicated in this movement of reversion, the reader is thus invited to turn back on Benjamin's own text the question it poses to the would-be expositors of Kafka's parables: "But do we have the doctrine which [these] parables interpret and K.'s postures and the gestures of his animals clarify? It does not exist; all we can say is that here and there we have an allusion to it. Kafka might have said that these are relics transmitting the doctrine, although we could regard them just as well as precursors preparing the doctrine" (122).

Whether it is because they come too early or too late, Kafka's parables— like Benjamin's essay—fail to present any doctrine. Rather than dissolving into a semantically transparent means of instruction, they remain cloudy and opaque.[5] As Werner Hamacher has observed,

> The mark of failure in Kafka's prose is what Benjamin calls on three different occasions the "cloudy spot" [*wolkige Stelle*] in his parables. In connection with the Potemkin anecdote toward the beginning of his essay he writes, "The enigma which beclouds it is Kafka's enigma." Later, he writes about the parable "Before the Law," "The reader who encountered it in 'A Country Doctor' may have been struck by the cloudy spot in its interior." And in the third section of his essay, Benjamin again takes up this strange metaphor: "For Kafka, there was always something that could only be grasped in the gesture. And this gesture, which he did not understand, constitutes the cloudy region of the parables [*die wolkige Stelle der Parabeln*]. From it emerges Kafka's literature."

Curiously enough, it is precisely by means of these "cloudy spots," which obscure more than they clarify, that Benjamin gets his bearings in Kafka's text. Through them, he is drawn not into heretofore uncharted regions but rather more deeply and ineluctibly into the very question of *bearings* itself; this term, it should be stressed, is to be understood in this context not only in the sense of a fixed point of orientation but also in the related sense of a supportive, weight-bearing structure.[6] As a way of gesturing to the fact that it is this particular question on which the entire essay bears, the text opens by invoking the stationary figure of Atlas shouldering the globe and closes with the moving image of a man on horseback: "Whether it is a man or a horse is no longer so important, if only the burden is removed from the back" (140). The strategic placement of these framing figures at the outset and end of Benjamin's text seems to suggest that the essay does not so much *pose* the question of bearings as *mobilize* it. The shift is worth emphasizing, since what is at stake is a particular volatilization of the question. Once set in motion, it is no longer posed in the static oppositional terms of bearer and borne. Instead, as it takes flight, there is a slight but decisive shift in accent from the back upon which everything is said to lie and depend to the pointedly ambiguous verb *aufliegen,* which itself begins to sound more like *auffliegen*: to fly up; such shifts are in turn accompanied by a gradual blurring of the distinction between Atlas and the globe he is supposed to carry. Mobilized, this spinning orb now sweeps its bearer up in its revolutionary flight through space. It is no doubt for this reason that Benjamin is drawn to the world of the "assistants" in Kafka, whom he describes as "falling outside the circle" of the family.[7] "None has a firm place in the world, firm inalienable outlines. There is not one that is not either rising or falling, none that is not trading qualities with its enemy or neighbor, none that has not completed its period of time and yet is unripe, none that is not deeply exhausted and yet is only at the beginning of a long existence. To speak of any order or hierarchy is impossible here" (117).

Here again it appears that as the question of bearings becomes increasingly volatile, imposing itself more massively and with an ever-increasing sense of urgency, identities come unhinged and in their place clouds of unstable, mercurial figures begin to form.[8] As these clouds gather, the question of bearings itself becomes more nebulous. Yet, as was stated earlier, it is paradoxically by means of these "cloudy spots" that Benjamin orients himself in Kafka's text—orients himself, that is, in the direction of a demanding revolutionary practice of perpetual disorientation. Needless to say, there is more to this practice than simply losing one's bearings in an otherwise stable structure, for it is a practice that also and perhaps above all involves listening to the stresses and accents, the props, supports, and weight-bearing structures of Kafka's text as they shift about and give way to unsettling movements of displacement.

With Benjamin's "interpretation" of Kafka as our guide, I would now like to return to the relationship of writing, death, and dilatory expedients with which I began and then move eventually to a reinterpretation of Kafka's *Metamorphosis,* which I propose to read as a singular metamorphic dislocation not only of Ovid's *Metamorphoses* but, moreover, of the very notion of metamorphosis.

Managing a Stagnant Economy

In section 3 of his essay, Benjamin observes that "in the stories which Kafka left us, narrative art regains the significance it had in the mouth of Scheherazade: to postpone the future [*das Kommende hinauszuschieben*]" (129). Before continuing this citation, it is not irrelevant to note that Benjamin here takes up the question of postponement as a way of introducing the life and death issues involved in the writing and execution of Kafka's own last will and testament—a document that, as is well known, was to have sentenced his unpublished literary offspring to destruction.[9] Benjamin continues:

> In *The Trial* postponement is the hope of the accused man only if the proceedings do not gradually turn into the judgement. The patriarch himself is to benefit by postponement, even though he may have to give up his place in tradition for it. "I could conceive [Kafka writes] of another Abraham—to be sure, he would never get to be a patriarch or even an old-clothes dealer—an Abraham who would be prepared to satisfy the demand for sacrifice immediately, with the promptness of a waiter, but would be unable to bring it off because he cannot get away [*weil er von zubause nicht fort kann*], being indispensable; the household needs him, there is always something or other to take care of, the house is never ready; but without having his house ready, without having something to fall back on, he cannot leave—this the Bible also realized, for it says: "He set his house in order." (129)

While Benjamin allows this passage to speak for itself, what draws him to it is apparently the connection made here between the house Abraham is preparing to leave and the economy (from the Greek *oikos*: house) of deferral which provisionally shelters the patriarch's offspring from the execution of the death sentence he is prepared to carry out. Here, as Benjamin implies, it is not only the judgment but "The Judgment" that is adjourned through the postponements of *The Trial*, through a singular recitation of the "trial" of Abraham. In Benjamin's reading of Kafka, deferral (*Aufschub*) thus seems to have two related components: first and more obviously, it involves a process of temporal postponement which, however, "may well last a whole life," as Kafka writes to Brod of the man sitting down to write his will shortly before hanging himself; second, and perhaps more importantly, it implies a suspension of narratives and narrative citations—in short, of *récits*—into and through one another.[10] To put it a little differently, deferral here involves a suspension within narrative of elements that effectively interrupt and relay each other in a way that upsets the order of the house, postpones closure, and manages a stagnating economy.

It is this very particular sense of stagnation as deferral and suspension that leads Benjamin to assert that Kafka's "novels are set in a swamp [*spielen in einer Sumpfwelt*]" (130). This remark is justified not only by the observation that "Kafka did not consider the age in which he lived as an advance over the beginnings of time" (130) but moreover by the way in which the very sense of narrative and historical progress is altered in Kafka's writings. Curiously enough, evidence of this alteration is to be found both in passages Benjamin cites from Kafka *and* in the odd narrative progression of his own text. Consider, then, the following sequence, which is adduced in support of Benjamin's claim that what is forgotten is not merely absent but rather is *actual* by virtue of this very oblivion: "An experience deeper than that of an average person can make contact with it. 'I have experience,' we read in one of Kafka's earliest notes, 'and I am not joking when I say that it is a seasickness on dry land.' It is no accident that the first 'Meditation' was made on a swing. And Kafka does not tire of expressing himself on the fluctuating [*schwankende*] nature of experiences. Each gives way and mingles with its opposite" (130).

Is it unreasonable to suggest that the final words of this citation refer both to the fluctuating experiences mentioned in the preceding sentence and to the very movement of the passage itself? Does the text, in other words, at this point stage a mode of experience which, because it is closer to the swamp of oblivion than to the ordered progress of conscious thought, actually present itself in a different narrative manner? As though moving through a number of determinate alterations of a muddled and indeterminate relationship, the passage proceeds from a particular experience of instability described as a seasickness on dry land, to an experience set in the shifting frame of a swing, to finally a reflection on the unstable, fluctuating nature of experiences. Rather than providing a sense of narrative progression, the passage has a way of turning back on itself as each momentary consolidation of this swamplike experience gives way to, mingles with, and becomes mired in the others.

Such a reading is supported by Benjamin's own subsequent analysis of the following lines from Kafka's "Knock at the Manor Gate," which follow directly on the heels of the passage cited above: "With my sister I was passing [*kam . . . vorüber*] the gate of a great house on our way home. I don't remember whether she knocked on the gate out of mischief or in a fit of absent-mindedness, or merely shook her fist at it and did not knock at all" (130).

Benjamin comments that the "very possibility of the third alternative [*Vorgang*] puts the other two [*die vorangehenden*], which at first seemed harmless, in a different light. It is from the swampy soil of such experiences that Kafka's female characters rise. They are swamp creatures" (130). Not only is much of the wit of Benjamin's commentary lost in Zohn's otherwise competent translation, its very point is obscured. For just as Kafka's text is concerned with what transpires as the narrator and his sister proceed past a particular gate, Benjamin is interested in the steps involved in a certain logical procedure. Slipping from the noun *Vorgang* to the etymologically related verb *vorangehen* in this passage, Benjamin playfully suggests that the footing gets especially slippery when the "alternative"—or more literally, the procedure—mentioned in the third place (*des an der dritten Stelle erwähnten Vorgangs*) allows the preceding ones (*die vorangehenden*) to *step forth* in a different light (*in ein anderes Licht treten*). What Benjamin refers to as the "swampy soil of such experiences" is precisely the absence of progress here, the inability of the reader to move through the competing versions mentioned and establish some order of priority, plausibility, or sense of temporal succession. So long as one is unable to order the alternatives presented in terms of a rational sequence, this swampy soil will remain a logical quagmire. Similarly, the swamp creatures who emerge from this soil are autochthonous heroines only insofar as they spring from a promiscuous mingling of opposites giving way to each other. Or as Benjamin suggests, they rise out of "the dark, deep womb, the scene of the mating 'whose untrammeled voluptuousness,' to quote Bachofen, 'is hateful to the pure forces of heavenly light and which justifies the term used by Arnobius, *luteae voluptates*'" (131).

Elsewhere, Benjamin remarks, "Not to find one's way in a city may well be uninteresting and banal. It requires ignorance—nothing more. But to lose oneself in a city—as one loses oneself in a forest—that calls for quite a different schooling."[11] If losing one's footing in the muddle of experiences described above is itself to metamorphose an uninteresting and commonplace sense of stagnation into a creatively altered mode of experience, one must learn how to proceed differently through logical alternatives that so obviously contradict and exclude one another. Felman's reading of the knotty figure of the dream navel in Freud, discussed in Chapter 3, and my own discussion of the kettle logic of dream censorship in Chapter 2 should prepare us to deal with these alternatives as threads of experience which run into and through one another in such a way as simultaneously to implicate, displace, and "unfold" each other as they go.

Learning how to trace the passage of these alternatives through one another certainly mires one more deeply in the *Sumpfwelt* of Kafka's novels. Yet, it also enables one to see how Kafka, who, as Benjamin says, "could understand things only in the form of a gesture," used such gestures to break through stable frames of reference into more fluid, unfamiliar spaces. Consider in this regard the unusually violent language Benjamin employs when describing the power of the gesture in Kafka: "Just as this bell [described by Werner Kraft in a commentary on 'A Fratricide'], which is too loud for a doorbell, rings out toward heaven, the gestures of Kafka's figures are too powerful [*zu durchschlagend*] for our accustomed surroundings [*die gewohnte Umwelt*] and break out into wider areas [*brechen in eine geräumigere ein*]" (121).

A little further down, Benjamin adds: "What Kafka could see least of all was the *gestus*. Each gesture is an event—one might even say, a drama—in itself. The stage on which this drama takes place is the World Theater which opens up toward heaven. On the other hand, this heaven is only background; to explore it according to its own laws would be like framing the painted backdrop of the stage and hanging it in a picture gallery. Like El Greco, Kafka tears open the sky behind every gesture [*reißt hinter jeder Gebärde—wie Greco—den Himmel auf*]" (121).

This paragraph then concludes: Kafka "divests [*nimmt*] the human gesture of its traditional supports [*die überkommenen Stützen*] and then has a subject for reflection without end [*die kein Ende nimmt*]" (122). As the reader will have noticed, in each of these three passages the violence is directed against some kind of support—be it the stable, orienting frame of familiar surroundings, the props and painted backdrop of the stage, or the traditional mainstays of the human gesture. In doing violence to these structures, which are apparently as burdensome as they are weight bearing, Kafka's gestures break—or rather tamper—with the very laws of gravity. They provisionally suspend these laws and, in doing so, open a different kind of space, one whose dimensions, Benjamin implies, can be measured only in negative and relativistic terms as particular movements of dislocation, distortion, and disorientation. The violence associated with these gestures is thus double-edged: for the very gesture that "breaks into wider areas," "tears open the sky," and "takes away traditional supports" is also the one that enables Kafka to grope his way in the unbearable lightness of such nebulous regions. I would suggest that it is Benjamin's incomparable feel for the tentativeness of these gestures that leads him to the paradoxical observation that "for Kafka, there was always something that could only be grasped in the gesture. And this gesture which he did not understand constitutes the cloudy part of the parables" (129).

THE METAMORPHOSIS

The gestures of Kafka's text thus provide a very particular sense of disorientation. For while they perhaps help one to lose one's bearings, they also supply in their stead—and in lieu of more familiar modes of cognition— a grasp that is not that of understanding, a grasp that instead dislocates understanding from within and makes of this creative *misunderstanding* a means by which to get a different hold on things. Nowhere in Kafka's work does this sense of disorientation or the question of bearings in general make itself felt with greater urgency than in the text of *The Metamorphosis.* Kafka's story abruptly begins with the famous words, "When Gregor Samsa woke up one morning from unsettling dreams [*aus unruhigen Träumen*], he found himself changed in his bed into a monstrous vermin" (3).[12] As though to emphasize the primacy of questions of orientation in this text, the calming effect and sense of reassurance which recognizably familiar surroundings may provide, and even the power of such surroundings to dissipate the hazy sense of inquietude left in the wake of unsettling dreams, Kafka draws an explicit contrast in the second paragraph between Gregor's dreams—his *unruhige Träume*—and the "room, a regular human bedroom, a little on the small side" which "lay tranquilly [*ruhig*] between the four familiar walls" (3).

Whereas readers of *The Metamorphosis* generally tend to focus on the fate of its central character; his sudden transformation from man to animal; and the altered relationship of this "vermin" to his profession, family, and self, I believe that before taking up such weighty issues it is necessary to dwell first on the more mundane matter of the text's physical setting. The stakes of such preliminary reflections are considerable. For, as I hope to demonstrate, it is only by orienting oneself in relation to the shifting spatial and temporal coordinates of Kafka's story that one can begin to discern another process of metamorphosis, one in which the very notion of transformation is metamorphosed from within—without, however, being changed into something else. It is this internal dislocation of metamorphosis, I will argue, that emerges only through an examination of the manner in which the seemingly tranquil setting of Kafka's text is repeatedly unsettled and upset. To appreciate the ways in which Kafka's singular *Metamorphosis* effects a displacement of more familiar notions of transformation and mobilizes the resources of metamorphic tradition only in order to deplete and divert them, it may be useful at this point to compare certain aspects of his text to Ovid's *Metamorphoses*.

In Ovid one finds no one definitive account of origins or sources. Indeed, precisely because there are so many competing creation stories presented in his text, it is impossible to find one string by which to pull all the others. In the absence of any single guiding thread, the reader is left to wind his or her way through stories of intricately woven tapestries, delicate webs, and sturdy nets. In lieu of any one cosmic weaver, there is only an incessant interlacing of connections, an endless spinning of yarns, and a fabulously self-reflexive fabrication of texts. Weaving mythical narratives into and through one another, Ovid's *Metamorphoses* raise and answer questions of motivation and causality by telling self-legitimating stories; that is, they present narratives that, in accounting for the existence of gods, mortals, and natural phenomena, also account for themselves. They contain their self-justification in their own telling—not in any one narrative but instead in the overall interconnectedness of narratives, in the fabric of their mutual and ever-mutating relations. Such a textual production as Ovid's *Metamorphoses,* or rather such processes of textual autoproduction, underwrite their own birth certificate as authorship and authority become effects the text itself produces.

In contrast to the plurality, heterogeneity, and interconnectedness of Ovid's *Metamorphoses,* the title of Kafka's text speaks of metamorphosis in the singular. As was noted earlier, its first line describes how a certain Gregor Samsa "woke up one morning from unsettling dreams, and found himself changed in his bed into a monstrous vermin" (3). In describing Gregor's change so immediately, Kafka seems to drain his metamorphosis of all the pathos and drama that typify Ovid's metamorphoses. Here it seems as if the metamorphosis—both Kafka's and Gregor's—had already come to an abrupt end by the conclusion of the first sentence.[13]

Whereas in Ovid transformations occur for some particular reason, Kafka's *Metamorphosis* simply begins with the inexplicable and unmotivated transformation of Gregor Samsa into a monstrous vermin. Yet, who is this person, and what indeed is a monstrous vermin? While some critics have attempted to domesticate this monstrosity by describing it in positive terms either as a gigantic cockroach or as an enormous dung beetle—Nabokov even tried to draw a picture of it in his essay on Kafka—the German text significantly calls it an *ungeheures Ungeziefer.*[14] As critics have often noticed, both terms begin with the negation *un-.* Moreover, unlike the detachable nose of Gogol's famous story, this prefix cannot be separated from the terms to which it adheres, since in German there is no such thing as a *geheuer* or a *Geziefer.*[15] Removing the negative prefixes from these signifiers does not restore them to some prior positive form, nor does doubling these negatives by combining them in the phrase *ungeheures Ungeziefer* yield any stable positive identity. Instead, the product of such a combination is only a kind of redoubled negativity. Etymologically, the noun *Ungeziefer* derives from a term formerly used to designate an unclean animal unsuited for sacrifice.[16] The adjective *ungeheuer,* which is rendered in English translations of *The Metamorphosis* as "gigantic" or "monstrous," also has the sense of something boundless, enormous, outrageous, and uncanny.[17]

Just as it is a little too easy to say that in rendering Kafka's *ungeheures Ungeziefer* as "monstrous vermin" much is lost in translation, it is equally misleading to imply that German is the only language that could accommodate such a doubly negative monstrosity.[18] For if we understand anything about Kafka's *Metamorphosis,* it is that this *Unding,* this monstrosity (formerly a traveling salesman), is not at home especially when in its own home—among family and familiar surroundings. It is significant in this regard that Gregor literally cannot even speak in his own mother tongue. Instead, his thoughts are communicated only through the medium of a narrator, about whom much remains to be said.

It seems, then, that this *ungeheures Ungeziefer* may be lost in translation even before it is explicitly translated from one positive language to another. Translation in a sense only redoubles its negativity. Recall that whenever Gregor tries to communicate directly, without the intervention of a narrator, translator, or interpreter, his voice is almost immediately engulfed in static noise—"as if from below, an insistent distressed chirping intruded, which left the clarity of his words intact only for a moment really, before so badly garbling them as they carried, that no one could be sure if he had heard right" (5).

Lost in translation, always in need of an interpreter, always a mistranslation in need of retranslation, the double negative that Gregor has become may itself be a creature lost in *metamorphosis*.[19] For just as there are unclean animals unsuited for sacrifice, so too perhaps are there monstrosities unfit for metamorphosis—for example, monstrous vermin that prey on the host body of a text or narrative contents that cannot be contained within the borders of a frame narrative. What I am suggesting is that certain monstrous forms of parasitism and incontinence here inhabit the very notion of metamorphosis and transform it from within. Yet, as was suggested earlier, they do so not by changing it into something else but instead by corrupting and corroding it. Like Gregor's fasting, this corrosion at the center of metamorphosis consumes and displaces the text from the inside out. One might consider in this regard the following entry from Kafka's diary written approximately ten months before he set to work on *The Metamorphosis*:

> When it became clear in my organism that writing was the most productive direction for my being to take, everything rushed in that direction and left empty all those abilities which were directed toward the joys of sex, eating, drinking, philosophical reflection and above all music. I atrophied [*magerte ab*] in all these directions. This was necessary because the totality of my strengths was so slight that only collectively could they even halfway serve the purpose of my writing. Naturally, I did not find this purpose independently and consciously, it found itself, and is now interfered with only by the office, but that interferes with it completely.... My development is now complete and, so far as I can see, there is nothing left to sacrifice; I need only throw my work in the office out of this complex in order to begin my real life.[20]

In *The Metamorphosis*, it is the verminous Gregor Samsa who grows thin through fasting. As his body parasitically feeds on itself, it loses volume and flattens out. More generally, it may be observed that in the course of the narrative the focus also shifts from three dimensions to two: from the interior space of Gregor's "regular human room, a little on the small side lying tranquilly between the four familiar walls" to the two-dimensional space of the walls themselves. In other words, as Gregor begins to climb the walls and ceiling, the emphasis shifts from voluminous interiors to flat, planar surfaces. In order to appreciate the full significance of these shifts, it is important to bear in mind the ways in which other related issues cluster around these coordinates. For example, it is no accident that at the beginning of the story there is a close relationship between the "four familiar walls" used by Gregor to get his bearings in space and the quarter-hour divisions of the clock by which he locates himself in time. This carefully calibrated coordination of time and space at the outset of the story is best captured in the numerous references to trains (where distance is but a relation of speed and time) and railway timetables (which, as his mother says, Gregor studies even on his days off). The precision with which these relationships may be measured and translated into each other is at this point also linked to the sharpness of the narrative eye. For instance, when describing Gregor's numerous little legs, which never stopped waving in all directions and which he could not control in the least, the narrator adds: "If he wanted to bend one [*Wollte er eines einmal einknicken*], the first thing that happened was that it stretched itself out; and if he finally succeeded in getting this leg to do what he wanted, all the others in the meantime, as if set free, began to work in the most intensely painful agitation" (7).

Here the futile effort to gain control over each individual leg and to coordinate its movements with those of the others is reflected on the level of the signifier through an emphatic repetition of the *morpheme ein.* As though sounding out the stresses and strains of individuation, the *ein* in *Beinchen* here insists in the phrase *Wollte er eines einmal einknicken.* Such details would hardly be worth mentioning were it not for the fact that, later on, the very same signifier is repeated in terms used to describe a movement in the opposite direction: a movement in which oppositions are neutralized as sharp contours blur and everything fades into a hazy shade of gray. This movement is summed up in a vision Gregor has at his window of "a desert [*eine Einöde*] where the gray sky and the gray earth were indistinguishably fused [*sich vereinigten*]" (29).[21]

What is important to bear in mind is the way issues of depth perception—in particular Gregor's ability to see things in relief as they stand out individually from their surroundings—are related to the matter of Gregor's own physical volume ("his domelike brown belly") and especially to his position relative to *his* surroundings—both physical and familial— at the outset of the story. It is not by chance, for instance, that Gregor's mother, father, and sister—each standing at a different door of his centrally located bedroom—communicate with each other through his space. Gregor may at this point be unable to take part in the conversation, but he is still the principal object of discussion, just as his room is literally the medium through which communication takes place.[22]

By contrast, when Gregor dies, his body is described as being "completely flat and dry" (55). This literal loss of volume reflects not only an atrophying interest in the world outside but also a decrease in the attention paid to him by others. Moreover, it accentuates an evacuation of the very opposition between inside and outside as the focus increasingly shifts to the tenuous borderland of writing and to a different, less stable articulation of spatiotemporal relationships. Here it should be recalled that even before Gregor is positively attracted to flat, planar surfaces, before he distracts himself by crawling over the walls and ceiling of his room, he begins to experience three-dimensional space—both the volume of his room and that of his own body—as oppressive. Thus, toward the beginning of the second section, the narrator describes in a kind of free indirect style how "the empty high-ceilinged room in which he was forced to lie flat on the floor made him nervous, without his being able to tell why—since it was, after all, the room in which he had lived for the past five years—and turning half unconsciously and not without a slight feeling of shame, he scuttled under the couch where, although his back was a little crushed and he could not raise his head any more, he immediately felt very comfortable" (23).

Gregor's agoraphobia, which one might describe as an anxiety about being in a voluminous, open space, is accompanied by a significant decrease in his field of vision: "from day to day he saw things even a short distance away less and less distinctly; the hospital opposite, which he used to curse because he saw so much of it, was now completely beyond his range of vision, and if he had not been positive that he was living in Charlotte Street—a quiet but still very much a city street—he might have believed that he was looking out of his window into a desert where the gray sky and the gray earth were indistinguishably fused" (29).

One can almost picture the horizons of visibility closing in on Gregor here as his myopia increases.[23] It is important to note, however, that the shallowing of his depth of vision and the weakening of his sense of sight is to some degree compensated for by a hyperdeveloped sense of smell and touch. More important, and something typical of Kafka's text, is the fact that Gregor's decreasing capacity to see shapes clearly and distinctly is accompanied by the increasing dissolution of his own shape. Long before his bodily space is literally violated when he is kicked through doorways or bombarded with apples, Gregor's space is defined not simply by the palpable contours of his body but by everything with which he comes into contact. Thus, for example, his sister does not dare touch the utensils used for feeding him. When, at the beginning of section 2, she retrieves a bowl of milk from his room, she "picks it up immediately—not with her hands of course but with a rag" (24). This touching taboo also extends to Gregor's very name, which is almost never used to contact him, and which is later replaced by the pronoun "it" when his sister exclaims, "I won't pronounce the name of my brother in front of this monster, and so all I say is: we have to try to get rid of it" (51). In short, as Gregor becomes more dependent upon his antennae and sense of touch, the taboo against touching *him* extends to almost everything with which he has come into contact. Such things can only be touched indirectly, if at all.

It is important to note, moreover, that what Gregor loses in clarity, depth of vision, and volume, he gains in extension and two-dimensional spread. In order to give him room to spread out and range across the floor and walls, his sister even attempts to remove all the furniture from his room. What comes increasingly to define Gregor are not so much his palpable physical contours or proper name, but everything he has touched and thereby contaminated. The dissolution of the protagonist as a particular three-dimensional character might thus be described as a movement from the space of Gregor, that is, his literal physical body, to Gregor's space, his room and whatever he comes in contact with, to finally something like Gregorian space, which might be defined as the way people move through space and the ways in which they posture and position themselves.[24] Gregorian space is defined not by *where* things are positioned but instead by certain gestures—by how they "assume the position," so to speak. Taking one example among many, consider the following description of Gregor's father. Notice in particular the upward mobility of the passage.

> Was this the same man who in the old days used to lie wearily buried in bed when Gregor left on a business trip; who greeted him on his return in the evening, sitting in his bathrobe in the armchair, who actually had difficulty getting to his feet but as a sign of joy only lifted up his arms; and who, on rare occasions when the whole family went out for a walk, on a few Sundays in June and on the major holidays, used to shuffle along with great effort between Gregor and his mother, who were slow walkers themselves, always a little more slowly than they, wrapped in his old overcoat, always carefully planting down his crutch-handled cane, and, when he wanted to say something, nearly always stood still and assembled his escort around him? Now, however, he was holding himself very erect, dressed in a tight-fitting blue uniform with gold buttons . . . ; above the high stiff collar of the jacket his heavy chin protruded.

And a little further down:

> He probably did not know himself what he had in mind; still he
> lifted his feet unusually high off the floor, and Gregor staggered
> at the gigantic size of the soles of his boots. (37–38)

Here the erect father stands in stark contrast to the totally prostrate
son.[25] The two could not be farther apart, nor could their contrary fates
be more graphically described. Nevertheless, for all the father's apparent
superiority, he still stands, paradoxically, under the shadow of what lies
below him. Certainly the roles have been reversed between father and son,
but the *terms* of the opposition remain the same and are still Gregorian.[26]
As if to hint at this state of affairs, the erect father in a way seems to be
held up only by virtue of a kind of exoskeleton not unlike Gregor's own
armorlike exterior. Not only is he corseted by his tight-fitting blue uniform,
but the only thing keeping his "protruding chin" up is the high stiff collar of
his jacket.[27]

Thus, as Gregor literally gets flatter and lower, his existence in the family
and his influence over it become more insidious and indirect, more nebulous
and diffuse. His reduction to the pronoun "it," while certainly depersonalizing
him in the extreme, at the same time assures, or at least confirms, his absorption
into—and contamination of—the very language of the text. Like a fresco that
fades into the wall on which it was painted, so too does Gregor's image fade
into the surface of the narration. And just as his weakened vision and insomnia
diminish his ability to differentiate dark from light as everything turns into an
indistinct and monotonous "desert where the gray sky and the gray earth were
indistinguishably fused" (29), and just as Gregor's initial attempts to e-nun-
ci-ate clearly fail as his words are engulfed in a "persistent horrible twittering
squeak . . . which . . . rose up reverberating around them to destroy their
sense," so too are the black islands of print in a sense absorbed into the white
background of the page. In short, as the spacing shifts, the monstrous vermin
becomes increasingly illegible as a particular unique mark or distinct unit of
meaning. He or "it" instead merges into the walls of the text, the flatness of
the page, and the surface of everyday language.

Finally, just as Gregor flattens out as he cleaves to the two-dimensional
surfaces described in the text, so too does the text itself metamorphose into a
wall. It is no coincidence in this context that the German word for wall, *eine
Wand*, is at the center of the word for metamorphosis, *eine Verwandlung*. In
the context of all the shifts from three to two dimensions which we have been
following—*and only in light of these displacements*—can one read the title a little
differently: as a becoming-wall of metamorphosis. This sounding out of the
Wand in *Verwandlung* is emblematic of the way Kafka's text metamorphoses

metamorphosis—not by turning it into something else, but by dislocating it from within, exposing the resounding wall in its midst.

Music of the Masonry

To readers of Ovid, this becoming-wall of metamorphosis should come as no surprise. For, as is well known, at the very center of *The Metamorphoses*, in the eighth book of a text consisting of fifteen books, Ovid places the story of another great wall, namely the convoluted enclosure of the Minoan labyrinth.[28] Returning to inspect the walls of book 8, one finds, in addition to the maze designed by Daedalus on the isle of Crete, the musical walls of the city of Alcathous to which King Minos had laid siege. Ovid describes these ramparts as follows: "Winged victory had long been hovering between the two sides, undecided. There was a tower belonging to the king, built on to those tuneful city walls where Leto's son, they say, laid down his lyre, so that its music was imparted to the masonry. Often in the days of peace Nisus' daughter had been in the habit of climbing up there, and flinging pebbles against the stones to make them ring."[29]

Without dwelling on these melodious walls or the various ways in which they continue to resonate throughout book 8, one might nevertheless recall how Scylla, Nisus' daughter, purportedly out of love for Minos, decides to open up the city gates to him, instead of waiting for his military strength to breach the city's fortifications. The obvious sexual imagery is made even more explicit later on, as Pasiphae, Minos's wife, opens up her gates to a bull through a hole in a walled enclosure constructed for her by Daedalus. It might also be recalled in this regard that Minos himself is said to be the offspring of an affair involving Zeus disguised as a bull and the mortal Europa. The tension here between real bulls and just a lot of bull, between literal and figurative language, between true and fictive accounts of one's origins, is compounded when the shunned Scylla questions Minos's own pedigree, claiming that his father was not Zeus masquerading as a bull, but in fact a real one. While the woman who had hoped to give herself so completely to Minos is left behind by him and is transformed into a bird known as a *ciris* by the father whom she has "castrated," her impertinent questions have an uncanny way of staying with the Cretan king. Like stowaways, these questions somehow manage to lodge themselves in his inner ear, where they continue to hover and fly about, unanswered and perhaps unanswerable. Unwittingly bearing these questions back home with him, Minos is confronted upon his return with the Minotaur, "the strange hybrid creature that revealed his wife's love affair. He determines to rid his home of this shameful sight, by shutting the monster away in an enclosure of elaborate and involved design, where it could not be seen. Daedalus, an architect famous for his skill, constructed the maze, confusing the usual marks of direction, and leading the eye of the beholder astray by devious paths winding in different directions" (183).

At this point in his description of the means by which an observer's eye may be led astray, Ovid curiously introduces nothing less than a visual aid for the reader as he goes on to compare this maze to the river Meander: "Just as the playful waters of the Meander in Phrygia flow this way and that, without any consistency, as the river, turning to meet itself, sees its own advancing waves, flowing now towards its source and now towards the open sea, always changing directions, so Daedalus constructed countless wandering paths and was himself scarcely able to find his way back to the entrance, so confusing was the maze" (183).

The irony of Ovid's image is striking, since what this comparison helps one to visualize is not so much a particular path as the devious ways by which the eye may be led astray. In other words, as a way of aiding the beholder of his text to picture an optical illusion, Ovid playfully offers the reader another one. One is thus left to consider whether this doubling of one *trompe l'oeil* by another actually helps to correct our vision, helps us to see through the illusion, or whether it merely redoubles the deception under the pretense of giving us a clearer picture of it.

In the guise of providing the reader with two images of a labyrinth, the passage instead seems to wander circuitously through labyrinthine figures. Instead of two pictures, the reader beholds an extremely convoluted picture frame—and a family picture frame at that. For just as the river Meander flows without any consistency and doubles back on itself, so too does the scandal involving the Minotaur flow back one or two generations, redound to Minos, and put his own pedigree in question. If Minos does not simply remove the monster by sending him away but instead keeps him in a kind of internal exile at home in the labyrinth, it may be because the king can neither adequately distance himself from nor sufficiently accustom himself to this stereophonic questioning of the legitimacy of his paternal line.

Beyond simply containing a Minotaur, the convoluted corridors of the labyrinth figure a crisis in lineage. At this point in book 8, both the story line and the paternal line double back on themselves, greatly disorienting the reader. Not only do the city walls of Alcathous resonate in all of Daedalus's walled constructions, but all of Scylla's questions regarding Minos's origins, which had formerly lodged themselves in the cochlea of his inner ear, seem once again to echo through the endless passageways of the labyrinth. Nevertheless, as complicated and convoluted as these labyrinthine walls may be, they do seem just barely to contain the Minotaur. They do give Minos just enough distance. Daedalus is just barely able to find his way back to the entrance, just as Theseus hanging by a thread is just barely able to do so later. Ovid is just barely able to contain this labyrinthine tale as the literal centerpiece and Medusalike aegis of his *Metamorphoses.* In Ovid, it seems, just barely is just enough.

In many ways, Kafka's singular *Metamorphosis* can be read as an unfolding of certain unresolved questions in Ovid. As in its predecessor, Kafka's *Verwandlung* literally has a wall, or *Wand,* in its midst. Yet, whereas in Ovid the walls of the labyrinth center his *Metamorphoses* and actually emblematize the complex interconnectedness of the many convoluted frame narratives that comprise the text, the walls of Kafka's *Metamorphosis* are labyrinths one enters without warning—just as Joseph K. awakens one morning to find himself ensnared in a seemingly endless web of legal complications in *The Trial.* If the Minoan labyrinth is a place of internal exile, a place recognizably foreign within a domestic setting, what is so disorienting about Kafka's *Metamorphosis* is the strange familiarity of it all. Here one finds no labyrinth as such, no clearly marked entrance or exit, and no real drama attached to it. What is so disconcerting is the familiar, everyday, utterly prosaic tone of it all.[30] There are no visible signs of labyrinthine walls, only an insistent shift from three- to two-dimensional space, only an increasing sense of claustrophobia, of invisible walls closing in, of myopia. In place of a maze, confusing the usual marks of direction, there is only a general sense of futility, of gray, unbroken monotony, the kind that makes one forget one was once human.

Whereas in Ovid the eye of the beholder is deceived by optical illusion, "by confusing the usual marks of direction," in Kafka's myopic world the spectator is not so much led astray as absorbed into a spectacle observed at dangerously close range. Here one might recall the scene Kafka stages in which Grete decides to remove all the furniture from her brother's room. Nowhere in the story does Gregor bear a greater resemblance to Ovid's Minotaur. While Grete clears the room, Gregor remains hidden under a couch, covered over with a cloth whose abundant folds conceal his hideous frame in the same way that the manifold walls of the Cretan labyrinth hide the Minotaur. Yet while the Minoan hybrid is literally half-man, half-bull, Kafka's *ungeheures Ungeziefer* is neither human nor animal. Instead, he or it is but a double negative suspended in metamorphosis. Were Grete to remove all the furniture, Gregor reflects, "he would be able to crawl around unhampered in all directions but at the cost of simultaneously, rapidly, and totally forgetting his human past. Even now he had been on the verge of forgetting, and only his mother's voice, which he had not heard for so long, had shaken him up" (33).

Gregor thus decides to break out of his semi-oblivion and salvage at least the souvenirs of his human existence. Yet in doing so, he attempts to rescue not just the memories of his human past but also and above all the activity of memory itself. As the *sound* of his mother's voice (which literally shakes him up) reminds him, he must remember to remember if he is to preserve anything of his human identity. Linking past and present, it is memory that makes possible the sense of continuity over time which conditions one's sense of self. By contrast, animal-like forgetfulness—at least in Nietzsche's parable of *On the Advantage and Disadvantage of History for Life*—involves a leaping from one present moment to another. "These animals," says Nietzsche, "do not know what yesterday and today are but leap about, eat, rest, digest and leap again."[31] Gregor's semi-oblivion is not a return to this "lost paradise" of discontinuous jumps from "now" to "now" but rather the unpunctuated, gray continuity of quotidian existence. Thus, Gregor finds that it was "the monotony of family life, combined with the fact that not a soul had addressed a word directly to him, [that] must have addled his brain in the course of the past two months" (33). Here in addition to seeing how monotony erodes memory as it "addles the brain," we also notice how the use of apostrophe actively calls its addressee to life. Thus, it is not by chance that the scene we are considering climaxes in Gregor's being directly addressed by his sister for the first and only time since the very beginning of the story. After breaking out from under the couch, he changes direction four times, not knowing what to salvage first, "then he saw hanging conspicuously on the wall, which was otherwise bare already the picture of the lady all dressed in furs, hurriedly crawled up on it and pressed himself against the glass which gave a good surface to stick to and soothed his hot belly. At least no one would take away this picture, while Gregor completely covered it up. He turned his head toward the living-room door to watch the women when they returned" (35).

Whereas Corngold's translation tells of how the glass "gave a good surface to stick to," in the German it is the glass that "had a firm hold" on Gregor and "held him fast [*das Glas, das ihn festhielt*]." In flattening himself against the glass, Gregor finds himself flush up against another two-dimensional creature, namely the picture cut out of an illustrated magazine of a lady whose fur-clad forearm is raised toward the spectator.[32] Here picture, frame, and an incredibly myopic beholder seem to merge in the flat, transparent fifth side of the frame, namely the glass.[33] The spectator is literally absorbed in an image that catches his eye and draws him in. As if following out the logic of this merger, the absorbed spectator in turn makes a spectacle of himself. For just as the lady in fur is said to gesture toward the viewer (*dem Beschauer einen schweren Pelzmuff entgegenhob*), so too does Gregor turn his head toward the doorway and cross glances with a subsequent spectator, his sister Grete, who in turn raises her fist toward the spectacle on the wall and cries out, "You, Gregor!" To which the narrator immediately adds, "these were the first words she had addressed to him since his metamorphosis" (36). Needless to say, both the fist raised toward Gregor and the calling out of his name repeat the ways in which the spectacle gestures toward the beholder. Grete's involuntary repetition of these gestures in turn absorbs her in the spectacle, which, like the glass of the picture frame, seems to have a firm hold on her as she beholds it. Thus, in contrast to the convoluted shape of Ovid's labyrinth, in which the eye of the beholder is led astray by devious and winding paths, Kafka's labyrinth is constructed as a flat, transparent surface, into which spectator and spectacle are mutually absorbed.

As was noted earlier, the actual metamorphosis of Gregor Samsa into an *ungeheures Ungeziefer* is described as a *fait accompli* in the very first sentence of the text. Yet, as Corngold argues, "in the process, it appears to accomplish still another change: it metamorphoses a common figure of speech. This second transformation emerges in the light of the hypothesis proposed in 1947 by Günther Anders."[34] According to Anders,

> All that Kafka has to work with is the common possession of ordinary language. . . . More precisely: he draws from the resources on hand, the figurative nature [*Bildcharakter*] of language. He takes metaphors at their word [*beim Wort*].
>
> For example: Because Gregor Samsa wants to live as an artist [i.e. as a *Luftmensch*—one who lives on air, lofty and free-floating], in the eyes of the highly respectable, hard-working world he is a "nasty bug [*dreckiger Käfer*]": and so in *The Metamorphosis* he wakes up as a beetle whose ideal of happiness is to be sticking to the ceiling.[35]

In claiming that Kafka "takes metaphors at their word [*beim Wort*]," Anders and others who have attempted to build on his hypothesis often fail to appreciate the extent to which Kafka also takes words at their word.[36] That is, in addition to literalizing metaphors, he literally disarticulates the signifying matter itself. This is apparent not only in the becoming-wall of *Verwandlung* but also in a term central to Anders's reading of Gregor's desire to live as a free-floating *Luftmensch*: namely, the word "ceiling." In the German text, Kafka uses the more common term *Decke* as well as the loanword *Plafond*, borrowed from French. Thus, he writes in the passage to which Anders's analysis refers,

> Eating soon stopped giving him the slightest pleasure, so, as a distraction [*zur Zerstreuung*], he adopted the habit of crawling criss-cross over the walls and the ceiling [*Plafond*]. He especially liked hanging from the ceiling [*Decke*]; it was completely different from lying on the floor; one could breathe more freely; a faint swinging sensation went through the body; and in the almost happy absent-mindedness [*Zerstreutheit*] which Gregor felt up there, it could happen to his own surprise that he let go and

plopped onto the floor.... His sister immediately noticed the new entertainment Gregor had discovered for himself—after all, he left behind traces of his sticky substance wherever he crawled—and so she got it into her head to make it possible for Gregor to crawl on an altogether wider scale by taking out the furniture which stood in his way. (31–32)

Using the synonymous terms *Decke* and *Plafond* in this passage, Kafka is able to avoid unnecessary repetition. Yet, more importantly, his use of the less common loanword *Plafond* in conjunction with his mention of the walls of Gregor's room marks a pivotal moment in the text. For just as the term *Plafond* condenses the roots *plat* and *fond* into a kind of oxymoron of profound superficiality, so too at this point is there a marked shift from the not so roomy interior of Gregor's bedroom and the shrinking volume of his body ("eating soon stopped giving him the slightest pleasure") to the flat surfaces of the ceiling and walls themselves. In order to gauge the extent of this shift, it might be recalled that Gregor's room is initially described as "a regular human room lying tranquilly [*ruhig*] between the four familiar walls" (3). The tranquillity of these walls, it might be remembered, stands in stark contrast to the agitation of Gregor's unsettling [*unruhige*] dreams. When Gregor becomes increasingly restless—perhaps haunted again by the dreams from which he first awoke—the walls in turn lose their familiarity.[37] No longer the four compass points by which he might orient himself in space, the walls and ceiling merely provide increased surface area for his "almost happy absentmindedness [*Zerstreutheit*]" (32).

While Corngold's translations of *Zerstreutheit* as "absent-mindedness" and *Zerstreuung* as "distraction" are certainly legitimate, taking these words at their word one also hears in them etymological resonances of "dispersion" and "dissemination," which are particularly relevant in this context. Repeating these signifiers in close proximity to one another, the text foregrounds a certain mode of fertilization—a kind of cloud seeding—as it sounds out yet another link to Ovid's *Metamorphoses* and the sexual overtones of its musical masonry. Whereas in Ovid Scylla opens her city's gates instead of waiting for Minos to breach its fortifications, and Pasiphae copulates with a bull through a hole in the wall of a device constructed for her by Daedalus, in Kafka it is the walls themselves, papered over in a floral pattern, that are clouded over and volatilized as Gregor absentmindedly leaves behind "traces [*Spuren*] of his sticky substance" (32). Rather than copulating *through* the walls, Gregor disseminates himself in them, thereby making himself into wall (*sich verwandeln*) as more walls are made. The scene thus anticipates the mutually absorbing spectacle later enacted on the fifth transparent side of the picture frame, on "the glass which gave a good surface to stick to and soothed [Gregor's] hot belly." If the sexual practices alluded to here are, to say the least, a little bizarre, it is perhaps because a different sense of pleasure and of reproduction is being articulated. As Corngold says, "In this story, writing reproduces itself, in the mode of allegory, as metamorphosis, literality, death, play, and reduction—the whole in a negative and embattled form."[38]

LOSING ONE'S BEARINGS: ON THE PLAFOND

For all its strangeness, Kafka's *Metamorphosis* is still very much a story of the workaday world. Indeed, the narrative has often been read as a gradual metamorphosis of the home into a workplace—as if it were not one already. In this sense, *The Metamorphosis* has always already taken place, for it takes place repeatedly, monotonously, senselessly without ever really taking place as such. The development the narrative traces is but a retracing. Thus, when Grete stands up at the end and stretches her young body, one has the sense that she is finally prepared to become what Gregor had been before the beginning—perhaps not a traveling salesman, but at least someone who could bring another meal ticket into the family. A good husband is what her parents seem to feel she is ready for.

As a traveling salesman, Gregor had ventured far from home for days at a time. When one morning he can no longer leave for work, the office suddenly comes to him with a vengeance in the person of the manager, whose presence occasions some of the funniest and most sardonic exchanges in the story. Soon after the initial crisis, all the familiar family roles are reversed as Gregor stays home while the other three go out to work. Mother and daughter even bring work home with them, while the father never even takes off his uniform. Indeed, the more the workplace enters the domestic space, the more the father's work clothes come to resemble the old bathrobe he never took off while staying at home. Finally, the family's living quarters do indeed become a second workplace when the three boarders move in.

The former center of the family, Gregor, through whose room the others literally communicated with each other at the beginning, is now displaced more and more to the periphery and served cold leftovers, while the strangers in the midst of the family are regaled with music and hot, steaming meats. Indeed, Gregor becomes so peripheral that by the end the family practically forgets to forget him. It could in fact be argued that he finally dies only in order to be remembered. His death seems to be almost a direct response to Grete's question, "But how can it be Gregor? If it were Gregor, he would have realized long ago that it isn't possible for human beings to live with such a creature, and he would have gone away of his own free will. Then we wouldn't have a brother, but we'd be able to go on living and honor his memory" (52).

As was noted earlier, Gregor's death is described as another loss of volume, another shift from three to two dimensions. As the narrator says,

"Then, without his consent, his head sank down to the floor, and from his nostrils streamed his last weak breath" (54). "Gregor's body was completely flat and dry" (55).

As I have tried to suggest, the scene of metamorphosis, the becoming-wall of *Verwandlung*, is played out on a number of uncannily "deep surfaces" ranging from the glass of the picture frame to all the floors, ceilings, and walls of the text, to the surface of everyday language, the plane of the printed page, and the general shift from three to two dimensions. To conclude, I would like to focus briefly on the narrating surface itself. If Gregor is a creature lost in translation and a mistranslation always in need of retranslation, a character who is almost never directly spoken to and one who never speaks for himself, it is the narrator who repeatedly translates, interprets, and speaks for him. The narrator, however, does not simply have another voice. For if he is the one who is most intimately in touch with Gregor, his voice is also the one most contaminated. Indeed, it is contaminated to the point where the reader often cannot distinguish Gregor's thoughts from the narrator's own editorializing comments.[39]

While the text is replete with examples of this fusion and confusion of voices, consider the following passage, in which the narrator describes Gregor's reaction to the cleaning woman's exclamation, "Look at that old dung beetle!"

> To forms of address like these Gregor would not respond but remained immobile where he was, as if the door had not been opened. If only they had given this cleaning woman orders to clean up his room every day, instead of letting her disturb him uselessly whenever the mood took her. (45)

Like the transparent glass of the picture frame in which spectator and spectacle are mutually absorbed, Kafka's frequent use of free indirect style confuses the unspeakable thoughts of an *ungeheures Ungeziefer* with the disembodied voice of a faceless narrator. And if we as readers, as beholders of *The Metamorphosis*, look closely and read myopically, we may in turn find ourselves absorbed in a narrative that from beginning to end is profoundly superficial. As such, Kafka's *Metamorphosis*, unlike Ovid's Minoan labyrinth, never quite lets one in—or out.

NOTES

1. The letter is in Franz Kafka, *Letters to Friends, Family, and Editors*, trans. Richard Winston and Clara Winston (New York: Schocken Books, 1977), 286–89. This volume is based on the collection of Kafka's *Briefe (1902–1924)*, ed. Max Brod (New York: Schocken Books, 1958). See also Gilles Deleuze and Felix Guattari's discussion of this letter in their

chapter "What Is a Minor Literature?" in *Kafka: Toward a Minor Literature*, ed. and trans. Dana Polan (Minneapolis: University of Minnesota Press, 1986), 16–27.

2. Kafka, *Letters to Friends*, 288; trans. mod.

3. For a book-length discussion of this essay, see Sven Kramer's *Rätselfragen und wolkige Stellen: Zu Benjamins Kafka-Essay* (Lüneburg: zu Klampen, 1991).

4. All further page references, which appear in parentheses in the body of the text, are to Benjamin's "Franz Kafka: On the Tenth Anniversary of His Death," in his *Illuminations*, trans. Harry Zohn, ed. Hannah Arendt (New York: Schocken Books, 1969).

5. The following discussion of the "cloudy spot (wolkige Stelle]" in Benjamin is greatly indebted to Werner Hamacher's unpublished essay "Failing Literature: (Benjamin's Reading of Kafka's Example)." See also his reading of "The Word *Wolke*—If It Is One," in *Benjamin's Ground*, ed. Rainer Nägele (Detroit: Wayne State University Press, 1988), 147–76.

6. Such structures, I would suggest, may also include the stress of an accent, the -phor of metaphor, or the *tragende* -fer of transference (*Übertragung*).

7. The notion of orbital paths such as those traced by the rings of Saturn also resonates in the German term used by Benjamin.

8. More generally, I would suggest that there is a certain structural affinity between the "cloudy spots" of the Kafka essay and the "crowded passages" of Benjamin's essay on Baudelaire discussed in Chapter 5. In both, a language of positing, positioning, and *Stellung* gives way at certain crucial points to more diffuse movements of displacement, disfiguration, and *Entstellung.*

9. It is no accident that the passages dealt with here belong to a section of Benjamin's essay whose introductory paragraph sets the tone for what follows. In it, Benjamin relates Knut Hamsun's reaction to the trial of a maid in a nearby town who had killed her infant child. "She was sentenced to a prison term. Soon thereafter the local paper printed a letter from Hamsun in which he announced his intention of leaving a town which did not visit the supreme punishment on a mother who killed her newborn child—the gallows, or at least a life term of hard labor. A few years passed. *Growth of the Soil* appeared, and it contained the story of a maid who committed the same crime, suffered the same punishment, and, as is made clear to the reader, surely deserved no more severe one" (127). Introduced by this story, the section never quite leaves the question of infanticide, which returns in various guises in the following pages.

10. See in this regard Derrida's essay "Devant la lox," trans. Avital Ronell, in *Kafka and the Contemporary Critical Performance*, ed. Alan Udoff (Bloomington: Indiana University Press, 1987), 128–49.

11. Walter Benjamin, "A Berlin Chronicle," in his *Reflections*, ed. Peter Demetz, trans. Edmund Jephcott (New York: Schocken Books, 1978), 8.

12. References are to Corngold's translation of *The Metamorphosis* (New York: Bantam Books, 1972) and appear henceforth in parentheses in the body of the text.

13. Commenting on the fact that Kafka's text reaches its climax by the end of the first line (whose last word is indeed the past participle of the verb *verwandeln*), Martin Greenberg notes, "a climax that occurs in the first sentence is no real climax." Greenberg, *The Terror of Art: Kafka and Modern Literature* (New York: Basic Books, 1968), 84.

14. In a letter of October 25, 1915, Kafka implores his publisher to allow the text of *The Metamorphosis* to appear without any depiction of the "insect" Gregor has become. "It struck me," he writes, "that Starke, as an illustrator, might want to draw the insect itself. Not that, please not that! I do not want to restrict him, but only to make this plea out of my deeper knowledge of the story, as is natural. The insect itself cannot be depicted. It cannot even be shown from a distance." *Letters to Friends, Family, and Editors*, 114–15.

15. That is, the adjective *geheuer* is employed only with the prefix *un-* or is preceded by the negation *nicht*, as in the phrase "*mir ist das nicht geheuer.*" Similarly, the noun *Geziefer*, which is in fact still to be found in the dictionary, is now employed primarily as a synonym for the term *Ungeziefer*, to which it was initially opposed.

16. In a provocative essay on labyrinths, Philip West notes that in the symbolism of the High Middle Ages a clean beast was one who knew how to interpret the Bible, whereas an unclean beast could not transcend the most mundane literalism. Philip West, "Redundant Labyrinths," *Salmagundi* 46 (Fall 1979): 78.

17. Willa and Edwin Muir translate the phrase *ungeheures Ungeziefer* as "gigantic insect" in *Kafka: The Complete Stories*, ed. Nahum N. Glatzer (New York: Schocken Books, 1976) 89, while Corngold renders it as "monstrous vermin" in *The Metamorphosis* (3). Reflecting on the problems involved in translating these terms, Corngold says, "what is remarkable in *The Metamorphosis* is that "the immortal part" [Adorno] of the writer accomplishes itself odiously, in the quality of an indeterminacy sheerly negative. The exact sense of his intention is captured in the *Ungeziefer*, a word that cannot be expressed by the English words 'bug' or 'vermin.'" Stanley Corngold, *Franz Kafka: The Necessity of Form* (Ithaca: Cornell University Press, 1988), 57.

18. Here one might wish to return to Kafka's letter to Brod and his discussion of *mauscheln*. "What we have here," he says, "is the product of a sensitive feeling for language which has recognized that in German only the dialects are really alive, and except for them, only the most individual High German, while all the rest, the linguistic middle ground, is nothing but embers which can only be brought to a semblance of life when excessively lively Jewish hands rummage through them. That is a fact, funny or terrible as you like." Such rummaging, I would suggest, is evident in the linguistic distortions of *The Metamorphosis*. For a further discussion of this famous passage, see Hannah Arendt's introduction to the English translation of Benjamin's *Illuminations*, 31–35.

19. That Gregor is always in need of an interpreter is confirmed not only "intratextually" by Kafka's use of free indirect style, in which the narrator's voice supplements that of the character, or, if one prefers, the character speaks through the voice of the narrator, but also "extratextually" by the enormous body of secondary literature which the text continues to elicit. See in this regard Stanley Corngold, *The Commentators' Despair: The Interpretation of Kafka's "Metamorphosis"* (Port Washington, N.Y.: Kennikat Press, 1973). In many ways the reading I propose here is an attempt to identify the structure of supplementarity and belatedness which will have been set in motion by *The Metamorphosis*.

20. *The Diaries of Franz Kafka (1910–1913)*, trans. Joseph Kresh, ed. Max Brod (New York: Schocken Books, 1948), 211.

21. I would further suggest that the blurry scene of *Vereinigung* described here be related to the vision of parental union recounted at the end of section 2, in which Gregor sees his mother force "herself onto his father, and embracing him, in complete union [*in gänzlicher Vereinigung*] with him—but now Gregor's sight went dim [*nun versagte aber Gregors Sehkraft schon*]—her hands clasping his father's neck, begged for Gregor's life" (39).

22. In contrast to Walter Sokel, who sees in this situation evidence that Gregor is now no longer treated as an adult or even as a man, since people talk through him rather than to or with him, I would argue that the scene draws attention both to Gregor's centrality in the family dynamic and in more literal and ironic terms to the strange capaciousness of his "regular human room, a little on the small side." Cf. Sokel, *Franz Kafka—Tragik und Ironie: Zur Struktur seiner Kunst* (Munich: A. Langen, 1964), 77.

23. In a superb discussion of *The Metamorphosis*, to which my own reading is greatly indebted, Heinz Politzer observes that as space closes in on Gregor, time also seems to dissolve. See his *Parable and Paradox* (Ithaca: Cornell University Press, 1962), 69.

24. As Adorno observes, "Gestures often serve as counterpoints to words [in Kafka]: the pre-linguistic that eludes all intention upsets the ambiguity, which like a disease, has eaten into all signification in Kafka.... Such gestures are the traces of experience covered over by signification. The most recent state of a language that wells up in the mouths of those who speak it, the second Babylonian confusion, which Kafka's sober diction tirelessly opposes, compels him to invert the historical relation of concept and gesture." Theodor W. Adorno, "Notes on Kafka," in his *Prisms*, trans. Samuel Weber and Shierry Weber (Cambridge: MIT Press, 1992), 249.

25. Despite appearances, Gregor's prostration is not altogether a bad thing. As Kafka writes in a letter to Felice Bauer, "Just as when lying on the floor one cannot fall, so, when alone, nothing can happen to one." Kafka, *Letters to Felice*, trans. James Stern and Elizabeth Duckworth (New York: Schocken Books, 1973), 176. This letter was written between January 29 and January 30, 1913. Kafka worked on *The Metamorphosis* from November 17 to December 7, 1912.

26. One might consider in this regard the following passage from Kafka's *Letter to His Father*: "My writing was all about you. All I did there, after all, was to bemoan what I could not bemoan upon your breast. It was an intentionally long-drawn-out leave-taking from you, yet, although it was brought about by force on your part, *it did take its course in the direction determined by me*" (emphasis added). *Dearest Father: Stories and Other Writings*, trans. Ernst Kaiser and Eithne Wilkins (New York: Schocken Books, 1954), 177.

27. See in this regard Politzer's illuminating discussion of the ensuing scene in which father and son do a kind of circle dance about one another. Politzer sees in the image of the circle a symbol of "the inextricable self-involvement of Gregor's fate." He continues, "With the consistency that characterizes Kafka's inspiration at its best, he now chooses a round object [an apple] to put an end once and for all to Gregor's aimless circular wanderings." *Parable and Paradox*, 73.

28. While Frederick Ahl unfortunately does not discuss the sections of book 8 devoted to the story of the Minotaur, one may infer from his brilliant study of *The Metamorphoses* that the seemingly frivolous attempt to sound out the resonant *Wand* in the midst of Kafka's *Ver-wand-lung* is in fact very much in keeping with Ovidian metamorphic tradition. Ahl's reading of *The Metamorphoses* is based on a hypothesis—which is carefully documented and, to my mind, persuasively proven in the course of his book—that Ovid "accompanies his descriptions of change in physical shape with changes in the shape of the words with which he describes those changes" (51). He argues that "for Ovid, as for Plato, the letters within words are the substrate, the shifting reality which establishes, undermines, redefines meaning at the verbal level. A sentence is a movable configuration of letters and syllables rather than of words" (54). Taking one example among many, Ahl observes how in "the first line of Ovid the Greek METaMORPHosis is itself changed into the Latin MUTatas ... FORMas. FORMa is a cross-language anagram of MORPHe and MUTatas even echoes the consonant patterns of the Greek." Frederick Ahl, *Metaformations* (Ithaca: Cornell University Press, 1985), 59.

29. Ovid, *The Metamorphoses*, trans. Mary M. Innes (London: Penguin Books, 1955), 179. Further references appear in parentheses in the body of the text.

30. See Hermann Pongs, "Franz Kafka—'Die Verwandlung' zwischen West und Ost," in *Dichtung im gespaltenen Deutschland* (Stuttgart: Union, 1966), 262–85.

31. Friedrich Nietzsche, *On the Advantage and Disadvantage of History for Life*, trans. Peter Preuss (Indianapolis: Hackett Publishing, 1980), 8.

32. Mark Anderson makes a compelling argument for reading this picture "as a coded reference to Kafka's own appropriation of Sacher-Masoch's narrative," *Venus in Furs*. See his fascinating book, *Kafka's Clothes* (Oxford: Oxford University Press, 1992), 136; see also his "Kafka and Sacher-Masoch," in *Franz Kafka's "The Metamorphosis": Modern Critical Interpretations*, ed. Harold Bloom (New York: Chelsea House, 1988). In order to make this argument, however, Anderson must treat the fifth side of the frame, the glass against which Gregor presses himself and which holds him fast, as a transparent medium that effaces itself and its own significance in order to allow one to see through it to the depths of the framed contents of the picture. This kind of approach, while certainly fruitful, nevertheless tends to look *through* rather than *at* the glass and by extension through a signifying surface that parasitically draws attention to itself as a sonorous and semi-opaque becoming-wall of metamorphosis. To observe this all too conspicuous foreground of *Die Ver-wand-lung*, I have argued that it is necessary to read in a pointedly myopic fashion, pressing oneself against the text's glassy surface as it in turn holds one fast.

33. As though to stress the importance not only of the frame but of the activity of framing, Gregor's mother explains to the chief clerk that "it's already a distraction for [her son] when he's busy working with his fretsaw. For instance, in the span of two or three evenings he carved a little frame. You'll be amazed how pretty it is" (20). Later on, when Gregor's room is being cleared out, it is said that the mother and sister were "depriving him of everything that he loved; they had already carried away the chest of drawers, in which he kept the fretsaw and other tools" (35). Even the first mention of the picture in the second paragraph of the text emphasizes the way in which Gregor "had recently cut [it] out of a glossy magazine and lodged [it] in a pretty gilt frame" (3).

34. Corngold, *Kafka*, 49.

35. Here I follow with slight modifications Corngold's translation of a passage from Anders's superb *Kafka, pro und contra* (Munich: Beck, 1952) rather than that of A. Steer and A. K. Thorlby, *Franz Kafka* (London: Bowes & Bowes, 1960). Cf. Corngold, *Franz Kafka*, 49. For a detailed discussion of the way Anders's hypothesis has been taken up and modified by Kafka criticism, see Corngold's chapter "*The Metamorphosis*: Metamorphosis of the Metaphor," 47–89.

36. Among the more notable exceptions to this approach are Werner Hamacher's "Failing Literature (Benjamin's Reading of Kafka's Example)," and Clayton Koelb's *Kafka's Rhetoric: The Passion of Reading* (Ithaca: Cornell University Press, 1989).

37. It is perhaps no coincidence that this process of defamiliarization reaches its uncanniest extreme in the scene in which Gregor mounts the picture on the wall. Finally tearing himself loose from the glass "to which he firmly adhered," he begins to crawl frantically "to and fro, over everything, walls, furniture, and ceiling" until the room itself seems to come unhinged: "the whole room," Kafka writes, "began to reel around him [*als sich das ganze Zimmer schon um ihn zu drehen anfing*]" (37; trans. mod.).

38. Corngold, *Kafka*, 85.

39. For an extended discussion of the relationship of narrator and protagonist in *The Metamorphosis*, see Roy Pascal, *Kafka's Narrators: A Study of His Stories and Sketches* (Cambridge: Cambridge University Press, 1982).

MARGIT M. SINKA

Kafka's Metamorphosis *and the Search for Meaning in Twentieth-Century German Literature*

Regardless of how often I lead discussions on Franz Kafka in my literature courses, I still find teaching Kafka a humbling experience. To "teach" Kafka seems, in fact, presumptuous. Even the Germanist Peter Heller says, in a wise article, that there is nothing in Kafka that he is sure of understanding sufficiently, since there are always possibilities of implications to lure him on and to dismiss him finally with a sense of failure. "This experience of incapacity to understand," adds Heller, "seems tantamount to understanding Kafka, at least in his essential and perennial message, the dramatization of a vast landscape of failures" ("On Not Understanding" 383).

Keeping in mind Heller's statement and my own failed attempts to attain conclusive meanings in Kafka, I find it presumptuous to state course objectives when Kafka appears on a class syllabus. Though Kafka insisted on the existence of a goal, he could never formulate it, and he stressed the absence of a way to reach it: "There is a goal but no way; what we call the way is mere wavering" (*Great Wall* 166). Instead of definite objectives that would seem hypocritical or, at best, highly inflated, this Kafka quote appears at the top of the syllabus for my third-year-level German course on modern literature.

There are, of course, both disadvantages and advantages to reading Kafka, as well as other authors, in German. Readily apparent disadvantages: some students have not yet bridged the gap between the different types

From *Approaches to Teaching Kafka's Short Fiction*. Edited by Richard T. Gray, pp. 105–113. © 1995 by The Modern Language Association of America.

of readings on the second- and third-year levels and thus have inadequate reading proficiency; others have only a slight interest in literature and sign up for the course mainly because of high oral proficiency in German attained while living abroad. Sometimes age differences become crucial, especially between the freshmen enrolled in the course because of high achievement on German placement tests and the juniors and seniors. The freshmen tend to balk at ambivalence; the older students are less threatened by it. Another disadvantage, perhaps not so apparent, is the shock some students who have been in my lower-level courses have to overcome: the shock at seeing their German professor, who once fussed about genders of nouns and stressed practical linguistic goals such as "oral proficiency," stray from language certainties on a functional level into ambivalent literary topics.

The most pronounced advantage, by contrast, is the possibility to spend more time on each work—and thus on its details—than would be justifiable in a survey course conducted in English. In the process of attempting to glean meaning, students concentrate more closely on language. Thus they frequently avoid facile solutions. Unfamiliar terrain seems, in addition, more acceptable to them if approached through a linguistic medium retaining foreign texture.

The Search for Meaning is the title and unifying theme of my third-year course on twentieth-century German prose before World War II. On the first day of the course, instead of starting with twentieth-century materials, we briefly step into the eighteenth and nineteenth centuries, discussing first Friedrich Schiller's "Ode to Joy" and then listening to Beethoven's rendition of the poem in his Ninth Symphony. Students thus sense the former belief in an anchored world—in short, the belief in meaning and the certainty in the values that provide meaning—so they are at least somewhat prepared to grasp the enormity of the changes that occur later.

Throughout most of the course, students read various chapters or excerpts from Stefan Zweig's *Die Welt Von Gestern* (*The World of Yesterday*), for Zweig demonstrates especially well how an age of certainty was transformed into an age of uncertainty. For additional background material, I lecture on Kant's and Schopenhauer's challenges to accepted ways of understanding the world. We then proceed to Gerhart Hauptmann's "Fasching," an example of naturalism, and afterward to Arthur Schnitzler's "Der Witwer," an illustration of impressionism. In conjunction with Schnitzler, we spend considerable time on the entire Viennese *fin-de-siècle* period and especially on artists and musicians (e.g., Gustav Klimt and Arnold Schönberg) who were accused of attacking the cherished ideals of rationalism and progress. At this stage, we also discuss Klimt's murals on "The Ode to Joy."

A unit on Sigmund Freud precedes Stefan Zweig's "Der Amokläufer," a tale in which the Freudian id can no longer be controlled. On subsequent discussions of Hugo von Hofmannsthal's and Rainer Maria Rilke's poetry, we proceed to Hofmannsthal's "Letter of Lord Chandos" and to an excerpt from Robert Musil's *Der Mann ohne Eigenschaften* (*The Man without Qualities*). Emphasis on the loss of belief in transmitted values and on the ensuing relativism leads to excerpts from Friedrich Nietzsche's *Also sprach Zarathustra* (*Thus Spoke Zarathustra*). In the next stage of the course we focus in detail on Hermann Hesse's *Demian*, which interweaves influences from Nietzsche and Carl Jung, and on Thomas Mann's *Tonio Kröger*. Kafka's *The Metamorphosis* then concludes the course.

At the outset of the three-week Kafka period, I assign the first chapter of Heinz Politzer's *Parable and Paradox*, a chapter providing numerous interpretations prompted by Kafkas ten-line parable "Give It Up." This selection not only enables students to read concrete examples of critical orientations such as the Freudian, the Jungian, the religious, and the Marxist but also demonstrates how previous background and subjective viewpoints determine the nature of the commentaries. Assured of student interest, I then discuss the whole problematic area of meaning in Kafka. Is it justifiable to think in reductionist fashion, to find only a single meaning in Kafka—one excluding all other interpretations? Or are all the many interpretations equally valid? Do they represent the accumulation of perspectives that Kafka once called the only possible truth? Or do all of the varied meanings cancel each other out and show that there is no meaning at all? Is it possible that Kafka's purpose was to demonstrate the absence of any meaning? Should one not stress instead that Kafka doggedly searched for a truth he sensed, even though he found its adequate expression impossible? At the end of this discussion, I tend to affirm Kafka's untiring quest for meaning. Because he cannot, he does not supply the "truth." But he always intimates its existence.

In the class period following the session on Politzer's chapter and possible ways of interpreting Kafka, I give students individual copies of many supplementary materials, most of them in English. While they include a long, excellent biographical article disseminated by the Austrian Embassy in New York, they consist mainly of book reviews or interpretive articles from major American magazines and newspapers directed at the general literate reading public (e.g., Auster, "Pages" and "Letters"; Roth; V. S. Pritchett; Steiner; Updike). The articles are not required reading, but they provide welcome aids for the particularly inquisitive.

Since I believe that no single Kafka work should be treated in entire isolation from the others, I pass out a list of Kafka quotes (mainly in German) gleaned from the entire spectrum of his writings. Examples: "A cage went in search of a bird" (*Dearest Father* 36); "What is laid upon us is to accomplish the negative; the positive is already given" (*Dearest Father* 36–37); "Theoretically there exists a perfect possibility of happiness: to believe in the indestructible element in oneself and not strive after it" (*Dearest Father* 41); "To reach clarity, it is necessary to exaggerate" ("Der Nachbar," in *Erzählungen* 346; my trans.); "I have no literary interest but am made of literature" (*Letters to Felice* 304). Individual students read some of the quotes out loud, and short discussions ensue. Sometimes I give only half of a quote, and students hypothesize about the rest of it.

Next, I spend two to three minutes reading titles of articles and books written on Kafka (e.g., "Moment of Torment"; "Kafka's Fantasy of Punishment"; "The Reality of the Absurd and the Absurdity of the Real"; "The Tragic Protest"; "The Alienated Self"). Then I provide students with a typed sheet of Kafka motifs (walls, doors, keys, food, the number three) and typical Kafkaesque developments (accelerated and terminated motion, decreasing appetite, frequent hiding and shrinking). To ascertain recurring patterns in Kafka, students refer to this sheet while they are reading.

During the last few minutes of the class, I mention Kafka's sentence "A book must be the axe for the frozen sea inside us" (*Letters to Friends* 16) and suggest that *The Metamorphosis* has become exactly the axe he was talking about. I then read its first sentence, probably the most famous beginning in all of twentieth-century prose. Rarely does a person hearing this sentence remain unaffected. In quick brainstorming, after a minute of appropriate silence, class members supply questions engendered by the sentence: Did Gregor truly become a beetle, or is he only dreaming? What could his "troubled dream" during the night have been? ("Troubled dream" is Vladimir Nabokov's translation of "unruhigen Träumen," generally rendered as "uneasy dreams" [256].) If Gregor has indeed turned into a beetle, how will he react? How will others react? What human traits, if any, is he likely to retain? Who turned him into a beetle? Does his beetle-self reflect his own feelings about himself? If so, how does he feel about himself? Will he be changed back into a human being? How will he have to change his manner of living as a result of being a beetle? How long can he live as a beetle? How will he change his perspectives on his spatial surroundings and on time? Not every class asks all these questions, and some classes ask other questions as well. In all classes, however, the first questions release a flood of others, especially since the students know that they are not yet expected to attempt responses.

With all reading assignments, students continue to formulate questions. At the beginning of the class hour, each student anonymously places a slip of paper with a question into a box. Either as a single group or in pairs, class members choose two or three of the questions at random and evaluate them, using criteria such as whether the answer is worth knowing and whether attempting to answer the question calls for genuine reflection. Later, students also provide possible answers. Through this process of producing questions and attempting answers, students become acquainted with *how* Kafka lures readers into his world of countless labyrinthine paths leading nowhere, least of all to explicit meaning.

Because students need help and time to accustom themselves to Kafka's style, I make the first reading assignment very short, not more than four pages. This brief text enables us to concentrate in class on how Gregor Samsa tends to follow, or be distracted by, most thoughts that occur to him. We scrutinize Gregor's rhetorical questions and quick self-justifications. We note how he avoids unpleasant thoughts by exaggerating the inessential and how the excessive details pertaining to inessentials hinder grasp of the essential. Students observe, moreover, how the prominent use of the subjunctive, the tense of conjecture and uncertainty, contributes to creating a world of ambivalence.

At this point I also find it necessary to inform the students of Friedrich Beissner's groundbreaking thesis, offered in 1952. There is no controlling authorial voice, says Beissner. We experience everything only from the viewpoint of the main character. Thus, instead of reaching conclusions about what is or is not real, we are doomed to floundering in the same indecisions and uncertainties as the main character does. To be sure, critics have contested the extent to which Beissner's thesis remains valid. In *The Metamorphosis*, for instance, the authorial voice enters not only in the conclusion (after Gregor's death) but also occasionally before then. Still, these episodes remain isolated instances, and I do not find it necessary to stress them to undergraduate students reading Kafka for the first time. It is more important I think, to emphasize how Kafka's dominant narrative mode contributes just as much to creating the Kafkaesque as do the metaphors—for instance, the human entrapped in a repugnant animal—which refer to nothing beyond themselves.

For the remaining seven days spent on Kafka, I find Nabokov's universal lectures on *The Metamorphosis* very useful, particularly his emphasis on visualizing. While I agree with Kafka that the beetle should never be drawn or appear as an illustration on a book jacket (see *Letters to Friends* 114–16), I think that readers do form an image of its appearance in their minds. Nabokov's observations, based entirely on Kafka's text, present a convincing case for the approximate size and shape of the beetle. Discussing student perceptions of the beetle's appearance along with Nabokov's can lead to lively class encounters and to careful scrutiny of the text. Equally helpful are Nabokov's illustrations of rooms and doors and his comments about where the family members are situated at various times. Through Gregor's perspective, readers find out how the physical appearances of the family members change and what spaces they occupy in the apartment (e.g., sofa, table, living room, kitchen). To ascertain the family's reactions to Gregor, the readers must activate their own visualizing capacities to a far greater degree. Nabokov, to my knowledge, is the only person who has emphasized that Gregor is always in a different spot when family members see him. Though Nabokov does not develop this point further, students find it interesting to hypothesize on the effects that Gregor's changes of location, as well as the changes in his appearance, may have on the family members. Then they begin to realize that the constant shifting of perspectives so prevalent in Kafka's works occurs largely because of the interplay of mental and physical dislocations.

The emphasis on visualization also leads to greater appreciation of Kafka's grotesque humor, an aspect not sufficiently stressed by critics or, I suspect, by professors. Students who have already read *The Metamorphosis* for English assignments (generally not more than two in classes ranging from twelve to twenty participants) seem unaware of it. Thus I highlight the comical absurdity of Gregor the beetle's preoccupation with the alarm clock, the difficulties he has getting out of bed (our own difficulties magnified a thousand times), his doomed attempts to placate everyone with arguments muttered in a voice that cannot be understood, the hilarity of his looking at his mother eye to eye on the floor, she being on his level because she has swooned, and the ridiculous juxtaposition of his present self with his former self (the Gregor dressed in military uniform in a photograph). It is, in fact, the constant coupling of his two irreconcilable selves—the inner human self and the exterior animal self, neither allowing the other to gain control—that conditions much of the grotesque humor of part 1 and consequently also the reader's vacillations in considering Gregor mostly human one minute, mostly animal the next. As Gregor behaves increasingly like an animal, even though his thoughts seem to remain human, much of the humor disappears. This development from a comically absurd world to a hopelessly bleak one should not, I am convinced, be overlooked.

In general, I place considerable emphasis on structure by discussing the development of certain motifs from part 1 through part 3. In the first part, for example, Gregor awakens from a troubled sleep; in the second from a deep, leaden sleep; but in the third part he barely falls asleep anymore, either during the day or at night. At the beginning of the first part it is morning; at the beginning of the second, dusk; but in the third part we find Gregor awake in an utterly dark room, in a sense no longer needing sleep to be plunged into darkness. Though this darkness starts to prepare us for his death, Gregor actually dies at 3:00 a.m., able to experience the beginning of dawn. Instead of waking up from "troubled sleep," Gregor sinks into death from a "vacant and peaceful" state (*CS* 135). The light here is not "the light on the flinching grimacing face" (*Great Wall* 174; trans. modified) that Kafka elsewhere called the truth but, rather, a noncommittal light, a light that makes it difficult for us to speculate about the possibility of an afterlife for Gregor.

I also stress structural development when concentrating on the aspect of motion. Part 1 shows us the difficulties encountered by Gregor (the traveling salesman!) to move at all; in part 2 we find him crawling avidly all over the walls and the ceiling, probably with the same senselessness characteristic of his travels as a salesman but actually with a greater joy, since he does not have to concoct any purpose for his constant movements other than their salutary capacity to distract him from self-analysis and from formulating plans of action for the future. In part 3 Gregor can no longer reach the walls and ceilings, but he does crawl happily amid all the garbage in his room. Yet these "wanderings," even more senseless and limited than his journeys on the walls and the ceiling, cause him to become "deathly" tired (49).[1] He moves constantly, to the point of exhaustion. His last trip outside his room and then back into it does, in fact, result in the total exhaustion leading to his death.

While time's restrictions on Gregor diminish (the alarm clock is not mentioned after part 1, and Gregor can't tell in part 3 whether Christmas has already occurred), the space available to him becomes increasingly restricted. To a certain extent, Gregor himself limits his space—for instance, when he squeezes into the darkness under the sofa and later arranges a sheet over the sofa to hide himself completely. Though he can still position himself at the window and crawl over walls and ceiling through most of part 2, toward the end of this section he does not even seriously consider escaping onto the walls, especially since the cutting edges and sharp points of the finely carved furniture provide only dangerous access to them. Whereas part 1 ends with Gregor kicked "far" into the room (19), part 2 ends with Gregor flattened on the floor, as if nailed down. In part 3 Gregor can no longer reach either the window or the walls, and he discovers—after his last return to his room from the family quarters—that he can neither see anything in the dark nor move anymore. With no space visible to him and his capacity for movement entirely gone, Gregor dies.

In the context of discussing structural development of movement and its termination, we also concentrate in detail on senseless circular movements and on the woundings that ultimately end all movement. Though not always (e.g., when Gregor is turning the key in the lock in part 1), to a large extent the circular movements are emphasized most when Gregor attempts to leave the family's quarters and return to his own room, and they are invariably connected with woundings. At the end of both parts 1 and 2, Gregor leaves his room in order to provide help: to detain the chief clerk, to help his mother. In each of these instances, the father chases him back into his room. In part 1, after Gregor slowly turns around, his flank becoming more and more bruised, his father shoves him back into his room. Gregor then bleeds heavily, but his wound heals quickly and leaves only a long scar by the beginning of part 2. At the end of part 2, though, the second apple thrown at Gregor by his father lands firmly in his back. This apple and the wound it causes remain, as stressed at the beginning of part 3.

Students hypothesize about why it is the apple in Gregor's body that causes his father to remember that Gregor is a member of the family and about why Gregor's wound starts to hurt whenever he hears his mother and sister crying. In contrast to medieval German epics, in which the hero's wounds are always cured by a physician, often the hero's beloved, no one dares touch Gregor to remove his apple and tend to his wound. To the others, Gregor is totally repulsive—entirely unlovable and untouchable. Inevitably, the more the apple rots in his body, the more quickly Gregor approaches death.

His deathly wound festering, Gregor no longer remains considerate of his family. Leaving his room in part 3, he does not seek to help others but, rather, pursues his own pleasure: listening to the music he did not appreciate in his human form but that now intimates the "unknown nourishment" he has been seeking (*CS* 131). Gregor's pursuit of this nourishment leads to his death. When his sister expresses her wish for his death, Gregor seems almost relieved. At this point we discuss in class the observation that his father no longer chases him back into his room. To turn around, Gregor frequently beats his head against the floor, thus inflicting his own deathly punishment. Surrounded by complete darkness, head and body completely wounded, entirely immobilized, his breathing failing him, and lacking any recourse for action, Gregor easily fulfills the sister's—and now his own— wish for his death.

Discussing the end, class members bring up on their own the two prevalent viewpoints stressed in Kafka criticism: Gregor dies at peace with himself and his family and enters a spiritual realm (suggested by his appreciation of music); with Gregor's death, the spiritual also dies and is supplanted by the physical vitality of Gregor's sister and the renewed energy of his parents. I remain bothered, however, by the exclusivity of each viewpoint and tend to stress Kafkas dissatisfaction with his ending. I cannot look positively at the family's vitality, nor can I really believe, on the basis of the text, that Gregor enters a more positive, spiritual world. Although Gregor claims to bear no grudges and appears to die peacefully, the end indicates to me the hopelessly trapped nature of some individual lives.

The number three, so often used in literature and art to suggest perfection and redemption, has an entirely different function in *The Metamorphosis*. Students note, of course, that Gregor leaves his room and returns to it three times, once in each chapter of the narrative. Pertaining to Gregor, the number three refers chiefly to actions leading to utter solitude and finally to annihilation. The number three suggests not perfection but merely completion. The role of the three lodgers, however, puzzles students the most. They remain unsatisfied by the explanation offered in Kafka criticism: the three lodgers reflect Gregor's parasitical behavior, and Gregor has to be removed just as the three lodgers are. Usually the students find my own conclusion more plausible (but perhaps only because I am their instructor): the three lodgers, who refuse to be intimidated by Gregor's father (unlike Gregor), function as a perfected entity of a threesome in the same sense that Gregor's father, mother, and sister act as a perfected threesome in no need of Gregor. As connected with the lodgers and Gregor's family, the number three is exclusionary: suggesting a complete solidarity impenetrable by others, it underscores Gregor's doomed isolation.

Gregor's isolation is far greater than the isolation of the protagonists in Hesse's *Demian* and Mann's *Tonio Kröger*, the two works discussed immediately before *The Metamorphosis*. Despite considerable self-doubt and pronounced alienation, Hesse's main character broadens his individual self until it contains aspects of the entire universe. While Mann's Tonio has a much more restricted self and remains alienated from society, he does affirm the love and the longing for normalcy that help condition his art. In Kafka's *Metamorphosis*, however, there are no redeeming ideas or redeeming love. Instead of representing the birth of a new man (*Demian*) or affirming his own self (*Tonio Kröger*), Kafka's Gregor Samsa dies and diminishes into nothing as he is swept out of the world. Kafka's *Metamorphosis* thus illustrates, at least in this course, the end of the so-called canon.

In their final essay for the course, generally ten pages long, students recognize this end by stressing the disappearance of values, both universal and self-created, that provide meaning in life. Though deeply affected by Kafka, most students envision a far more satisfactory life for themselves and continue to formulate specific goals related to future professions and to happiness with people. Still, Kafka's "landscape of failures," to use Peter Heller's words again, continues to haunt them.

Note

1. I use the Norton edition of *Die Verwandlung* in my classes, and page references are to that edition.

MICHAEL ROWE

Metamorphosis:
Defending the Human

Introduction

In Franz Kafka's *Metamorphosis*, Gregor Samsa, a commercial employee who lives with his parents and sister and is the family breadwinner, suffers a sudden, terrible misfortune. The opening sentence of this novella must be one of the most striking in all of literature. Here is Willa and Edwin Muir's translation from the German: "As Gregor Samsa awoke one morning from uneasy dreams he found himself transformed in his bed into a gigantic insect."[1] Reactions from Gregor's family members and others move from shock, outrage, concern, and grief, through emotional and financial adjustment and a growing recognition of the burden Gregor represents, toward anger at his betrayal of them, disgust with his condition, and finally, complete neglect of him. At the end of the story a charwoman removes the flat husk of Gregor's body after his death. His family members, rejuvenated by their release from him, look forward to their new lives.

Kafka's *Metamorphosis* can be interpreted on many levels: as a satire on the stifling proprieties of bourgeois life, as a story of psychological estrangement and alienation, and as a parable on the fragility of human empathy and solidarity, among many others. My purpose, however, is to draw on certain themes in the story as they relate to prolonged critical illness and especially as they concern the relationships between people who are ill and

From *Literature and Medicine* 21, vol. 2, pp. 264–280. © 2002 by The Johns Hopkins University Press.

those—family members, other loved ones, and medical professionals—who care for them. The question at the heart of this essay is: How can we defend individuals' humanity, as we acknowledge and know it in our relationships and interactions with them, when long-term critical or chronic illness seems to have changed them utterly?[2] In defending the ill person's humanity, caregivers must resist acting upon their own feelings of horror or disgust and help others to resist acting on such feelings too. (Horror and disgust may be inevitable in the face of the transformations of grave illness.) The task, then, is not to avoid having negative feelings toward the ill person but to keep those negative feelings from provoking acts of cruelty or neglect.

In discussing the imperiled humanity of those with long-term critical illness or other debilitating or disfiguring illnesses, I will draw on a few incidents that occurred during the hospitalization of my son, Jesse, who died at age nineteen in 1995 after a liver transplant. These incidents brought me face to face with what I will call the "Gregor Samsa problem"—the potential that exists within family members, friends, and medical professionals to slowly walk down the path that Gregor's family took as they allowed their shock and disgust with his transformation to taint their care of him in passive ways, such as decreased contact with him and neglect of his wounds, and in active ways, such as physical assaults. I will also discuss factors that helped to counteract those forces, keeping those who cared for Jesse from compounding the misfortune of his illness by dehumanizing both him and themselves. I suggest that when the Gregor Samsa problem emerges, it does so as a crisis within, not an inevitable condition of, the relationship between ill people and their caregivers.

I realize that my approach to Kafka's story may seem naive or unduly instrumental. Art resists our attempts to pigeonhole it, and if great art always speaks to the human condition, it does so in a way that defies its use as a prescription for personal or social ills. One could argue, too, that there is a *specific* folly in looking to Kafka for pointers regarding how caregivers should confront critical illness. David Egenswiller warns that what we gain through applying Kafka's *Metamorphosis* to our real-life problems, we lose in appreciation of the elusive quality that makes it great literature.[3] But great art can teach without ceasing to be art. It speaks to us in our lives,[4] not from an Olympian distance, and it may elicit interpretations that reflect the full range of our experience.[5] Conversely, our life experience can shape our understanding of the work of art, as Mary Lefkowitz has shown in depicting her changing appreciation of Homer's *Odyssey*.[6] It seems to me, then, that no great damage is done in using literature for such practical ends as I propose here, on two conditions. First, we should not demand such practicality of it (but can seize its potential for illuminating the "real world" when we can hardly ignore that illumination). Second, we should acknowledge our practical use of art without claiming that we have exhausted its meaning or essence. That the view of life and human relationships reflected in the *Metamorphosis* is tragic seems evident to me. Each gesture of mercy in the story is smothered in an act of cruelty. Love and hatred, mercy and the exercise of overwhelming power are intermingled, adventitiously it seems, in the place where many of us look first for acceptance and safety—the home. To take up the story's challenge is not to deny tragedy, though, but to respond to it, as we respond in other ways to art that moves and challenges us.

ART: *METAMORPHOSIS*

In the first chapter of Kafka's novella, Gregor, a commercial salesman, wakes up to find that he has turned into a gigantic insect. Slowly, he recognizes the immediate limitations this transformation has imposed: he has trouble persuading his many legs to move his large, bulky body around and his voice squeaks, insect-like, when he speaks to his family members and employer. When, finally, he manages to open his bedroom door—still intent on getting to the oppressive sales job he has maintained since the failure of his father's business—his parents and sister and the chief clerk from his office discover his condition. The clerk flees in terror, Gregor's mother faints, his father chases him back with a stick, and Gregor injures himself in the clumsy process of returning to his room.

In the second chapter, Gregor, albeit hobbled by an injury to his legs, begins to get accustomed to his physical transformation. He uses his room as an animal lair, scuttling under the sofa for comfort and walking upside down on the ceiling for amusement. His sister, Grete, the family member to whom Gregor feels closest and whom he dreams of sending to the music conservatory, becomes his caretaker, leaving him scraps of spoiled food that, Gregor now finds, are more to his taste than his previous human favorites. The family cook leaves her position in horror of him. Gregor, overhearing one of the early conversations that always center on him, learns that his father has saved some money from the collapse of his business and that this, along with what they have set aside from Gregor's earnings, will help the family scrape by. As time passes, his sister's ministrations become oppressive to Gregor. When she tries to move out Gregor's bedroom furniture so that he can move around more freely, he emerges from under the sofa to defend his possessions. His mother faints again and his father, more powerful now than he has been since the failure of his business, attacks Gregor, throwing an apple that breaks through his shell and lodges in his back.

At the beginning of the third chapter, Gregor's parents and sister are paying less and less attention to him and more and more to their own misfortune. The servant girl leaves, and a charwoman takes over Gregor's care.

Each of his family members has now taken a job. Finally they take in boarders, and Gregor's bedroom becomes a junk room for extra furniture and other discarded objects. One evening Grete plays her violin at the lodgers' request. Gregor is drawn to the sound and its association with his dream of being his sister's protector and sponsor. The lodgers see him and give notice on the spot. Grete announces that they must get rid of Gregor, who is no longer Gregor in any case, she says, but a creature that is ruining their lives. Gregor crawls back to his room to die. In the morning, the charwoman sweeps out his body. Gregor's parents and sister take a family outing and contemplate their new and brighter future.

The critical literature on *Metamorphosis* is voluminous and wide ranging. Themes in the story include, among myriad others, incest, rebellion against the father, and family shame;[7] socioeconomic and social class critiques;[8] and isolation and alienation.[9] More relevant for this essay are discussions by such writers as R. D. Luke, Paul Landsberg, and Robert Coles about the story's symbolism, in which physical transformation may metaphorically represent psychological or spiritual transformation.[10] Illness threatens not only the individual's physical integrity but also the individual's identity and sense of self in the world, as Eric Cassell writes: "Persons do things. They act, create, make, take apart, put together, wind, unwind. . . . When illness makes it impossible for people to do these things, they are not themselves."[11] Not only are those who fall ill "not themselves" from their own point of view; they are not themselves to others, or, at the very least, others have trouble seeing the "self" they have known in the past in the ill person they see before them in the present.

Although becoming an insect is not quite a disease, Gregor's transformed identity, in which his taken-for-granted life is suddenly disrupted,[12] may be likened to the onset of serious physical or mental illness. Serious illness damages the person not only in fact but also in self-perception when others confirm this damage without giving comfort or demonstrating their acceptance of the changed person (or even, perhaps, when they do). As a result of both self-perception and perception of others, the person experiences the "spoiled identity" of the stigmatized,[13] in the words of Erving Goffman, and becomes an "other."

Also relevant for this essay are those commentaries on the actions of Gregor's family members. As Coles writes, "*Metamorphosis* asks us to consider not only Gregor's deadly transformation but our own continuing experience as survivors: Do we profit handily from the human degradation of others? Is our comfort earned at the expense of terrible suffering? If so, what happens to us, what metamorphosis falls upon us?"[14] Luke suggests that the story "casts dreadful and tragic light on human incapacity to appreciate disaster."[15]

Four themes in *Metamorphosis* are particularly relevant to my concerns. The first is a dual sundering of Gregor's humanity and of his function within his family and society due to his inability to maintain his employment. Gregor's humanity, to the extent that his parents and sister acknowledge it, is inextricably tied to his function as economic provider. When his metamorphosis makes it impossible for him to perform his job, his humanity, in the eyes of those closest to him, is threatened as well.

The second is the power and ambiguity of the function of caregiver, a theme that is likely to give pause to readers who have stood on either side of the patient–caregiver relationship. Grete, closest to Gregor in the family, naturally assumes the position of his caretaker, but she is also the first to rebel against the burden that Gregor's transformation has imposed on the family and to put up a barrier between him and any mercy he might hope to receive from his parents. For his part, Gregor is, at first, grateful to his sister for her ministrations; then he resents his dependence on her and later resents her neglect of him. In addition, Gregor has fantasies of stealing her away from the others and becoming her sole protector. This fantasy, whatever sexual connotations it has, also involves reversing the power relationship between them.

The third thematic concern is the temporal nature of the changes precipitated by Gregor's illness. While Kafka's portrayal of family relationships in the novella is almost uniformly grim, there is a *gradual* movement away, and finally an exclusion of Gregor, from the family circle. This inexorable movement is prompted in part by economic concerns, since Gregor's family members have to turn much of their attention to bringing in income to replace his, but it is largely an emotional movement away from him and a growing denial of his humanity.

The fourth thematic interest is Gregor's continued efforts toward autonomy. Gregor's attempts to escape his dependent role—first when he tries to protect his furniture from his sister's zeal and later when he leaves his room—precipitate his injury and, finally, death. Even the most loving of caregivers might wince at this description, recognizing the difficulty of alternating between roles of "total caretaker" and equal partner.

LIFE: ILLNESS, MEDICINE, AND CAREGIVERS

My favorite photograph of Jesse sits on my desk. It was taken in the fall of 1994 around the time of his nineteenth birthday. He sits on the front steps to our house, wearing a Buffalo Bills sweatshirt and sweatpants, and looks off to the left, half-smiling. He has medium-brown hair and olive-colored eyes behind wire-frame glasses. On closer inspection you can see that his face is pale, his shoulders are a bit narrow under his sweatshirt, and his fingers are thin and bony. He is five foot four. At the time the photo was taken, Jesse suffered from the chronic and growth-inhibiting disease of ulcerative colitis and the ravaging effects of slowly advancing cirrhosis of the liver. Despite his gauntness, he is a handsome young man, and his paleness only accentuates a certain shy vulnerability that is evident in the photograph.[16]

The flip side of Jesse's shy vulnerability, which caused many people, especially women, to be protective of him, was his maddening, sometimes infuriating refusal or inability to reveal himself to others by talking about his hopes and fears. He was a quiet child and young man, but he could be witty, too. He and his younger brother Daniel tape-recorded Abbott and Costello-like routines in which teenage ducks could commit drive-by paintings that transformed houses from polka dot to scandalous blue, cars could swim, Martians might pass unknown among us except that they mistook toast for lemonade and lemonade for toast, and hospitals could be turnips, as in, "I'm sorry, sir, but since your infection hasn't responded to antibiotics, we're going to have to admit you to the turnip." And Jesse was an artist. He drew in both black and white and color and completed thousands of drawings that tended toward either caricature, inspired by his droll sense of humor, or the heroic, inspired by comic books, science fiction, and any accounts of ancient myths he could lay his hands on.

In 1991, at age fifteen, Jesse was diagnosed with ulcerative colitis, an intestinal disease that causes blood loss, prevents absorption of nutrients from the intestine, and often requires both medical and surgical treatment. In 1992 he was diagnosed with sclerosing cholangitis—scarring and narrowing of the bile ducts going into the liver. In 1993 an arteriogram performed before his upcoming operation for colitis revealed early-stage cirrhosis. In 1994 he was placed on a waiting list for liver transplantation, and in May 1995 he received a liver transplant. Four days later he was taken back into surgery with a rising fever and abdominal pain even with frequent high doses of Fentanyl, a narcotic for pain. This second operation revealed a perforation in his intestine, inadvertently caused during transplant surgery by the difficult task of cutting through adhesions, or scar tissue, that had built up during the two years since his colitis surgery. Peritonitis had already set in, to be followed swiftly by sepsis, or severe infection, and multiorgan failure. Against all odds and predictions he rallied and received a second transplant, but another perforation, this time as a result of his weakened condition, another bout of sepsis, more downturns and rallies, followed. He died in August 1995 after a total of thirteen operations, including two liver transplants.

During all but the first few days of this hospitalization, Jesse was unable to speak because he had, first, a breathing tube in his mouth and later, a tracheotomy, connected to a respirator that sat to the left of his bed. These rendered communication between Jesse and others difficult, of course, although our lip-reading improved over time. He also had several intravenous lines—for antibiotics, for pain medications, and for administering blood products—and a big IV line to a vein in his groin for dialysis. He usually had one or two chest tubes to drain excess fluid into a thin aquarium—divided into vertical cells of equal size—that sat on the floor. Medicines and blood hung from poles at the corners of his bed. A red light clipped to his index finger was attached to an oxygen monitor. Electrodes on his chest measured heart rate and blood pressure. His nurses suctioned blood and fluid from his lungs, making a vacuum with the thumb on a piece of plastic tube that went to the respirator and snaking a second connected piece down his breathing tube to pull up blood clots in stops and starts with the thumb, probing as deep as possible without damaging his lungs or stirring up blood and bacteria.

More dramatic than machines and lines and tubes, though, were the physical transformations that illness wrought upon Jesse. As a response to sepsis, or systemic bacterial infection, his antibodies attacked the bacteria but also altered the permeability of his blood vessels and capillaries, causing water and protein and electrolytes to leak into his tissues, his abdomen, his lungs, his hands, and his feet. Fluid in his belly pushed up and crowded his lungs. His lungs pushed up on his heart. Fluid and blood seeped inside his lungs. Externally, the effects of sepsis were massive weight gain and bloating from accumulated fluid. Jesse's doctors, taking into account the twenty or thirty pounds of muscle mass he had lost to critical illness, calculated that his heart was pumping for an extra seventy pounds of fluid in his body. Six weeks later, the sepsis apparently gone but its damage done, he was emaciated. His attending hepatologist, Dr. Lanier (a pseudonym, as with other medical personnel in this essay), pointed at him one day and said, "The jaundice looks bad but the facial thinness is worse. That's one of the last areas of the body to go. He has a concentration-camp look." At the end, though, sepsis returned with a vengeance, turning Jesse into a bloated parody of a Sumo wrestler as blood was poured into him to keep his blood pressure from dropping like a stone.

During Jesse's 1995 three-month hospitalization there was not a single day that his mother (my ex-wife), our spouses, or I, and usually two or more of us, were at his side, encouraging him and advocating for him with his doctors. Although I think I could forgive myself for passing emotions of horror or disgust at seeing the physical wreck of Jesse's body, I do not recall having them. Perhaps my reserves of love and affection for Jesse saved me from having to confront such feelings about my own child, perhaps it was the mutual support of parents and stepparents, or perhaps it was Jesse's Phoenix-like partial recoveries that rewarded my hopes and allayed my despair. I saw no visible reactions of disgust from his mother or stepparents. (I did see the quickly stifled looks of shock on the faces of friends and extended family members who came to visit.) Nor did I see such reactions from his professional caregivers, except for one time, two days before Jesse's death, when a technician came in to check his respirator settings and looked at Jesse with disgust and disbelief and at us with disapproval, apparently for not putting Jesse out of his misery. It is noteworthy that this technician was a newcomer to the unit who had not cared for Jesse over time.

I do recall feeling angry with Jesse once or twice for not getting better. If his near recovery helped me to avoid the horror that Gregor's family felt toward Gregor, then the ups and downs, the "almost betters" followed by relapses, the two steps forward and two or three steps back that characterized Jesse's struggle during the latter half of his three-month hospitalization may have prodded my anger. A small wave of this anger had passed over me shortly before the following incident took place.

After weeks in which we were grateful to get a hand squeeze or detect a wiggle in Jesse's left foot, he woke up, both literally and figuratively. We, his parents, felt as though we finally had him back, and more, that he was reaching out to us and others, giving of himself, in a way we had seen only in isolated moments in the past before it was hidden in his shadows again. Still, mixed in with my elation and hope was my frustration—with myself, with Jesse's doctors, and with him for not being able to cross the invisible border that separated illness from wellness.

On this particular day, Jesse was complaining of belly pain. His nurse, Terri, gave him a bolus of pain medication, but he remained alert and in pain. Terri then drew off blood through his nasogastric tube into a beaker to see how much fresh and how much old blood was in his stomach. A few minutes later we looked at the blood in the beaker. It had congealed like Jell-O. Terri said she'd seen this only once before, with another liver patient. Then he started to bleed from his mouth. We slipped into normal crisis mode, grabbing towels and blue pads to help Terri soak up the blood. Standing near the foot of the bed on the window side, I tossed a towel to land on Jesse's chest for Terri to use. It landed on his face and covered it.

I cursed myself. I did not "intend" to throw the towel over Jesse's face, but I was horrified, feeling as though my bad aim might have been an unconscious, but deliberate, toss. I removed the towel immediately in the midst of the flurry of activity that went with this crisis, and it caused Jesse no physical harm. The only crisis here was my own, unless he, too, wondered about my motives. If he did, he hid it well.

A second incident, really more of a prompt for my reflections than an incident, involved one of Jesse's nurses. The nurses loved Jesse and fought over who would take care of him, but even they had their moments of frustration and anger with him when he pulled out his nasogastric and respiratory tubes out of his own frustration and despair. Marian, for instance, was his usual 8 P.M.-to-8 A.M. nurse. One evening around this time I helped her move Jesse up on his bed. I looked at him, now stick thin where, a few weeks ago, he had been heavy with accumulated fluid. I saw the sadness, the pity, and the frustration in Marian's eyes, and thought of the famous photograph of the Japanese mother bathing her daughter some years after the bomb had been dropped on Hiroshima. The girl's spastic limbs and face are contorted from radiation, and, I suppose, from the fear of being dropped in the water or of slipping into it. I wondered if one of Jesse's caregivers might think, perhaps not consciously, that it was best for all this to end, and I thought that, merciful or not, Marian's exhaustion or frustration might influence her actions, if such a thought came to her mind.

For the most part, Jesse's doctors treated him with respect and often with affection. There was a series of incidents, however, around the same time as the incident with the towel, that led us, his parents, to wonder whether they were subtly withdrawing from him as a lost cause. Over the Fourth of July holiday, Jesse bled profusely from his surgical wound on his belly and into his ileostomy bag. The attending surgeon sent word that there was no surgical solution for the bleeding. Back on the unit the next day, Jesse's chief surgeon, Dr. Dorand, read in Jesse's chart how much blood he had been given to replace what he was losing, and ordered him back into surgery. A difference of opinion, perhaps, but we wondered about the other surgeon. That afternoon we sat in the surgical waiting room anticipating a visit from still another surgeon (not Dr. Dorand or the previous night's attending). For the first time among ten surgeries, no one came. The surgeon did call the unit in the evening and told us she hadn't realized we were there, but again we wondered. Two days later, Dr. Dorand partly acknowledged our fears when I talked with him about them. "People can sometimes back away from a depressing situation," he said. "Now we have to do better."

No physical or, from what I can discern, emotional harm was done to Jesse during any of these incidents. Rather, they aroused for me the fear that, with more time and further exhaustion, with more hopes raised only to be dashed again and again, harm might be done.

The final incident I want to relate took place about three years after Jesse's death. We had decided to turn his room into a family room. I looked around the room. The bed, the bureau, the bookcase, and the end tables would be discarded. The couch upstairs would come down here when the new one arrived for the living room. Those objects that Jesse cared about—his Buffalo Bills sling chair, his Buffalo Bills bedspread, the Buffalo Bills and St. Louis Cardinals pennants pinned to the wall above his bed, the newspaper clippings about the new Star Wars movie that George Lucas was making and about Kurt Cobain's suicide, and the poster advertising Fat Dog Mendoza comic books—would remain. I wondered what life would have been like for Jesse if he had survived the wreckage of his body. Would he have been bedridden, too weak to draw, getting out only to be carted back and forth to doctors or helped onto a lounge chair on the deck during good weather? Would his mother and I have fought over who would take care of him? And would we have fought to assume that care or to be relieved of it? While this incident involves the tug of guilt that any parent might feel in going on after the death of a child, the content is consistent with the incident and themes above.

DISCUSSION

Despite the potential for dehumanization and neglect in the face of such horrendous illness and with all the terrible things that happened to my son, he was, in fact, never mistreated or dehumanized. This "success" is not to be taken for granted; rather, it represents an effective response to a crisis of Jesse's humanity and of ours.

Social, professional, and institutional practices and shared values regarding the worth of human life, specifically regarding the care of children, helped to minimize the threat of dehumanization during Jesse's illness. For parents, these values include the willingness to sacrifice many things—career opportunities, nights out, time for oneself or intimacy with one's spouse—for the sake of one's child and to advocate for and defend that child when he or she falls ill. Such normal expectations and values do not automatically make us good parents, and they may be affected by other factors, such as having other children to care for, being a single parent, or lacking the income or time off from work to be with the ill child full-time at the hospital, but they are powerful influences nonetheless.

Physical, intellectual, and social characteristics of patients may make them more or less attractive to their caregivers and either boost or drain their endurance in the worst of times. Jesse, for example, was young and, until the transformations that illness brought, good looking. In addition, the shy vulnerability that had drawn others to him in the past drew his caregivers to him now, whether he was conscious or unconscious.

Professional and institutional values and standards help to protect patients' dignity as well as their bodies. Nurses pride themselves on caring for the person, not the illness. Doctors are criticized for focusing on diagnosis and cure at the expense of attending to the person, yet they draw on their own ideals, including the Hippocratic injunction to first do no harm, for their relationship with the patient. Within Jesse's liver transplant program, there was an explicit principle that "once we have a patient, we stay with the patient." This principle was both an articulation of a commitment that justified giving a precious second liver to Jesse when a patient waiting for his first would have a better chance of success and an ideal that helped the liver team carry forward with a difficult case.

Standards of care that accrediting bodies enforce and hospital policies designed to assure quality medical care, even if they are created largely to reduce the chance of lawsuits, can protect vulnerable patients from neglect that might otherwise occur.

Still, even with professional and institutional norms, dire situations can lead the participants in grave illnesses away from them. Jesse's illness, and our response to it, made me reflect on bulwarks against the Gregor Samsa problem. These include awareness of the potential for moral exhaustion, representation and memory, and witnessing.

Moral exhaustion, by which I mean a loss, however temporary, of one's normal caring and empathic attitudes and reactions to the ill person, is a primary threat to the patient's humanity. Enlisting moral exhaustion in defense against itself, then, is an apparent contradiction. Yet moral exhaustion as a momentary sounding of the depths can serve as a wake-up call to the caregiver. The thought of what we *might* be capable of doing may bring us back to what is best in us. While I do not believe I had exhausted my moral and empathic reserves at the time of the incident with the towel, it did get my attention and, I believe, made me call on those reserves. I also think that my conversation with Dr. Dorand about what we had observed as a flagging of the doctors' attention and resolve may have served as a reminder of moral exhaustion for him and, through him, for the transplant team as a whole. A more cynical view would hold that Dr. Dorand was placating us in case Jesse didn't survive, thus hoping to fend off a lawsuit pursued out of anger or grief. I see no reason, however, that a doctor's self-interest in avoiding a lawsuit and his empathy for a patient cannot coexist.

In Gregor Samsa's case, his family members seem, at times, to relent from their cruelty toward him. Chapter III begins immediately after the incident in which Gregor's father has injured him with an apple that lodged in Gregor's back:

> The serious injury done to Gregor, which disabled him for more than a month—the apple went on sticking in his body as a visible reminder since no one ventured to remove it—seemed to have made even his father recollect that Gregor was a member of the family, despite his unfortunate and repulsive shape, and ought not to be treated as an enemy, that, on the contrary, family duty required the suppression of disgust and the exercise of patience, nothing but patience.[17]

It is difficult to conceive of a more grudging and qualified "relenting" than this one. Gregor, it seems, cannot count on a reserve of empathy and compassion that we might hope to exist, even in a contentious family, for a stricken member. He is not close to either parent and the travel associated with his work has kept him away from home. The two points in his favor—his becoming the family breadwinner after his father's business failed and his protective, big brother relationship with Grete—also count against him. His father, apparently, resents him for usurping his proper role, and Grete's adolescent push to establish her own identity contributes to her need to distance herself from Gregor (whose name so closely resembles her own).

Representation and *memory*, as I use them, are closely related and sometimes overlapping terms. Representation has a dual meaning here. In the first, parents or others represent patients who cannot represent themselves, advocating for them and doing what they think the patients would do if they could act on their own behalf. In the second, these same caregivers provide representations in their actions—by way of symbols, images, and other cues—that contradict or complement, and that add poignancy to, the image of the patient on the hospital bed. The image of the patient and the image of the person, then, are juxtaposed. They point back and forth to and confirm each other: "This is who he was, and therefore, still is; that is who he is, and cannot be divorced from who he was."

Representation, in the first sense, requires little explanation—in Jesse's case, we constantly made our presence as advocates and defenders known to his doctors. Representation in the second sense took several forms. Our interactions with Jesse (who also represented himself well when he was alert) and his caregivers demonstrated who Jesse was to us as a person. Other actions supplemented this caregiving. For example, we taped get-well cards and photos of Jesse on his walls and next to the chart taped to his door that showed the progress of his liver enzymes. One day Dr. Dorand came by on rounds and saw a photo of Jesse holding his new electric guitar, a Christmas present from the previous year. The photo was taped under the liver chart on his door that told the story of his illness—in numbers crowded into boxes that ran the width of the door and, as the days passed, down its length from eye to waist level—in terms of liver enzymes, clotting time, and other blood values. We talked about the fact that Jesse was playing left-handed, and how unusual that was. "I play guitar," said Dr. Dorand. "I could play for him." Two days later he came onto the unit with his guitar and played and sang for Jesse. Who knew how much of this was a response to "representation," how much was guilt or sorrow looking for an outlet, how much was Dr. Dorand just wanting to do something for Jesse when nothing else had worked? The fact that some of his doctors, including Dr. Dorand, had known Jesse as an outpatient may have enabled them to respond more easily to our representations of him and to represent him to those on the liver team who had not known him before his hospitalization.

In Gregor's case there is little representation of either sort. Grete's insistence on caring for him seems to have as much to do with adolescent petulance and willfulness as it does with concern for her brother. She does honor his human appetites and human bedroom at the outset, but she adjusts quickly, too quickly (albeit with good, practical reasons) to his new insect habits and inclinations. Gregor's mother honors her image and memory of him by fainting when he shows his metamorphosed self, but she might have helped him more if she had demonstrated in her demeanor and actions that she still believed there was a human being underneath the insect his body proclaimed him to be.

Memory is closely related to representation in the second sense. Each invokes and can be a form of the other. Memory, though, involves creating a story about the individual. It provides a fuller and rounder representation of the person and locates him or her in a web linked with family, others, and the world at large. Examples of memory creation, in Jesse's case, might include stories we told the nurses about him or examples we gave of his wit, or even information about our own lives, complementing and locating his own. Transcending representation, in memory the storytelling takes place over time, with a gradual accumulation of images and facts and everyday details. Memory shrinks the distance between the person with a life outside the hospital and the patient-as-body who is not equipped to represent himself or herself. These memories made available to doctors and nurses may also trigger "memory by analogy," reminding them of their own children or other loved ones and thus narrowing the gap between their patient and them.

In Gregor Samsa's case there is scant memory for his family members to call upon and no attempt to create one. Gregor spent little time at home until his transformation, always on the road and only staying the night when he was in town. There is little family story beyond that which involves grudging fulfillment of obligation on his part and an unreflective acceptance of that obligation by his parents, or at least Kafka decides not to provide it. There is the irony that Gregor, in his transformation, becomes the center of the family story for which he had been only the machine that kept that organization running.

To witness is "to be with and for," in Alan Mermann's words.[18] Discussing health care professionals and their work with survivors of state-sponsored violence and trauma, Stevan M. Weine writes that "to witness is to see, to know, and to be engaged with another's experience of traumatization."[19] Another form of witnessing—videotaped or other recorded survivor testimony—formalizes the act and process of witnessing, which starts when the survivor tells his or her story, extends to the primary listener, then to the community of listeners that supports the testimony and assists in its documentation, and finally to the human community at large.[20]

Witnessing, in Jesse's case, took all these forms. His parents stood "with and for" him physically and psychologically both when he was awake and communicating and when he was unconscious. We "knew and were engaged with" his trauma through our presence and involvement in the intimacy of his personal disaster. Witnessing, in the third sense, occurred through Jesse's silent witnessing and "telling" of his own trauma as it unfolded, through his family "listeners" and the doctors and nurses who attended upon this trauma, and continues to occur now in my telling of it to the larger community. This witnessing involves creating a framework of meaning within which representation and memory can do their work. Within this framework, the local story of unlucky patient and stricken parents, while retaining its particularity, gives witness to the story of the human community, which is linked in part through suffering and death and in part through its ability to represent, remember, and witness these same facts of the human condition.

In Kafka's *Metamorphosis* there are only two witnesses: the reader and the charwoman who cares for Gregor efficiently, without empathy or repugnance, and who witnesses "death's honesty" when it falls upon him.[21] Perhaps it is unreasonable to apply the concepts of representation, memory, witnessing, and the promptings of moral exhaustion to Gregor Samsa's family members, whom Vladimir Nabokov rightly derides for their cruelty and stupidity in "the house of disaster and dust."[22] Yet the lack of emotional connection evident in Gregor's family, economic worries, and the absence of a network of family or friends to support them might threaten the humanity of a family with even greater moral and emotional resources than theirs.

CONCLUSION

Kafka's *Metamorphosis* represents a challenge to the notion of a shared humanity and solidarity that accepts an obligation to protect its most vulnerable members, including those with life-threatening illness. As such, it cannot help but have resonance for those who confront that challenge in their lives. The story continues to ask a question about our humanity, or our lack of it, long after we have put the book back on the shelf. In this way, the dichotomy of the instrumental nature versus the "in-itself-ness" of literature is bridged: the work resonates in our lives, affecting, perhaps deepening, our response to our lived experience, and in turn informing our understanding, and next reading, of Kafka's great cautionary tale of human suffering. Our humanity is not a given. It can wear away. We maintain it by drawing on structures that nourish it and undertaking conscious efforts that may help to keep the milk of human kindness flowing.

NOTES

1. Franz Kafka, *Metamorphosis and Other Stories*, trans. Will and Edwin Muir (Mitcham, Australia: Penguin, 1961).

2. "Humanity" has complex and contested meanings, but it also evokes generally shared ideas about our individual and collective being as people, including what Michael Ignatieff, referring to individuals living in extreme poverty, calls the respect that "is owed a human being as a human being" (*The Needs of Strangers* [London: Chatto & Windus, Hogarth Press], 43).

3. David Eggenschwiler, "*The Metamorphosis*, Freud, and the Chains of Odysseus," in *Franz Kafka*, ed. Harold Bloom (New York: Chelsea House, 1986), 199–219.

4. Klaus Köhnke, "On Gregor Samsa, Kafka's 'Good Sinner'," in *Kafka: The Metamorphosis, The Trial, and The Castle*, ed. William J. Dodd (London: Longman, 1995), 72–78.

5. Robert Coles, "On Kafka's *Metamorphosis*," in *The Mind's Fate: A Psychiatrist Looks at His Profession* (Boston: Little, Brown, 1995), 306–312.

6. Professor Lefkowitz describes the metamorphoses of her views of the *Odyssey* over twenty-five years of teaching it, from her first view of it as the archetypal journey of the hero, to seeing it as a lesson that Odysseus must learn about others before he can discover his true identity, as an exposition of the difficulty of understanding how others see us, and finally as a rendering of the perspectives of those whose lives Odysseus destroys (Mary Lefkowitz, "2,800 Years Old and Still Relevant," *The New York Times*, August 21, 1999, sec. A.13).

7. See F. D. Luke, "*The Metamorphosis*," in *Franz Kafka Today*, ed. Angel Flores and Homer Swander (Madison: University of Wisconsin Press, 1958), 25–44; Richard H. Lawson, *Franz Kafka* (New York: Ungar, 1987); Paul L. Landsberg, "*The Metamorphosis*" in *The Kafka Problem*, ed. Angel Flores (New York: Octagon, 1963), 129–140; Köhnke; and Eggenschwiler.

8. Ritchie Robertson, "On *The Metamorphosis* and the America Novel," in *Kafka: The Metamorphosis, The Trial, and The Castle* (London: Longman, 1995), 157–163; Coles; and Landsberg.

9. Vladimir Nabokov, "Franz Kafka: *The Metamorphosis*," in *Vladimir Nabokov: Lectures on Literature*, ed. Fredson Bowers (New York: Harcourt Brace Jovanovich, 1980), 251–283; Martin Greenberg, *The Terror of Art: Kafka and Modern Literature* (New York: Basic, 1968); Hartmut Böhme, "Mother Milena: On Kafka's Narcissism," in *The Kafka Debate: New Perspectives for Our Time*, ed. Angel Flores (New York: Gordian Press, 1977), 80–99; Köhnke; Lawson; and Landsberg.

10. See Luke; Landsberg; Coles. See also Jack Coulehan, "Franz Kafka: The Metamorphosis," *Medical Humanities: Literature, Arts, and Medicine* website, http://endeavor.med.nyu.edu/lit-med/lit-med-db/webdocs/webdescrips/kafka98-des-.html (New York University, 1997).

11. Eric J. Cassell, *The Nature of Suffering and the Goals of Medicine* (New York: Oxford University Press, 1991), 41.

12. Böhme; Landsberg.

13. Erving Goffman, *Stigma: Notes on the Management of Spoiled Identity* (New York: J. Aronson, 1974).

14. Coles, 311–312.

15. Luke, 33.

16. I describe most of the incidents in this section in my memoir, *The Book of Jesse* (Washington, D.C.: The Francis Press, 2002).

17. Kafka, 44–45.

18. Alan Mermann, M.D., Chaplain and Clinical Professor of Pediatrics, Yale School of Medicine, gave this definition during his February 10, 2000 Faculty Bioethics Workshop presentation at the Yale Institution for Social and Policy Studies.

19. Stevan M. Weine, "The Witnessing Imagination: Social Trauma, Creative Artists, and Witnessing Professionals," *Literature and Medicine* 15 (1996): 167–182.

20. See, for example, Dori Laub's discussion of witnessing and testimony in "Bearing Witness, or The Vicissitudes of Listening," in *Testimony: Crises of Witnessing in Literature, Psychoanalysis, and History*, ed. Shoshana Felman and Dori Laub (New York: Routledge, 1992), 57–74.

21. Bob Dylan, "It's Alright Ma (I'm Only Bleeding)," in *Bringin' It All Back Home* (New York: Columbia Records, 1965).

22. Nabokov, 271.

Michael Rowe is Associate Clinical Professor of sociology at the Yale School of Medicine, Department of Psychiatry and Co-Director of the Yale Program on Poverty, Disability, and Urban Health. He is the author of *Crossing the Border: Encounters Between Homeless People and Outreach Workers; The Book of Jesse: A Story of Youth, Illness, and Medicine;* and a number of articles on homelessness and mental illness and community behavioral health services.

Chronology

1883	Franz Kafka is born on July 3 in Prague, a provincial capital of the Austro-Hungarian empire. His father, Hermann Kafka, is a hardworking and successful merchant. His mother, Julie Löwy Kafka, is from an old and affluent Prague family. Kafka is the eldest of six children, with two younger brothers, Georg and Heinrich, who die at the ages of fifteen months and six months, respectively, and three younger sisters, Gabriele ("Elli") (1889–1941), Valerie ("Valli") (1890–1942), and Ottilie ("Ottla") (1891–1943). Running the family business, both parents were absent from the home, and the children are largely cared for by Czech-speaking household servants.
1889	Kafka begins attending the German school and, as a result, he speaks more German than Czech.
1893	Kafka enters the Alstädter Deutsches Gymnasium, the German preparatory school in Old Town, where he proves to be an excellent student.
1901	Kafka enters the German Karl-Ferdinand University in Prague where he registers for chemistry and one semester in Germanics, but then switches to law.
1902	On October 23, Kafka meets Max Brod at Charles University. Brod had given a lecture at the German students' hall on Schopenhauer. Brod will become Kafka's most celebrated friend and, later, his literary executor.

171

1904	Begins *Description of a Struggle*.
1906	Starts working in a law office as a secretary. Receives his law degree. Embarks on a year of practical training at the Prague law courts.
1907	Writes "Wedding Preparations in the Country." Takes a temporary position with Assurazioni Generali.
1908	Eight prose pieces are published under the title *Betrachtung* (*Meditation*). Starts his diary. Accepts position with Workers' Accident Insurance Institute.
1909	Two sketches (originally part of *Description of a Struggle*) are published. Trip to Riva and Brescia (with Max and Otto Brod). "*Die aeroplane in Brescia*" is published.
1910	Five prose pieces are published under the title *Bectrachtung* (*Meditation*). Takes a trip to Paris (with Max and Otto Brod) and later visits Berlin.
1911	Official trip to Bohemia. Travels with Max Brod to Switzerland, Italy, and France, writing travelogues. He becomes interested in Yiddish theatre and literature.
1912	Starts working on *Amerika*. Visits Leipzig and Weimar with Max Brod. Now a frequent guest at Brod's parents' home, Kafka meets his future girlfriend and fiancée Felice Bauer, cousin of Brod's brother-in-law, Max Friedmann. He writes "The Judgment" and *The Metamorphosis*. *Meditation* is published. In May, Brod and Kafka publish one chapter from an attempted travelogue, for which Kafka writes the introduction, in the journal *Herderblätter*
1913	"The Stoker" is published. He visits Felice Bauer in Berlin. "The Judgment" is published. He travels to Vienna and Italy.
1914	Engagement to Felice Bauer, which is soon broken off. He visits Germany. He starts *The Trial* and writes "In the Penal Colony."
1915	Reconciliation with Felice Bauer. *The Metamorphosis* is published.
1916	Resumes writing after two years' silence: the fragments of "The Hunter Gracchus," "A Country Doctor," and other stores later included in *A Country Doctor*.
1917	In July, Kafka agrees to marry Felice Bauer and live in Berlin as soon as the war is over. Five months later, the engagement is called off. Kafka is on medical leave with pay

from his insurance company, living with his sister, Ottla, and her husband on their farm in Zürau. He is also busy writing numerous stories and parables, among them "The Country Doctor," "A Report to an Academy," "The Great Wall of China," and "The Hunter Gracchus," all the while harboring doubts about the quality of his work

1918   Kafka contracts influenza, part of the worldwide pandemic. He continues to stay in bed for three weeks and receives additional medical leave from his job while recuperating in the countryside of Schelesen, north of Prague. While at Schelesen, Kafka meets and becomes engaged to Julie Wohryzek, the daughter of a shoemaker and synagogue official in Prague. Kafka's father is angered by this proposed marriage to a socially and economically inferior family. Though Kafka continues to see Julie, the wedding planned for November 1919 does not take place because Kafka, once again, gives in to his fear that marriage will have an adverse effect on his ability to write.

1919   "In the Penal Colony" and *A Country Doctor* are published. Writes "Letter to His Father."

1920   Begins correspondence with Milena Jesenská. Intermittent stays at sanatoria.

1921   Resumes employment with the Workers' Accident Insurance Institute. "The Bucket Rider" is published.

1922   Writes *The Castle*, "A Hunger Artist," and "Investigations of a Dog." Breaks off relations with Milena Jesenská. He retires from Workers' Accident Insurance Institute. "A Hunger Artist" is published.

1923   Meets Dora Dymant and decides to live with her in Berlin. Writes "The Burrow."

1924   Moves back to Prague and writes "Josephine the Singer." Moves to Sanatorium Wiener Wald near Vienna. Dies at Sanatorium Kierling also near Vienna. Buried in Prague. The collection *A Hunger Artist* is published shortly after his death. Upon his death, Brod preserves his unpublished works from incineration despite Kafka's stipulations in his will. Brod defends his decision, stating that, "Franz should have appointed another executor if he had been absolutely and finally determined that his instructions should stand."

1925–27   Brod begins to edit Kafka's papers, with the publication of
             fragments of Kafka's novels. During the 1930s Brod will
             edit and publish six volumes of Kafka's collected works.

1937   Brod writes the first biography of Kafka: *Kafka, eine
             Biographie*.

Contributors

HAROLD BLOOM is Sterling Professor of the Humanities at Yale University. He is the author of 30 books, including *Shelley's Mythmaking, The Visionary Company, Blake's Apocalypse, Yeats, A Map of Misreading, Kabbalah and Criticism, Agon: Toward a Theory of Revisionism, The American Religion, The Western Canon*, and *Omens of Millennium: The Gnosis of Angels, Dreams, and Resurrection. The Anxiety of Influence* sets forth Professor Bloom's provocative theory of the literary relationships between the great writers and their predecessors. His most recent books include *Shakespeare: The Invention of the Human*, a 1998 National Book Award finalist, *How to Read and Why, Genius: A Mosaic of One Hundred Exemplary Creative Minds, Hamlet: Poem Unlimited, Where Shall Wisdom Be Found?*, and *Jesus and Yahweh: The Names Divine*. In 1999, Professor Bloom received the prestigious American Academy of Arts and Letters Gold Medal for Criticism. He has also received the International Prize of Catalonia, the Alfonso Reyes Prize of Mexico, and the Hans Christian Andersen Bicentennial Prize of Denmark.

JAMES ROLLESTON has been a professor in the department of Germanic languages and literature at Duke University. He is the author of *Narratives of Ecstasy: Romantic Temporality in Modern German Poetry* (1987), *Rilke in Transition: An Exploration of his Earliest Poetry* (1970), and editor of *A Companion to the Works of Franz Kafka* (2002).

JOHN WINKELMAN has been a professor in the department of Germanic and Slavic studies at the University of Waterloo in Ontario, Canada. He is the author of *Goethe's Elective Affinities: An Interpretation* (1987).

J. BROOKS BOUSON is a professor in the English department at Loyola University, Chicago. He is the author of *Jamaica Kincaid: Writing Memory, Writing Back to the Mother* (2005), *Quiet as It's Kept: Shame, Trauma, and Race in the Novels of Toni Morrison* (2000) and *Brutal Choreographies: Oppositional Strategies and Narrative Design in the Novels of Margaret Atwood* (1993).

ALLEN THIHER is Curator's Professor of French literature and professor emeritus of French at the University of Missouri-Columbia. He is the author of *Fiction Refracts Science: Modernist Writers from Proust to Borges* (2005), *Fiction Rivals Science: The French Novel from Balzac to Proust* (2001), and *Revels in Madness: Insanity in Medicine and Literature* (1999).

KEVIN W. SWEENEY has been a professor at the University of Tampa. He is the author of "Alice's Discriminating Palate" (1999), "Lying to the Murderer: Sartre's Use of Kant in 'The Wall'" (1985), and coauthor with Steven Jay Schneider of "Genre Bending and Gender Bonding: Masculinity and Repression in Dutch 'Thriller' Cinema" (2005).

MARK M. ANDERSON has been an associate professor of German and comparative literature at Columbia University. He is the author of "Die Kinder under der Holocaust: Eine amerikanische Geschichte" (2005), "The Shadow of the Modern: Gothic Ghosts in Stoker's *Dracula* and Kafka's *Amerika*" (2002), and editor of *Hitler's Exiles: Personal Stories of the Flight from Nazi Germany to America* (1998).

ROBERT WENINGER has been a professor in the department of German, King's College London. He is the author of *Gewalt und Kulturelles Gedächtnis: Repräsentationsformen von Gewalt in Literatur und Film seit 1945* (2005), *Streitbare Literaten: Kontroversen und Eklats in der deutschen Literatur von Adorno bis Walser* (2004), and *Framing a Novelist: Arno Schmidt Criticism 1970–1994* (1995).

MICHAEL G. LEVINE has been a professor of German at Rutgers University. He is the author of *The Belated Witness: Literature, Testimony, and the Question of Holocaust Survival* (2006).

MARGIT M. SINKA has been a professor of German at Clemson University. She is the author of "After the Odes of Joy: The First German Dramas Responding to the Fall of the Wall" (1996), "Genre and Meaning: Wolfdietrich Schnurre's Die Tat in Its Novelle and Kurzgeschichte Versions" (1987).

MICHAEL ROWE is associate clinical professor of sociology at the Yale School of Medicine, department of psychiatry and codirector of the Yale Program on Poverty, Disability, and Urban Health. He is the author of *Crossing the Border: Encounters Between Homeless People and Outreach Workers*; *The Book of Jesse: A Story of Youth, Illness, and Medicine*; and a number of articles on homelessness and mental illness and community behavioral health services.

Bibliography

Barry, Thomas F. "On the Parasite Metaphor in Kafka's 'The Metamorphosis.'" *West Virginia University Philological Papers*, vol. 35 (1989): 65–73.

Binion, Rudolph. "What the *Metamorphosis* Means." *Symposium* 15 (1961): 214–220.

Breen, Margaret Sönser. "Reading for Constructions of the Unspeakable in Kafka's *Metamorphosis*." *From Understanding Evil: An Interdisciplinary Approach*. Amsterdam, Netherlands: Rodopi (2003): 43–53.

Brod, Max. *Franz Kafka: A Biography*. New York: Schocken Books, 2nd ed., 1960.

Brooks, J. Bouson. "The Repressed Grandiosity of Gregor Samsa: A Kohutian Reading of Kafka's *Metamorphosis*." *Narcissism and the Text: Studies in Literature and the Psychology of Self*. Edited by Lynne Layton Lynne, Barbara Schapiro and Leo Goldberger. New York: New York University Press (1986): 192–212.

Bruce, Iris. "Kafka's *Metamorphosis*: Folklore, Hasidism, and the Jewish Tradition." *Journal of the Kafka Society of America*, vol. 11. nos. 1–2 (June–December 1987): 9–27.

Cantrell, Carol Helmstetter. "The *Metamorphosis*: Kafka's Study of a Family." *Modern Fiction Studies* 23 (1978): 578–586.

Corngold, Stanley. *The Commentator's Despair: The Interpretation of Kafka's* Metamorphosis. Port Washington, NY: Kennikat, 1973.

———, ed. Introduction to his critical edition of *The Metamorphosis*. New York: Bantam (1972): 11–22.

————. "Thirteen Ways of Looking at a Vermin: Metaphor and Chiasm in Kafka's *The Metamorphosis.*" *Literary Research* (vol. 21, no. 41–42 (2004): 59–85.

D'Haen, Theo. "The Liberation of the Samsas." *Neophilologus* 62, no. 2 (1978): 262–278.

Dodd, W.J. "Varieties of Influence: On Kafka's Indebtedness to Dostoevskii." *Journal of European Studies*, (14:4 [56]), December 1984, 257–269.

Friedman, Norman. "Kafka's *Metamorphosis*: A Literal Reading." *Approach* 49 (1963): 26–34.

————. "The Struggle of Vermin: Parasitism and Family Love in Kafka's *Metamorphosis.*" *Forum* 9, no. 1 (1968): 23–32.

Golomb, Jacob. "Kafka's Existential Metamorphosis: From Kierkegaard to Nietzsche and Beyond." *CLIO*, vol. 14, no. 3 (Spring 1985): 271–286.

Goodman, Paul. Preface to *The Metamorphosis by Franz Kafka*. New York: Vanguard, 1946.

Holland, Norman. "Realism and Unrealism: Kafka's *Metamorphosis.*" *Modern Fiction Studies* 4 (1958): 143–150.

Jofen, Jean. "Metamorphosis." *American Imago*, vol. 35 (1978): 347–356.

Kuna, Franz. *Literature as Corrective Punishment*. Bloomington: Indiana University Press (1974): 49–63.

Leadbeater, Lewis W. "Aristophanes and Kafka: The Dung Beetle Connection." *Studies in Short Fiction*, vol. 23, no. 2 (Spring 1986): 169–178.

Ryan, Michael P. "Samsa and Samsara: Suffering, Death, and Rebirth in *The Metamorphosis.*" *German Quarterly*, vol. 72, no. 2 (Spring 1999): 133–152.

Stine, Peter. "Kafka and Animals." *Contemporary Literature*, vol. 22, no. 1 (Winter 1981): 58–80.

Winkelman, John. "The Liberation of Gregor Samsa." *Crisis and Commitment: Studies in German and Russian Literature*. Edited by John Whiton and Harry Loewen. Waterloo, Ontario: University of Waterloo Press (1983)

Yehoshua, A.B. "Civilization and Its Discontents." *Queen's Quarterly*, vol. 112, no. 2 (Summer 2005): 169–181.

Acknowledgments

James Rolleston, "The Metamorphosis" from *Kafka's Narrative Theater:* pp. 52–68. © 1974 The Pennsylvania State University. Reprinted with permission.

John Winkelman, "The Liberation of Gregor Samsa" from *Crisis and Commitment: Studies in German and Russian Literature in Honor of J.W. Dyck,* edited by John Whiton and Harry Loewen: pp. 237–246. Copyright © 1983 University of Waterloo Press. Reprinted with permission of John Whiton.

J. Brooks Bouson, "Insect Transformation as a Narcissistic Metaphor in Kafka's *Metamorphosis*" from *The Empathic Reader: A Study of the Narcissistic Character and the Drama of the Self:* pp. 51–63, 177–178. Copyright © 1989 by the University of Massachusetts Press. Reprinted with permission.

Allen Thiher, "'The Judgment' and 'The Metamorphosis'" from *Franz Kafka: A Study of the Short Fiction,* pp. 33–50, 157–165. Copyright 1990 by G.K. Hall and Co.

Kevin W. Sweeney, "Competing Theories of Identity in Kafka's The Metamorphosis." This article originally appeared in *Mosaic, a journal for the interdisciplinary study of literature,* vol. 23, issue 4, (Fall 1990), pp. 25–35.

Mark M. Anderson, pp. 123–144 from "Kafka's Clothes: Ornament and Aestheticism in the Habsburg Fin de Siecle" (1992). Reprinted with permission.

Robert Weninger, "Sounding Out the Silence of Gregor Samsa: Kafka's Rhetoric of Dys-Communication," from *Studies in 20th Century Literature*, vol. 17, no. 2, Summer 1993, pp. 263–286. Reprinted by permission of STTCL.

Michael G. Levine, from *Writing Through Repression: Literature, Censorship, Psychoanalysis,* pp. 149–177, 207–212. © 1994 The Johns Hopkins University Press. Reprinted with permission of The Johns Hopkins University Press.

Margit M. Sinka, reprinted by permission of the Modern Language Association of America, from "Kafka's *Metamorphosis* and the Search for Meaning in Twentieth-Century German Literature," from *Approaches to Teaching Kafka's Short Fiction*, edited by Richard T. Gray: pp. 105–113. © 1995 by The Modern Language Association of America.

Michael Rowe, *Metamorphosis: Defending the Human. Literature & Medicine* 21:2 (2002), pp. 264–280. © The Johns Hopkins University Press. Reprinted with permission of The Johns Hopkins University Press.

Every effort has been made to contact the owners of copyrighted material and secure copyright permission. Articles appearing in this volume generally appear much as they did in their original publication with few or no editorial changes. In some cases, foreign language text has been removed from the original essay. Those interested in locating the original source will find the information cited above.

Index

Adorno, Theodor
  on *The Metamorphosis*, 44
Also sprach Zarathustra (*Thus Spoke
  Zarathustra*) (Nietzsche), 147
Althusser, Louis, 70
Amerika
  writing, 50
Anders, Günther
  on *The Metamorphosis*, 18, 78, 88,
  102, 137
Anderson, Mark M., 176
  on the aesthetic autonomy in *The
  Metamorphosis*, 77–94
Angress, Ruth K.
  on *The Metamorphosis*, 24
Angus, Douglas
  on *The Metamorphosis*, 43
Art Forms of Nature (Haeckel),
  80

Bakhtin, Mikhail, 63
Bauer, Felice, 92
Beckett, Samuel, 2
Beck, Evelyn T.
  on *The Metamorphosis*, 23
Beethoven, Ludwig von, 146
"Before the Law" (parable), 120
Beissner, Friedrich, 149

Benjamin, Walter
  "Frank Kafka: On the Tenth
  Anniversary of His Death,"
  119–125
Bergmann, Hugo, 81
Bible
  parallels to, 24, 28, 36, 49–50, 122
Binder, Harmut
  on *The Metamorphosis*, 24–25
Bloom, Harold, 175
  introduction, 1–3
Bölsche, Wilhelm, 80
Bouson, J. Brooks, 176
  on Gregor's need for attention in
  The Metamorphosis, 35–46
Brentano, Franz, 66
"Brief an den Vater," 31
Brod, Max, 47, 81–82
  letter to, 117–119, 122
  religion, 97

Cantrell, Carol
  on *The Metamorphosis*, 43
Cassell, Eric, 158
Castle, The
  language of, 62
Celan, Paul, 95
Cersowsky, Peter, 91

chief clerk (*The Metamorphosis*)
   arrival of, 9, 65–66, 86, 110, 151
   departure, 11, 157
   rage, 59, 61, 70
cleaning woman (*The Metamorphosis*),
   157
   brutal, 24–25, 78
   disposal of Gregor, 29, 140, 158
Coles, Robert, 158
Commentator's Despair, The
   (Corngold), 98
Corngold, Stanley
   The Commentator's Despair, 98
   on *The Metamorphosis*, 23, 43–44,
     55, 74–75, 78, 109, 136–139
   "The Metamorphosis of the
     Metaphor," 78
Counterfeiters, The (Gide), 50
"Country Docotor, A" (parable),
   2
   language in, 120

Darwin, Charles
   On the Origin of Species, 81
   theory of evolution, 80–81
David Copperfield (Dickens), 23
Deleuze, Gilles, 63
Demian (Hesse), 147, 153
"Der Amokläufer" (Zweig), 146
Der arme Spielmann (Grillparzer), 23
Der Mann ohne Eigenschaften (Musil),
   147
"Der wilde Mensch" (Gordin), 23
Descartes, René
   Discourse on Method, 65
   personal identity theories, 64–65,
     67–68
Diaries
   writing in, 75, 86, 96, 128

Dickens, Charles, 58
   David Copperfield, 23
Die Geschichte der jungen Renate Fuchs
   (Wasserman), 24
Die weißen Blätter (Wolf), 79
Die Welt Von Gestern (*The World of
   Yesterday*) (Zweig), 146
Discourse on Method (Descartes), 65
Dostoevsky, Fyodor
   The Double, 23
   Notes from Underground, 35, 117
Double, The (Dostoevsky), 23

Edel, Edmund
   on *The Metamorphosis*, 24, 43
Egenswiller, David, 156
Emrich, Wilhem
   on *The Metamorphosis*, 2, 19, 44, 55
Erlich, Victor
   on *The Metamorphosis*, 23

"Fairytale of the 672nd Night"
   (Hofmannsthal), 81
fantasy
   in "The Judgment," 53
   in *The Metamorphosis*, 6, 8, 35–36,
     40, 57–58, 62, 66, 72, 74, 82,
     159
"Fasching" (Hauptmann), 146
Flaubert, Gustave, 49, 58
"Frank Kafka: On the Tenth
   Anniversary of His Death"
   (Benjamin)
   Kafka's writing style in, 119–125
Freud, Sigmund
   allegory, 56
   and psychoanalysis, 118
   reality principle, 2
   theories, 86, 99, 124, 146–147

Georg Bendemann ("The
  Judgment"), 24, 87
  alienation, 5–7, 13, 20
  consciousness, 7, 11, 50
  death, 7, 11, 17, 54, 90
  destruction, 7, 9
  exploitation of family, 5, 13, 52
  father, 7, 12, 52–54, 61
  letter writing, 51–52
Gide, André
  The Counterfeiters, 50
"Give It Up" (parable), 147
Gnostic interpretation
  of *The Metamorphosis*, 1
God
  death of, 49
  and the Law, 1
  Second Commandment, 2
Goethe
  Metamorphosis of Animals, 80
  Metamorphosis of Plants, 80
Goffman, Erving, 70, 158
Gogol, Nikolai
  "The Nose," 23
Gordin, Jakob
  "Der wilde Mensch," 23
Gottwald, Adolf, 81
Gregorius (Hartmann)
  influence on *The Metamorphosis*,
    23–24, 27–29, 32
  Prologue, 27
Gregor Samsa (*The Metamorphosis*),
  23
  anger, 40–41, 98, 108, 155
  attempts to move, 8–10, 37, 54–55,
    60, 63, 82, 129, 138, 150–151, 157
  consciousness, 1–2, 5–7, 11, 13,
    15, 38, 55–56, 63–65, 67–69, 74,
    91, 168

death, 2, 6–7, 12, 17–18, 27–29,
  40–43, 54, 57, 73–74, 89–92, 102,
  107, 130, 139–140, 149–153,
  155,
  158–159, 168
dreams, 126–127, 150, 155
dual identities, 63–76, 158
employer, 1, 59, 61, 65–66, 70, 86,
  104, 151, 157
father, 5–6, 25–26, 31, 37–39, 41–
  42, 55–57, 60–62, 66–68, 71–72,
  84–85, 89, 102–107, 109–112,
  129,
  132, 139, 151–153, 155, 165–166
God's forgiveness, 28
and Grete, 5–8, 10, 12–16, 24, 29,
  31, 38–42, 56, 59, 61, 68, 70–71,
  73, 102–106, 108–109, 129–131,
  135–136, 138–139, 155, 157–
  159, 166
imagination, 14, 17
metamorphosis into bedbug, 1–2,
  6–8, 12–14, 16–19, 28–32, 35–
  39, 43–45, 55, 58–59, 61, 63–64,
  66–67, 69–71, 73, 77–79, 82–83,
  85–86, 88, 90–92, 99, 102, 104,
  106–110, 112, 126–131, 136–
  137, 139–140, 148, 155–159, 167
mother, 7, 25–26, 28, 37–42,
  56–61, 65–66, 68, 70–71, 77, 79,
  82, 85–87, 90, 102–106, 109, 129,
  131,
  135, 139, 150–151, 155, 157, 167
need for attention, 35–46
outcast, 1, 6, 20, 24, 40, 54–55, 78,
  85, 111, 153, 155, 158
outlook, 5
past, 64–66, 84, 87, 135–137,
  150–151, 167

quest for identity, 6–20, 29, 35,
  63–64, 66–69, 85, 87–89, 105,
  110, 149, 158
room, 26, 28, 37–38, 41–42, 55,
  58, 61, 63–66, 68, 70–72, 77, 87,
  105–106, 126, 129–130, 135,
  138, 149, 151–152, 157–159
sexuality, 57–58, 86
speech, 65–66, 70, 98, 102–105,
  108–111, 127–128, 130, 157
sufferings, 29–32, 42, 52, 66, 109,
  168
tormented vision, 1, 14
transgressions, 24, 30, 88, 91
traveling salesman, 1, 24–25, 28,
  31, 37, 39, 55, 58, 83–84, 139,
  150–151, 155, 157, 159, 165
Grete Samsa (*The Metamorphosis*)
employment, 25
interpretation, 62, 79
maturation, 24, 26–27, 43, 57–58,
  71, 73, 85, 87, 90, 105–106
music, 28, 31, 41–42, 60–61, 72–
  73, 89, 109, 152, 157–158
normality, 8
relationship with Gregor, 5–8, 10,
  12–16, 24, 29, 31, 38–42, 56, 59,
  66, 68, 70, 73, 102–105, 108–109,
  129–131, 135–136, 138–139,
  155, 157–159, 166
role, 6–7, 12–14, 18
weeping, 10
Grillparzer, Franz
Der arme Spielmann, 23
Guattari, Felix, 63
guilt theme
in "In the Penal Colony," 30
in "The Judgment," 30, 61
in *The Metamorphosis*, 30–32, 61, 107

Haeckel, Ernst
Art Forms of Nature, 81
The Riddle of the Universe, 81
Hamacher, Werner, 120
Hauptmann, Gerhart
"Fasching," 146
Hartmann von Aue
Gregorius, 23–24, 27–29, 32
Hayman, Ronald, 66
Hegel, 69, 95
Heller, Peter, 145, 153
Heselhaus, Clemens, 16
Hesse, Hermann
Demian, 147, 153
Hofmannsthal, Hugo von, 82, 146
"Fairytale of the 672nd Night," 81
"Letter of Lord Chandos," 147
Hölderlin, Friedrich, 95
Homer
Odyssey, 156
Honig, Edwin, 43
"Hunger Artist, A" (short story), 2,
  90
near-starvation theme in, 52, 54,
  56
"Hunter Gracchus, The" (short story),
  2

"Imperial Message, An," 53
impressionism, 146
incest theme
in *The Metamorphosis*, 28
"In the Penal Colony" (short story),
  29
death, 18
guilt theme in, 30
writing, 120
"Investigations of a Dog" (short
  story), 90

Jewish
 law, 1
 literature, 23, 27
 memory, 2
 modern tradition, 2
 writers and the German language,
  117–118, 127, 132, 145–147
"Josephine the Singer" (short story),
 90
Joyce, James, 50
"Judgment, The" (short story), 24, 29
 autobiographical, 30
 falsely based individuality in, 5–6, 9
 friend from Russia in, 6–7, 51–53
 guilt theme in, 30, 61
 language and narrative of, 47,
  49–52, 54–55, 122
 setting, 51
 structure of, 6, 19–20
 window imagery in, 51
 writing of, 50
Jung, Carl, 147

Kafka, Elli, 30
Kafka, Franz, 1
 childhood, 100–101, 112
 chronology, 171–174
 death, 119
 education, 23, 81
 family, 30–31, 96–97, 99–102, 110,
  123
 guilt, 31–32
 language, 47–62, 65, 78–79, 137
 narratives, 2, 11, 24, 27–28, 35–36,
  44–47, 49–62, 64–67, 73–74, 79,
  95–115, 117–125, 139
Kafka, Janouch, 30
Kafka, Ottla, 31
Kafka, Valli, 31

Kant, Immanuel, 146
Kleist, Ewald Jürgen Georg von 95
Klimt, Gustav
 "The Ode to Joy," 146
"Knock at the Manor Gate" (parable),
 123
Köhnke, Klaus
 on The Metamorphosis, 24
Kohut, Heinz, 36, 39
Kraft, Werner, 124
Kubin, Alfred, 82
Kuna, Franz
 on The Metamorphosis, 24, 43

Landsburg, Paul, 158
Lefkowitz, Mary, 156
"Letter of Lord Chandos"
 (Hoffmannsthal), 147
"Letter to His Father" (short story),
 54
 cockroach in, 82
 relationship with father in, 97–99,
  101–102, 110, 112
Levine, Michael G., 176
 on The Metamorphosis compared to
  Ovid's Metamorphoses, 125–138
 on Walter Benjamin and Kafka's
  writing style, 117–140
"Little Fable, A" (short story), 2–3
Locke, John
 personal identity theories, 64–65,
  68
Lukács, John, 11
Luke, R.D., 158

Mallarmé, Stephane, 95
Mann, Thomas, 91
 Tonio Kröger, 147, 153
Margolis, Joseph, 75

Marty, Anton, 66
Marx, Karl, 70, 147
Mead, George Herbert, 70
Mermann, Alan, 167
Metamorphoses (Ovid), 121
    Kafka's *The Metamorphosis*
        compared to, 125–138
    narrative, 126
    sexual imagery in, 133–134
Metamorphosis, The, 147
    aesthetic autonomy in, 77–94
    illustration for, 2, 79, 149
    influences on, 23–33
    narrative and language of, 24,
        27–28, 35–36, 44–45, 55–60, 62,
        64–67, 73–74, 78–79, 85–86,
        100, 102,
        121, 129, 137, 139, 152
    publication, 78
    servant girl in, 25, 157
    structure of, 14, 19, 36, 57, 78, 86,
        97–98, 110, 150–151, 168
    writing of, 25, 31, 78, 100, 128
Metamorphosis of Animals (Goethe), 80
"Metamorphosis of the Metaphor,
    The" (Corngold), 78
Metamorphosis of Plants (Goethe), 80
modernism
    artwork, 91
    literature, 49, 79, 92
    narrative, 96
Muir, Edwin, 155
Muir, Willa, 155
Musil, Robert
    Der Mann ohne Eigenschaften, 147

Nabokov, Vladimir
    on *The Metamorphosis*, 69, 127,
        148–150, 168

naturalism, 146
near-starvation theme
    in "A Hunger Artist," 52, 54, 56
    in "The Judgment," 52, 54, 90
    in *The Metamorphosis*, 28, 38,
        41–42, 54, 56, 59, 67, 74, 90, 128,
        152
Nietzsche, Friedrich, 49
    Also sprach Zarathustra (*Thus Spoke
        Zarathustra*), 147
"Nose, The" (Gogol), 23
Notes from Underground
    (Dostoevsky), 35, 117
Novalis, 95

"Ode to Joy" (Schiller), 146
"Ode to Joy, The" (Klimt), 146
Odyssey (Homer), 156
On the Origin of Species (Darwin), 81
"On Parables" (parable)
    self-referential metalanguage in,
        47–50
Ovid
    Metamorphoses, 121, 125–138

Parable and Paradox (Politzer), 147
Parry, Idris F.
    on *The Metamorphosis*, 23
Pascal, Roy
    on *The Metamorphosis*, 43
Plato
    Republic, 69
Politzer, Heinz
    on *The Metamorphosis*, 23–24, 101
    Parable and Paradox, 147
Pritchett, V.S., 147
Proust, Marcel, 50

Quinton, Anthony, 64

Rattner, Josef
on Kafka, 97–98
realism
in fiction, 49–50
Rennet, Alan
on Kafka, 96
Republic (Plato), 69
Riddle of the Universe, The (Haeckel),
81
Rimbaud, Arthur, 95
Rolleston, James, 175
on Gregor's quest for identity in
The Metamorphosis, 5–22
Romantic
literature, 79–80
Rowe, Jesse
illness of, 156, 159–168
Rowe, Michael, 176
on humanity in *The Metamorphosis*,
155–170
Ryan, Lawrence
on *The Metamorphosis*, 6

Sacher-Masoch, Leopold von
Venus im Pelz, 24, 86–87
Satire
in *The Metamorphosis*, 2
Schiller, Friedrich
"Ode to Joy," 146
Schönberg, Arnold, 146
Schopenhauer, Arthur, 146
Schubiger, Jürg, 17–18
Shakespeare, William
characters, 1
Sinka, Margit M., 176
on teaching Kafka, 145–153
Skulsky, Harold, 66
social-constructionist theories of self,
69, 72–74

Sokel, Walter, 96
Sontag, Susan, 95–96
Spann, Meno
on *The Metamorphosis*, 44
Spilka, Mark
on *The Metamorphosis*, 23, 37
Starke, Ottomar, 79
Steiner, George, 95–96, 147
Steinmetz, Horst
on Kafka, 97–98
"Stoker, The" (short story), 30
Karl Rossmann in, 5–6, 19–20, 54
structure of, 19–20
Sweeney, Kevin W., 176
on Gregor's dual identities in *The
Metamorphosis*, 63–76

temporal reference
in *The Metamorphosis*, 26
Thiher, Allen, 176
on "The Judgment" compared to
The Metamorphosis, 47–62
on Kafka's language, 47–62, 97
Tonio Kröger (Mann), 147, 153
Trakl, Georg, 95
transcendentalism, 2, 53
Trial, The
language of, 62
postponement in, 122
window imagery in, 51

Updike, John, 69, 147

Venus im Pelz (Sacher-Masoch), 24,
86–87
Verlag, Kurt Wolff
on *The Metamorphosis*, 29
Vietta, Silvio
on *The Metamorphosis*, 44

Wagenbach, Klaus
    on *The Metamorphosis*, 23
Wasserman, Jakob
    *Die Geschichte der jungen Renate
    Fuchs*, 24
"Wedding Preparations in the
    Country" (short story), 96
    Eduard Raban in, 83
    transformation in, 83
Weinberg, Kurt
    on *The Metamorphosis*, 24
Weine, Stevan M., 167
Weninger, Robert, 176
    on Kafka's narrative, 95–115
Wiese, Benno von
    on *The Metamorphosis*, 11, 44

window imagery
    in "The Judgment," 51
    in *The Metamorphosis*, 51, 86, 97,
    129
    in *The Trial*, 51
Winkelman, John, 175
    on the influences on *The
    Metamorphosis*, 23–33
Wolf, Kurt
    Die weißen Blätter, 79

Zweig, Stefan
    "Der Amokläufer," 146
    Die Welt Von Gestern (*The World of
    Yesterday*), 146